Dirt & Spirit
A History of the Red Dirt Music Scene

Tonya Little

Little Okieland Publishing - Midwest City, Oklahoma

Copyright © 2025 by Tonya Little

All rights reserved.

No portion of this book may be reproduced in any form without written permission from the publisher or author, except as permitted by U.S. copyright law.

Published by Little Okieland Publishing, LLC.   ISBN: 978-1-7352703-8-8

Little Okieland Logo designed by Trigger Latimer of Tattoos by Trigger.

Cover Designed by Ragan Parkerson with Table Zero Productions.

Front photo of the Skinner Brothers Band provided by Mike Shannon (L-R: Mike Skinner fiddle, Mark Lyons guitar, Tony Harrison drums, Tom Skinner guitar & vocals, Mike Shannon pedal steel & guitar, Craig Skinner bass, Tim Smalley bass. Photo taken in 1980).

Back cover photo provided by Sage Powell, LaFave Musician's Reunion party at the farm on the porch (Photo taken in late 80's).

Contents

Dedication	1
Acknowledgements & Sponsors	3
Foreword by Rick Reiley	5
Notes From The Author	7
Introduction: What is Red Dirt Anyway?	11
1. Stillwater: The Genesis	17
2. Early Contributors	30
3. Coming Together	43
4. The Mid-Seventies	57
5. Stillwater Expansion	71
6. Connections & Collaborations	84
7. An Influx in Stillwater	97
8. The First Three Albums	110
9. The Eighties Begin	121
10. Red Dirt Finds a Home	135
11. Festivals & Fightin'	148
12. Growth & Expansion	161

13. Moving Out of Oklahoma	174
14. Musician Reunion & Santa Fe	186
15. Nashville Adventures	200
16. Austin & Three More Albums	212
17. Newcomers	225
18. Wrapping up the Eighties	238
19. Passing the Torch	250
20. The End of the First Era	262
Resources & Reference	275
Author Page	278

Tiny Tom Skinner. Photo provided by Craig Skinner

Sometimes you gotta have faith like a blind man, standing in the middle of the road – Tom Skinner

TONYA LITTLE

This book would have never existed without all the amazing help, encouragement and support I received from everyone who contributed and were my cheerleaders throughout the creation. Especially those that didn't give up on me even though it took a decade to get here. So, this book is dedicated to you. Ya'll know who you are.
This book is also dedicated to all those we have lost along the way that were a part of the fabric of it all. You live on in the stories and the music, and we are forever grateful for that and you. We know who you are, and we will never forget.

And while he falls into both of those categories above, a special dedication goes to Chad Sullins, as well as the rest of the Last Call Coalition, who led me down the Red Dirt rabbit hole, treated me like family from day one, and let me experience the Red Dirt community of love firsthand. Without them, I would have never been inspired to write this book. Thank you, Chad, Josh, Jeremy, Jerry, Mike, and Jesse. You'll forever and always be "my" band.

Acknowledgements & Sponsors

There are so many people to thank for all of their help along the way, I'm sure I'm going to miss some, please forgive me. First and foremost, thank you to all the contributors of this book and for trusting me with your stories. Thank you to Sage Powell, Stan Woodward, Craig Skinner and Chuck Dunlap for contributing all the photos. Thank you to Trigger Latimer for his work on the Little Okieland logo. Thank you to Ragan Parkerson for his awesome cover art design and graphics help. Thank you to Jayson Starkey for all the amazing graphics help, he restored flyers and photos into usable resolutions and sizes like a champ. Thanks to my parents, Dennis & Kathie Reynolds for all of their unwavering support, love and just being who they are. Thanks Missy Miller Doggett, Leah Romeros, Shelley Owen, Robert Thornton, Rachel Jones, Carol Gordan and John & Erin Thornton, Brandi Smith and Clint Stayton for jumping in and sponsoring the book. I really appreciate you guys.

The book is also sponsored by Kicker Performance Audio, School of Rock of New Braunfels, Tumbleweed Dance Hall, The Dirty Rooster, and Mile 0 Fest, thanks everyone for all of your support!

Foreword by Rick Reiley

I first met Tonya Little about 15 years ago in the early days of the Tuesday Night Music Club.

About TNMC: Gene Collier and I began playing outdoors in Centennial Park in downtown Cushing on Tuesday evenings and the late Sean Kelly soon joined us. It was Sean who later dubbed it the Tuesday Night Music Club. Kelly was then owner of KUSH Radio in Cushing as well as a competent singer/songwriter.

Later, DJ Duncan invited us to move out of the weather, to her living room, indoors where she became the official hostess, serving up hot coffee, encouragement, a welcome smile and snacks to all who entered. TNMC (2009-2020) served a music hub for connecting musicians from all over the area to meet and greet and sing and trade stories. Folks from all over this part of the country joined the circle and we traded songs and licks for hours. It was a good run and we saw hundreds and hundreds of musicians come through those doors to share their gifts.

Tonya was a part of that first, colorful, meandering entourage of music aficionados who first appeared when the Damn Quails and others from the Norman/OKC area and further reaches began dropping in. Many lasting connections were made in that living room.

Tonya's interest and passion in the red dirt scene only deepened. Consequently, this self-confessed Red Dirt Queen of Hearts began documenting the history of the music as her adopted mission. Now the book has arrived!

Many years and hundreds of hours have gone into this project. Many late-night conversations in campgrounds, after hours behind the scenes at festivals, concerts, house concerts, chance meetings on the street. Phone snippets, emails, texts and photos have all come together to tell the story of Oklahoma red dirt music as told by those who helped create, nurture and love into being.

You'll read stories of the legendary Farm west of Stillwater where many of those red dirt seeds were planted, bloomed and blossomed. You'll read about the ever-evolving live music scene on The Strip in Stillwater. You'll read stories of life on the road and tales of how it all came to pass. (Some of them true!)

This is a kaleidoscope of red dirt memory from those who witnessed it as it happened. Stories threaded and woven together as a true labor of love by one who has truly loved, lived and breathed the subject for a good long while!

Long may the red dirt spirit live! Enjoy!

~ Rick Reiley

Notes From The Author

What a fantastical, weird and wacky trip down the Red Dirt rabbit hole this has been over the last decade or so. I've met some of the most magical characters along the way, and it's changed my life in the best ways possible. I fell into this scene by accident, in 2009, and quickly became immersed in all things Red Dirt. It led to some freelance writing gigs, with my penchant for penning, and I was working for Red Dirt Nation in 2015 when I realized there wasn't much of anything out there in the way of a history for the scene. There were bits and pieces here and there, some projects that could be dug up. But nothing easily accessible at all at that time, to help explain and preserve the history of this amazing scene. I wanted to change that. So, in 2015 I wrote a couple of articles explaining Red Dirt. Which spurred me on to want to write a book.

    I have been collecting stories and talking to anyone who would talk to me since then, in an effort to create this book. It's been a long time coming, but I just kept finding more people, more stories… more history. I had a hard time drawing the line and deciding when it was really done. I wanted this to be as complete of a collection as possible. I wanted it to pay homage and tribute to these amazing artists and the path they carved into the musical realm. I wanted to do it justice in the best possible way. I'm not sure if I did or not, but I promise you that it wasn't for a lack of trying.

    As much as the Red Dirt artists have poured their heart and soul into their music, I wanted to pour mine out into honoring them. This is not my story, I was just lucky enough to be able to collect it, compile it, and organize it to be shared. I feel extremely honored to have been a part of this journey and am grateful to every single person who took the time to share their story with me. While I tried hard to keep it in chronological order to the best of my ability, there will be overlapping chapters and stories. I also have come to accept the fact that I may not have every story, every artist, every venue and every scrap of history here in this book. For anyone or anything that I missed, I apologize profusely. If there are any stories I am missing, I'm including my contact information here. Feel free to reach out and share your stories with me. I've already decided to break this book up into a series, who knows how many books I can create out of this one musical niche? There may need to be an updated version of this book once more stories start to pour out.

I have rearranged, edited, changed around and reorganized this thing a dozen times trying to make sure I offered it up in a way that made the most sense, and would hold the attention of the reader. Please note that I have combined different parts of interviews into one quote to make it more organized, without adding any ellipses to indicate it was not all said together, just because it made it "cleaner". The quotes are what contributors said, just maybe not in the order they said it necessarily. I also left grammatical errors and jargon in quotes to help show more personality. I tried to use as many quotes as possible and limit just using my own words to tell the story, because I feel like this makes it all more genuine and authentic. My ultimate goal is to share their stories, not my own words. When I say this project has been a labor of love, trust me that the labor part was just as intense as the love part. I paralyzed myself for a long time with getting it published, afraid I wasn't doing it justice, afraid I was missing something, afraid it wouldn't be complete. But I finally bit the bullet and decided it was time. Well past time really, to get these stories into your hands. It's been so much fun collecting them, following these artists, researching, meeting new people and tracking down as much content as I possibly could for everyone. But it's definitely been work. Don't even get me started on how many hours went into transcribing the countless interviews. I had to break it into multiple books because I just had too much, and I didn't want to cut any of it out.

My whole goal with this project is to help give the Red Dirt scene its own history books, so when someone asks, "What is Red Dirt Music anyway?", there is a reference. But not in a cut and dried fashion of just facts, I wanted all the colorful stories collected straight from the sources. I wanted the whimsical journeys and hilarious backdrop that went into making this scene what it is. I wanted you to get to know the characters of this scene in the rich tales they themselves, as well as their friends and cohorts, shared about them. Almost everything I have collected for this book was given to me from the people who lived it- the ones who were there to remember. I trust their memories and stories are as true as they can be. There's no fact-checking when there isn't a history to be found, so these stories are as fact-checked as possible from the sources. If anything is incorrect, I'll chalk it up to hazy memories and entertaining embellishments, which I think they are all entitled to none the less. These are their stories; I just want to share them.

I eventually want to write additional volumes and include everyone I possibly can from the time it started until this very day, because these are my friends. I have made some amazing music family connections through the years, and we have such a plethora of fantastic artists around Oklahoma who pour out their hearts and souls into what they do. My goal has never been just to feature and recognize the "bigger" names that have broken out of the Oklahoma music sphere and made larger names for themselves. I wanted to get much more granular, and into the little pieces of Red Dirt. To introduce you to the ones you may never have had a chance to learn about, so you can look them up, check them out, and appreciate the music they have to offer. I wanted to give the unsung heroes their moment of recognition and their place in history. If I can bring one person on as a fan to any of my music friends, it will be worth it to me. It's all about spreading the dirt, and I am glad to do my part. I encourage you to search out the names in this book and find their music and art however you can and dig in.

This journey has changed the whole trajectory of my life really. Along the way I created my website, LittleOkieland.com where I strive to provide content about all things Oklahoma. It also led to my self-proclaimed title of Red Dirt Queen of Hearts, and to the podcast I co-host with Leah Rae- the Queen of the Silver Dollar- called Backstage Queens. This music scene isn't just a music scene to me; it's my world, it's my family. The plan is for this to just be the first book in a series of Red Dirt books. I've got big goals, big dreams. What else could you expect from the Red Dirt Queen of Hearts?

This first book is mostly just to pay homage and respect to the early musicians, venues, patrons and fans who created this scene. These may include names you have never heard of before, but the part they played is just as important as any of the names you have heard of. They may not all have gotten their "15 minutes of fame" or the recognition they deserve, but my goal is to make sure they have a spot in history. They earned it.

There is a Dirt & Spirit photo album where you can see the photos from this book in full color, as well as so many others that wouldn't fit into the book, on my website at Littleokieland.com.

So, that all being said, dive in and enjoy. I hope you have just as much fun with these stories and these characters as I did. Thanks for getting your hands on this book.

Tonya Little
Tonya@Littleokieland.com

Introduction: What is Red Dirt Anyway?

It is widely known that the state of Oklahoma is characterized by its red, clay-like dirt that permeates the state. Which is a big reason why the name Red Dirt music was created as a regional moniker given to musicians that played genre-blending music filled with spirit, stories and community. This is also why 'Dirt and Spirit' is a great way to describe the Red Dirt movement. The music seems to be more spiritual in nature, although not in a religious way- as spirituality and religion can mean different things. These songwriters write about what they know; songs that come from their soul, not manufactured songs created for the masses. These are songs written by people simply living their lives and singing about it. The music of Red Dirt artists is natural, honest, and about real life. The culture of Oklahoma; the grit, perseverance and independence- is found laced throughout the Red Dirt movement.

While Woody Guthrie was clearly a folk singer, he had a huge influence on those that came to create the Red Dirt scene, along with other Oklahoma musicians that pre-date the Red Dirt movement, or are included in other genres; like Wanda Jackson, Leon Russell and JJ Cale, to name just a few. These musicians greatly influenced those who came later and are a stepping-stone towards Red Dirt in the history of Oklahoma music. There are others that may have not been born in Oklahoma but ended up here and shaped the musical landscape as well. For instance, Byron Berline, who was born in Kansas but came to Oklahoma in college, helped shape the bluegrass scene in Oklahoma. Berline was also a part of The Flying Burrito Brother's Band, which is often cited by Red Dirt artists as having an influence and impact on their musical tastes. He earned his place in the Red Dirt music scene even if he wasn't born here and was mostly in the bluegrass world.

Then there are those like Ray Wylie Hubbard, who was born in Oklahoma but ended up moving to Texas as a child and becoming a part of the Texas Country fabric. His influence on the Red Dirt scene is also prominent, along with many other Texas artists. While closely related, like cousins from the same family tree, Texas Country and Red Dirt often get combined as one genre, which isn't really the case. Both have distinct beginnings with different sounds and styles, both have been born out of different cultures and philosophies. They are each regionally different in a variety of ways. While the evolution of the two seems to have cross-bred and cross-pollinated in many ways, they still are distinct musical scenes with their own flavors. Much like peanut butter and jelly, they may mesh well together as one menu item, but they are significantly different on their own.

Oklahoma music had its fair share of musical success long before the Red Dirt movement was ever born, and many of these artists had a major influence on the Red Dirt movement, including all the names mentioned above and more. These artists, among many others, would come to shape and form the way Red Dirt musicians perceived and made music years down the road.

Jesse Ed Davis, an Oklahoma Native American musician, released a song called *Red Dirt Boogie Brother* in 1972. Which may be the first time Red Dirt was used or placed in a musical reference. His amazing talents and career are often revered and praised by those in the Red Dirt scene. While his career pre-dates the Red Dirt days and wasn't a part of the scene, he no doubt inspired and motivated those in it.

If you are immersed in the Red Dirt scene it just becomes a way of life- you learn the ins and outs and figure it out by being around it. But those on the outside looking in often wonder, what is Red Dirt anyway?

When asked to explain what Red Dirt music is by anyone in the scene, there is a likelihood that you will get many different and varying answers from both the musicians and fans.

"It's rock-n-roll, it's country, folky, bluesy, but mostly the heartfelt lyrics being sung to be listened to and not just a catchy phrase to be played and heard by the masses on 'the man's' radio stations," said musician Patrick D. Winsett, of the Foolish Pride Band.

"Its music that rattles you with a perfect blend of several genres, based on strong songwriting, clever yet basic instrumentation, and is very approachable as it is music for the everyday man or woman and often tells relatable stories," described music lover Drew Watson.

"Its music made by kids that grew up listening to Merle Haggard and Metallica. Kids that went their own way. It has a unique feel. It's not Texas country, it's damn sure not Nashville. It is what happens when you put old school country, rock, blues, folk and whiskey into a blender," said Trigger Latimer, who has worked with many bands in the scene.

Chad Sullins and The Last Call Coalition would always say "We're a rock band that plays country music. We're too rock to be country and too country to be rock," during their shows. That sums it up well. However, this is just scratching the surface of the dirt.

Once upon a time, the term Red Dirt was created to give name to a group of Oklahoman musicians who didn't really fit in anywhere else; a name for bands who did their own thing without care for the "rules" of the big music game- commonly found in the Nashville area. While these musicians were far from being the first to blend different sounds and styles, they still used that model to create their own niche. Outlaw country was breaking the rules of Nashville around the same time the Red Dirt genesis was being formed, and western swing mixed genres before that. If you look back at the history of any music genre and scene, you can find those who decided to layer the sounds and styles to create something entirely new. Red Dirt music is just one of many that was formed in this way.

In the popular podcast Cocaine and Rhinestones, which breaks down the history of country music in the nineteenth century, Tyler Mahan Coe said this about genres that borrowed from one another, when describing music by Rusty and Doug Kershaw.

"Now I've talked a lot about western swing this season, so you may hear that and think it's just western swing with Cajun-French vocals. It's not really that simple. Because western swing is just what happened when country musicians played swing jazz, and jazz was practically invented in New Orleans. So, what you've got is Texas and Oklahoma borrowing a cup of flour from Louisiana, and Louisiana borrowing a cup of sugar from Texas and Oklahoma. It's all neighborly." – (CR013- Rusty & Doug Kershaw: The Cajun Way)

That sentiment sums it up quite nicely about how genres tend to blend and borrow, and the creation of the Red Dirt scene was no different in this aspect. But although Red Dirt may have been used to describe a certain sound and style of music at one point, the term is loosely used not to describe a musical sound, but instead to describe a community and philosophy of like-minded musicians who create music from their soul. In simplistic terms, it is a regional musical moniker for those who hail from the land of the red dirt, who play music that doesn't quite fit into any other category, using lyrics that are genuine and heart-felt. Red Dirt musicians focused on the song above all else.

There are artists who are performers, who focus on flashy stage presence, costumes, fancy lights and more to convey their art and talents. Then there are artists who are singer/songwriters, who focus on the music alone to carry their art. Red Dirt artists are primarily singer/songwriters, not performers. While there is nothing wrong with performers and how they do things, there is a distinct difference in how they put on a show. Dolly Parton probably started out more as a singer/songwriter but now is a performer, and everyone knows how brilliant she is. So, this is not to say there is anything wrong with being a performer versus a singer/songwriter in the philosophy of music and live entertainment. They are just different parts of the same game. There are even some in the music world that manage to combine both philosophies and pull it off well. Which is the whole point of art; to express yours in the way that makes the most sense for you, regardless of what anyone else is doing.

To really understand something, you have to go back and look at the roots and where it all began. The history of the Red Dirt music scene spans several decades and is full of people and places. Unfortunately, at this time it carries on mostly as just an oral history from the people who were around at the time. Sadly, some of those people are no longer around with us, but thankfully the people that still are share the stories and carry on the Red Dirt legacy. This book is a collection of their stories and a way to honor that legacy.

The sounds and songs of the first Red Dirt pioneers were folksy and bluesy, a tinge of rock and a tinge of country. They were mixing up genres in a way that made sense to them and their love of different musical influences. This set the foundation for the large Red Dirt umbrella it became, where so many people fit into yet may not sound anything alike. Red Dirt became a melting pot of genres, a way to synthesize all the different musical tastes that they all had at the time. It was a way to stretch and grow and try new things. More importantly, Red Dirt is a culture based on community, collaboration and staying true to yourself. This book is just a snapshot of where it all began.

Stillwater: The Genesis

Many people wrongly believe that Red Dirt music started in the '90s, when names like The Great Divide and Cross Canadian Ragweed made it more popular, but really the foundation for it all started twenty years before that. The birth of the Red Dirt music scene started in the '70s in Stillwater, Oklahoma, which was known to be a loud and raucous college party town. The most popular place in town seems to be on 'The Strip', four blocks located on Washington Ave. between University and Sixth St. The Strip features bars, restaurants and other establishments, and is within walking distance from the OSU college campus. Stillwater was even home to what was known as "Streak night", which started in 1974 and lasted about a decade. The Thursday before Spring break became known as the designated date. T-shirts were made, and people came out in droves to see who would tear off their clothes.

Daring young people could be found running naked down the Strip, many of them finding themselves arrested for the adventure. This perfectly encompassed the free for all, let it loose, party vibe of the town during this time. This tradition continued for several years into the late 70's and early 80's. While the local police tried to get these shenanigans to stop, it took several years before they were successful. Part of that plan included changing the legal drinking age from 18 to 21 in 1984 and creating a law to make it illegal to carry beer on the street. While these laws certainly made it harder for the party crowds, it didn't entirely stop them all.

Not only were there streaker nights, but locals also made a tradition of stealing the giant bull that was displayed outside of the Sirloin Stockade on the strip. A few brave, and probably drunken, souls would break the chains holding the bull, which was on a trailer. They would then ride it down Washington St., sometimes in the nude. Many times, it ended up in Theta Pond on campus and would have to be fished out. This was the environment and culture that pervaded when Red Dirt music formed its genesis.

There were a few musicians on the scene by the early '70s, but most of the pioneers of the movement found their way there by the end of the '70s and '80s. Within that short time, a whole tribe of like-minded musicians happened to be in the right place at the right time to create what is known as Red Dirt music today. Somehow, they all managed to find one another, like the gravitational pull of planets to a star. They came to Stillwater and discovered they had found their tribe of people, and together they paved a path that has rippled out and grown through time.

Steve Ripley, who was born in Idaho but grew up in Oklahoma, was a part of one of the first bands to use the term Red Dirt when his band Moses put out a self-titled album and named their label Red Dirt Records in 1974. Printed on that album it says, "Red dirt is a hue of funk, a shade of sound, a basic spirit embodied in music." Thus, giving us our first definition of Red Dirt, which has held true through the years. It's widely commented that the Red Dirt music scene isn't about the sounds or styles created by the musicians- it's about the spirit of the music and the music family they are connected to. It's about their Okie roots and the soul; dirt and spirit.

Steve Ripley was most likely one of the first ones onto what would become the Red Dirt scene, although it would take almost two decades before the scene was labeled and recognized. Ripley wore many hats over his long career. He wasn't just a founding member of the Red Dirt movement, but as a musician he had a huge influence on those that came after him. Ripley was not only a songwriter, but also a record producer, studio engineer, guitarist and an inventor during his lifetime. He is a legend among Oklahoma musicians and did more in his career than most people can hope for. Ripley grew up in Pawnee County and started playing in bands in junior high and continued to do so all the way through college. He graduated from Oklahoma State University with a communications degree. Ripley recorded with his band at the Hi Fi studio in Oklahoma City, owned by Gene Sullivan, in the '60s. This was the same studio where Oklahoma legends J.J Cale and Leon Russell had made some of their first recordings as well.

Steve Irby was also a musician in the area, and a member of Moses with Ripley. Irby learned to play piano from his mother and grandmother as a child, progressing to taking lessons in the second grade up until his freshman year of high school. It was then he transitioned into playing keys in rock and roll bands. Irby was a freshman in 1964, the same year The Beatles did their US tour, which started a fever in young people who wanted to play music. In 1965, Irby and some friends started a garage band called The Innkeepers. "The first band was called the Innkeepers. There was a song out called, the In Crowd. Like I'm with the in crowd. I go where the in crowd goes. So, we were the Innkeepers, you know, we were cool. So that was the name, but also the Holiday Inn, their motto was 'we are the Nation's Innkeepers'. So, our kind of mascot on our business cards was the little fat man holding the key, as the innkeeper. A little goofy but we thought it was kinda cool," said Irby.

In about 1967, the Innkeepers' bass player moved, and the band was left looking for a replacement. Through a friend of a friend, they were referred to Steve Ripley, who lived in Glencoe, which is a small town near Stillwater. They asked Ripley to come over and audition, and he brought a bass and a bass stand that probably had been borrowed from the music store in town. "We practiced and boy, he was really good. We were really impressed. We said, yeah, we want you in the band. Kind of interesting story years later- I mean, like 30 years later- I was talking to Steve. I was going, man, we were so impressed with you when you came over that day to play. He said, yeah, I'd never played bass before. Said, I was actually playing lead on the bass. That's why he was so fast. He never played bass. But we were impressed, we didn't know the difference and he was really fast. We just thought, oh, my gosh, this guy's awesome," said Irby.

Not long after that audition Ripley transitioned to playing guitar and singing, and Irby started playing keyboard bass. At that time, they called it Steve Ripley and the Innkeepers. They were all still in high school and this continued throughout their high school years and into college. "I quit playing in the band for about a year in college. I was not doing well in college. Then when we kind of reformed, we came up with the name Moses. Just sitting around trying to think of names and somebody said Moses. We all thought, well, that sounds kind of cool. No religious affiliation actually, it was just a cool name. We had a business card that had a kind of a picture of this white-haired man with a long white beard holding up his hand, like Moses or something. And that was the band," said Irby.

Moses originally included Steve Ripley, Steve Irby, Dow Simank on drums, and Robert Hatfield on bass. Later when Simank went to law school, Bruce Houston, who had been in another band called Toad, joined Moses as the drummer.

Moses Promo. Photo provided by Steve Irby

Moses played fraternity parties on campus, high school proms, and other local events. Ripley quickly began befriending the DJs at the radio stations KOMA and WKY to form connections and help the band. That led to the band being invited to play teen sock hops with Danny Williams and Ronnie Kay, DJs out of Oklahoma City. Moses played teen sock hops all over the state, as well as a few in Kansas and Texas. They made their way into clubs like the Town House and The Late Show as the house band. Soon they had a regular gig at a ski resort in Vale, Colorado where they would play at least twice a year for a couple of weeks at a time throughout the late 60's and early 70's. They were invited to play on The Scene, a dance television show, out of Oklahoma City with Ronnie Kay.

"It was kind of like American Bandstand, but it was local. We would record, and it was lip synced. We would go into the studio in Oklahoma City, the Sullivan studio, and record our songs. Then we would be on The Scene and play our songs. I'm not sure we played any original songs. They were pretty much covers of popular songs. We did that, played on that show a number of times. We also played on another show called Danny's Day, which is a kind of a noon time talk show. Danny Williams was a DJ out of WKY. We played on his show several times and it was more sedate; it wasn't like a dance show. But that was fun. We were still in high school when we did that," said Irby.

While Moses was the first band on the scene that eventually paved the way for the Red Dirt movement to form, there were others like Gene Collier- who penned what would later become a Red Dirt Anthem, *Boys from*

Oklahoma- who were playing small gigs around Stillwater as early as 1968. Collier would play anywhere that he could, sometimes little gigs around town, and sometimes just sitting around a campfire somewhere picking out songs with others. Collier, like many of the early singer-songwriters, just loved to play and played more to entertain himself than anything else. "I never did get really good, I just liked to play. I just play for myself, just write a song or work on something, that's how I wind down for the evening," explained Collier.

Collier had a rock and roll band by the age of 16 in the '60s called The Lords of London. They played gigs from the Civic Center in Tulsa for large crowds, to small sock hops all over the state for much smaller crowds.

Gene Collier. Photo provided by Craig Skinner

"I bet I've played around a million campfires and with everybody in this state that was playing back then. I played with them somewhere sometime. It was just a great experience and wonderful stuff," said Collier. Collier got high for the first time the day they put a man on the moon in 1969 while he was still in high school. It would be a few years later that Collier wrote the song *"Boys from Oklahoma"* in 1972. He had made his way to a party over in Nella Valley Arkansas, way off the beaten path near Mina, Arkansas. He recalled having to be led into the party for nine miles just to find it and having to be led out again afterwards. It was a weekend-long shing-dig, where Collier saw the wildest, craziest people he had ever seen at this point in his young life. "Hillbillies coming out of the woodworks and partying", was how he described it.

"We were trying to roll out a joint and I kept turning them out like- they just wouldn't hold together- and that's where that line comes from. I was just so embarrassed writing that song, it was like it was the stupidest song in the world. I sat on it for 20 years, from the '70s to the '90s," said Collier. Little did he know at the time that the song he felt embarrassed for writing would become an anthem for the Red Dirt scene for the next generation, over 20 years later.

Another hidden Okie treasure is Rick Reiley, who befriended Collier in 1968 and created a lasting friendship. Collier had spent the day in Stillwater and was hitchhiking back home. He found himself about 5 miles east of Stillwater on Highway 51 with his thumb in the air when he noticed a 1950 Chevy zigzagging and doing about 70 mph coming down the road. The driver hit the brakes, barely missing hitting Collier. He then slid off through the ditch and back up on to the top of the field, hitting about 12 fenceposts along the way. Then he went right back onto the highway about 80 yards ahead. Collier immediately thought. "oh crap, I don't know if I'll get in with him". However, despite his initial hesitation, Collier walked up to the car. He introduced himself to Rick Reiley and his friend and graciously accepted the ride. That began a lifelong friendship that involved playing together for decades. "We'd just play every chance that we got, and I just love that guy like he's my brother. I'd do anything for him, he's just that good of a friend of mine. We have a lot of memories, we've played around many a campfire, good times," said Collier about Reiley.

Reiley had started playing guitar at the age of 12, took a year of lessons, and decided it was beyond his scope and gave up. In 1970, his drummer friend Mike Holloway invited him to come listen to his new band practice. Reiley was excited about it and showed up to hear them. They had a drummer, a bass player, two guitar players but no one was singing. Reiley asked who was singing, and Holloway threw him a microphone and said- you are. While they couldn't quite agree on a name that they liked, they agreed on one they didn't quite like and called themselves the Handsome Rabbits. The band played a few fraternity dances in Stillwater, and Reiley decided it was time to pick the guitar back up. He formed a band around that time with Collier who played rhythm guitar, and Reiley started writing songs. He had always been somewhat of a writer from an early age, mostly poetry, so it was a seamless transition into songwriting. "My first experience in Stillwater with homegrown music came in 1968 at the Saturday night coffee house held in the basement at the old Wesleyan Center. My friend, and Cushing High School graduate, Hal Greenwood performed there along with another guy named Barry -who looked and sounded like Art Garfunkel. Wild hair. He wielded his Gibson guitar like a magic wand. I could close my eyes and feel like I was in Greenwich Village with the folk masters of my generation. It was an eye-opening experience and made me realize the magic of music can happen anywhere," said Reiley.

Chuck Dunlap is one of the next earliest pioneers of the Red Dirt music scene in Stillwater. He was also one of the first of the Stillwater singer/songwriters to hit the ground running, creating a path for others to follow along. Dunlap came to Stillwater in 1972 and was playing the coffeehouse circuit at the time. He had been playing music for years already at that point, and by the time he got to Stillwater was doing more folk music than anything else. As soon as he got to Stillwater, he also began hitting up Oklahoma City and Tulsa to find little coffeehouses to play. At that time in Stillwater there weren't many places that had just acoustic music. There were clubs and bars that hosted bands, mostly dance bands, but he had a hard time finding coffeehouses that featured acoustic music. Dunlap eventually found a guy named Greg who owned a little restaurant called the Venusberg on the strip and asked if he had ever thought about having music in his place. Greg thought it sounded like a good idea and offered to pay Dunlap $25 to come play a half hour set during the dinner hour. Dunlap said that was perfect because that's about how many songs he had anyway. They got it set up and Dunlap played the half hour dinner set for about a month when other business owners on the strip saw what Greg was doing with just a little bit of acoustic music. The idea spread and soon several other places started having acoustic music too. It quickly caught on, and soon many musicians like Dunlap, folk musicians who played a blend of everything, began having more places to play. They knew the chords to play, which were everything from country tunes to whatever rock and roll they could play on an acoustic guitar, to whatever they had written themselves. That was Dunlap's first experience with acoustic music in Stillwater.

The early music scene was just starting to get some traction at this time. Steve Ripley opened his own studio there, Stillwater Sound Studio, in 1973. Ripley and his band Moses were a big deal in town, and many people would come out to watch them play. Ripley befriended many Tulsa musicians and created a link between Tulsa and Stillwater with his studio. The musical atmosphere of Stillwater in the early 70's not only included Steve Ripley with his band Moses playing around town, but also a big band with a horn section called Harlem Riot, which was one of the biggest draws in town. There were a handful of other local bands holding their own as well, that were in college in Stillwater, as Dunlap remembers. "I imagine that was their draw to be there and together. There were quite a few of those that came and went and migrated. People would graduate and leave town, and other players would step in because they didn't want to break up the band. That had a lot to do with the ability of the musicians to flow with what was happening and not really take it personal when somebody left or somebody new joined- because we just played with whoever was available. They knew someday down the road they might need to play with them again. Everyone was about keeping it friendly," said Dunlap.

Chuck Dunlap 1978 - photo provided by Chuck Dunlap

The college of course was a major influence on the music scene, constantly providing local venues and bars with a steady stream of young people who wanted entertainment, as well as new talent who attended the college themselves.

In Their Own Words

Gene Collier - Well I got involved really early, in 1956, I think. My mom got my dad a Gibson les Paul electric guitar, and boy I mean I wanted to play it instantly. My dad he wasn't going to let his boys play it too much, ya know? Of course, we didn't have electricity so to play an electric guitar without it is a pretty quiet thing to do. Finally, after about 3-4 years- I was probably about 8-9- he finally let us start playing his guitar. He was a really great player. I had a cousin who had gotten a guitar and started playing and when we come up to Oklahoma and see him- we lived way out in the desert in west Texas when I was a little kid. I started playing right then, the minute he (dad) turned loose of that guitar and let us boys start playing. He would sit around in his underwear with his boots sticking out and a cowboy hat just playing El Paso or some of those old songs, and my grandma would always send us records. Of course, we didn't have any electricity so to play the records we had a little bitty record player that we would spin with our fingers and then get really close. I still got all those old records too, Johnny Horton stuff, I mean way back there, Cheb Woodly and Purple People Eater type music. So, I got to hear it, but I didn't get to hear it with very much volume. All the guys in the desert - we had a few of them that had electric- on the days that Johnny Cash would come out with a new song, we would all go get in the back of the pickup and go to Wayne Murphy's house because he had electric. We would set the amplifier out and all the men- my dad and all his friends- would sit around and work on that new tune. I remember Folsom Prison Blues the day it came out, us boys would wrestle and have fun. By having that spark to play by the time I was 10, I was trying to teach myself something. My first song I played on the guitar was Ghostriders in the Sky. My guitar by that time- they had finally gotten me an acoustic guitar- it had one string on it. I would learn how to play all a song on one string. Top to bottom, it was a pretty violent workout to get all of that on it. We played and we kids got into rock and roll about the time The Beatles had been out about two years. I was probably about 12-13. By the time I was 15-16 we had our own rock and roll band and boy we had a really great lead electric guitarist named Dave Ferguson. We got us some Beatle boots and Beatle coats and looked like the Beatles, ya know? But not really. We didn't sound like them, but we played rock and roll for the longest time. The insurance group, the Lloyds of London, they insure very wealthy people's stuff, so we called ourselves the Lords of London. We played all over the place. We played over at the Civic Center in Tulsa in front of big crowds and then all the sock hops and things. I probably played in- I want to say 1968- doing gigs in Stillwater, little bitty tiny things where you could sit and play a little bit. But that was pretty much where I come from, the beginnings of it all.

Chuck Dunlap: When one person takes their guitar and has the guts to step in front of people and play a song that they have written, no matter how shakily they may do it- that's the musical essence of what red dirt music is right there. It's just having the guts to do it that first time. After that it gets easier and you get everything else that comes into it; the crowd you are playing to, the enjoyment of getting to experience it yourself, getting better as a musician, learning chords and playing with people and all of that comes after you step out for the first time. On a porch, or wherever it is; just singing a part, singing the harmony or just beating on a block or whatever. But to include yourself in this thing we call music- that is like nothing else. It touches you like words can't, visions can't. Music reaches into you and gets you on some kind of vibrational level, man, that you can't ever reproduce with anything else.

Early Contributors

It was around this time that Rick Reiley, Steve Ackley and Mac Bolerjack had a trio that they called the Bread and Water band, because they couldn't think of a better name. They had guitar, harmonica, and the bass player also played mandolin. Reiley said it was an odd combo, but they played on the strip in Stillwater all the same. He recalled that they played at Wet Willie's, Wild Willy's, Bill's Italian restaurant, The Family Dog, and Spavs. The high point of their playing days was performing at the Mid Ark Rock Festival in Benton Arkansas in 1975. The headliners were the Nitty Gritty Dirt Band and a group called Zorro and the Blue Footballs. "We had no idea what we were doing but Mac got us the gig. We were the opening act on Sunday morning. Long after the main acts had done their magic and moved on down the road. There we were, waking up hundreds of hungover, spaced-out campers wondering what planet they were on. I broke a big E string on my D35 on the downstroke. But we managed to finish our set without being massacred. Fun times," said Reiley.

The band found out quickly that they had some major competition when it came to booking gigs. "We did an audition at Spavs, that used to be a place once north of Stillwater. We were terrible, but anyhow we would play a lot over there. Was probably just one summer and one fall. We went in one night to hear Chuck Dunlap, see what the competition was we were up against. I hated Chuck Dunlap. He was tall and handsome, very talented, had a great PA system and he could do a whole show by himself. He didn't need two other guys hanging out. We used to approach bars, and they would say, 'what can you do that Chuck Dunlap doesn't do?' We would say 'what do you mean?' They would say 'Well he's a one-man show. He can come in and is good looking and all the women show up. Then all the men show up for the women and we all have a wonderful time, and we make a lot of money. Can you do that?' and we said 'No, no we can't do that. but but but....'" said Reiley with a good-natured laugh.

Reiley's adventure took him away from Stillwater for a time. Like most musicians, he decided he needed to be in Nashville to make anything of value happen with his career, however that decision led him to Seattle instead. "That's always been my mode of operation- whatever seems logical, do directly the opposite of it- for some reason. Bolerjack, our harmonica player, had gone to Los Angeles and had some contacts with RCA up there. So, Ackley and I followed him out there in our yellow panel truck and we were going to do an interview with RCA. We got out there and it turns out Bolerjack really was just blowing smoke. I think he really just met the janitor at RCA, and she was going to let us in to look at the cigarette machine or something. We spent the night in St. Louis, on Bisbell Street and played out there on the street, had a great time out there," said Reiley. Somehow Ackley and Reiley then decided that they would drive to Seattle, and that's where their money ran out. They ended up spending the winter there. They played on the street corner, and they played at the Pike Place market during the fall and winter, made a few dollars a day as a street musician. It cost one dollar to get a street permit there at the time.

After some time, they made their way back home. "In 1973 I did some recording at Leon Russell's Shelter studio in Tulsa, and they offered me a six-year writing and recording contract that I did not sign. Then when

I decided I should sign it, they said never mind, we're going in a different direction. That was when the Gap Band, Phoebe Snow, and Willis Ellen Ramsey, they were in that catalog at the time. Anyhow it wasn't too long after that they folded up shop and Shelter went out of business. That was kind of my brush with the big time, but it was very fortunate that it didn't happen because I wasn't writing anything then that anybody would want to hear. I could do verse after verse after verse in A minor, the oh woe pitiful me shit, which sometimes it works and sometimes you better just shut up until you really have something to say," said Reiley.

While Red Dirt was nowhere near an official genre at this time, it wouldn't be what it is today without these guys paving the way and laying the foundation. Another pivotal moment happened when the first official Walnut Valley Festival was held in Winfield, Kansas in 1972. It's mostly just referred to as Winfield with everyone who attends the festival. Founded by Stuart Mossman, Joe Muret and Bob Redford, it started as a two-day flat-picking contest. While this festival was of a Bluegrass nature, it would serve as a meeting ground for many of the aspiring Red Dirt artists that began to carve out the genre. Many of them started out attending the festival and meeting others who had the same passion and motivation to create genuine and heartfelt music on their own terms.

Byron Berline, while a Bluegrass legend and not a Red Dirt one, was also important to the Oklahoma music scene and played a large part in teaching, mentoring, and inspiring those that would later be prominent members of the Red Dirt scene. Berline was born in Kansas in 1944 and started playing fiddle by the age of five. He won the National Old time Fiddlers' Contest Championship in Idaho in 1965, 1967 and 1970. He graduated from OU in 1967 with a teaching degree and joined the Bluegrass Boys band the same year. He had to leave the band later that year when he was drafted into the Army. When he returned in 1969, he joined Dillard & Clark before moving to California. Berline was asked to record on the Rolling Stone's song *Honky Tonk Women*, which launched his career. He joined The Flying Burrito Brothers in 1971, which was a band heavily mentioned as being inspirational to the forming Red Dirt Movement.

Of course, Tulsa legends like JJ Cale and Leon Russell heavily influenced and inspired the musicians of this time as well. As well as drummer Jimmy Karstein, who toured and recorded with musicians such as JJ Cale and Gary Lewis and the Playboys. From Tulsa, Karstein moved to California in the '50s and '60s and worked with names like Eric Clapton, Joe Cocker and the Everly Brothers. He would eventually make his way back to Tulsa and join up with some of the Red Dirt artists later in his career. He was a hero and legend among the Oklahoma crowd.

Another Tulsa musician who was involved in that scene at this time was David Teegarden Sr. who played drums with a variety of musicians including JJ Cale and Leon Russell. He opened a studio near the Church Studio in Tulsa, but his career would take him to LA and Detroit before coming back to Tulsa. He has had a very successful music career in his own right. Later down the line, it would be his son, also named David Teegarden, also a drummer, who would enter the world of Red Dirt.

Even though Stillwater gets credit as the birthplace for Red Dirt music, rightfully so, there were still other areas and musicians who were starting around the same time in different places that would converge and join the Red Dirt movement and are just as important to the whole picture. Not everyone who became a part of the Red Dirt scene came from or started their music careers in Stillwater but would still find themselves there helping to weave the fabric together to create the Red Dirt roots. One of these early pioneers was Terry "Buffalo" Ware, who had started playing music in high school in the '60s in Norman, Oklahoma. While Ware's musical career doesn't start in the Red Dirt scene, later in life he does become an integral part of it all. After graduating college in 1972, he moved from Oklahoma to Red River, New Mexico where he was playing with Bill and Bonnie Hearn, who were icons in the Texas Music scene. He met Ray Wylie Hubbard there in a band called Three Faces West, which was considered a central folk group in Texas at the time. There was a little coffee house in Red River where Three Faces West played every summer, staying there for the season then traveling on and playing elsewhere in the fall and winter months. When Ware came upon them in Red River, two of the Three Faces West band members had just decided they no longer wanted to travel and instead wanted to stay in Red River, and Hubbard was going to go out on his own. That's when Ware decided to join him.

Ware and Hubbard began traveling around as a duo, playing many Midwest states but also a lot in Texas. They were traveling so much, they were rarely ever in Red River, so in 1973 Hubbard decided to move back to Dallas. Ware didn't have any interest in moving to Dallas, so he came back to Norman as his homebase, but continued to travel to play with Hubbard. "I didn't play in Oklahoma that often. I mean, when I was with Ray in the '70s. We'd play Cain's Ballroom, and a great place called the Prairie Lady in Oklahoma City that we used to play. They had people like Emmy Lou Harris, just all sorts of folks. And so that was my Oklahoma experience back then, was kind of coming in as a touring musician even though I lived here," said Ware. At that time, the backing band for Hubbard was called the Cowboy Twinkies, and the entire band besides Hubbard was from Norman, Oklahoma. Ware continued to play in that band until 1979. He then formed a band called the Sensational Shoes which played locally out of Norman, playing the occasional gig with Hubbard when he would call and ask him to.

Randy Crouch is also a well-known Red Dirt icon that got his start outside of Stillwater. Crouch is known as the world's best rock fiddler, among other things. His unique fiddle playing can be attributed to the fact that he learned how to play the instrument using a mandolin instruction guide, tailoring it to the fiddle. This resulted in him being a bit of a fiddle wizard. However, that's not all he plays and does. While Crouch might be best known for his distinctive fiddle playing, he also is a guitarist and plays electric, acoustic, pedal steel and dobro. He also plays piano, keyboards, banjo and mandolin. Crouch likes to experiment with different instruments and their sounds, such as using his harmonica like a synthesizer. In addition to his instrumental wizardry, he's also an incredible blues singer and highly prolific songwriter. Crouch enjoys testing the boundaries of sounds, styles and songwriting topics. He has even created a country rock opera about aliens coming to catch flying horses, which is also how he got the name of his band. He's a mystical wizard, a musical guru, a modern-day hippie.

"I think the first time I saw Randy, he was playing with his Flying Horse Opera band, and this must have been 73-74. I look up across this crowd of people and I see this guy on stage and he's grabbing the mic stand and he's playing slide guitar with the mic stand. That got my attention. Then I worked my way closer. I gotta kinda see what this guy is doing. By that time, they are doing another song and he's playing pedal steel. He grabs his folding chair, and he gets it up on his strings. Playing pedal steel with a folding chair, and that was my introduction to Randy. He was a mystic spirit that didn't even have a box to think out of. He lived outside of everybody else's box," said Chuck Dunlap in a Red Dirt Nation interview (Youtube : *Chuck Dunlap: Meeting Randy Crouch for the first time*, Red Dirt Nation).

Crouch was born on April 1st 1952 in Dallas, Texas and moved around West Texas during his youth. His father, Hurbert Crouch, was a Methodist preacher and moved the family from town to town every few years as he moved to different churches. Crouch credits his family with his musical upbringing, giving him a solid musical foundation with piano lessons, followed by picking up the ukulele and then a guitar. He said when he started learning how to play guitar and sing that Woody Guthrie was his hero, and someone he aspired to be like. Crouch's grandfather played the fiddle, which had a big influence on him as well. "We always had music in our family. Grandad was a fiddle player. The first thing I ever picked up was a ukulele, those are fun to play. I advise everyone to play one. I think playing the ukulele was what got me hooked. There was always music in our town when we got together, that was my education. Rock and roll," said Crouch.

Crouch joined a band as a freshman in high school in Canadian, Texas where the family moved in 1962. They then moved to Crosbyton, Texas where Randy finished high school. Crouch first came to Oklahoma to attend Oral Roberts University but later transferred to the University of Tulsa before dropping out and hitchhiking to Boulder, Colorado, to "learn everything that you can't learn in school." Crouch returned to Oklahoma, where he got plugged into the music scene and helped plow the way in the Red Dirt movement being formed at the time. Crouch got turned onto bluegrass music when he attended the very first Winfield Festival in 1972, which is when he decided to learn how to play the fiddle, using a mandolin teaching guide.

Kevin Warren Smith and Randy Crouch. Photo provided by Kevin Warren Smith.

Crouch has always had a bit of spunk and fire in him, using his music much in the way Woody Guthrie did; to highlight social injustice and to spark reform. Crouch likes to refer to his songs as "Oklahoma protest music". He spent a large chunk of his youth and musical career protesting for the environment. In 1973, when the Public Service Company of Oklahoma announced they would be building twin black nuclear power plants, named Black Fox 1 and 2- Crouch and many other Oklahomans took action, and a protest movement began. Crouch performed over 50 'Stop Black Fox" events around Oklahoma. He was blackballed by music promoters in and around the Tulsa area for a time period after his involvement in the protests.

"I decided pretty early on that I wanted to rock and roll. It's a challenge. There's never been a better time to rock and roll, the world needs it. I call any kind of good music rock and roll. I'm not very good at putting a boundary on it. I've tried to get better over the years. I've tried to play songs that wanted to say something. It does seem like I had better things to say when I wasn't trying to say anything. I said it better when I wasn't trying too hard. I try to keep a song in my head until it comes out or it doesn't. I would have gone to school for a rock and roll degree if they would have made one," said Crouch.

In 1973 Crouch moved to a former landfill site on 80 acres in Tahlequah, in an electricity-free geodesic dome that he built. He and his wife Liz have lived there, mostly off the grid, ever since. They got by through the electricity free years using a car battery, a propane refrigerator, a generator, and wood burning stoves for heat. Crouch has always believed in and brought attention to environmental concerns through his music and his lifestyle. He didn't just talk the talk, he walked the walk as well.

Jim Downing who was from Tulsa, would come to Stillwater when he was still in High school in the late '60s. His band would play fraternity parties. "I don't know if they really had their own scene going at that time because a lot of the Tulsa bands would go over there and play for the college kids. Tulsa was a hotbed of musical activity. It always has been, no one seems to be able to explain why," said Downing. He met Randy Crouch in about 1970. There was a place in downtown Tulsa called Living Arts, where the Performing Arts center would later be. It was an old furniture store, and one of the professors from Tulsa University, Chuck Tomlin, made a deal with the city to rent the building for a dollar a year because it was slated for demolition and urban renewal. Tomlin allowed artists to come in and build their own studios in the three-story building. People divided it up into individual spaces. Artists of all media could build their own enclosures within the building, which was two stories and had a full basement. There were many sculptors and painters and a couple of music studios. The front portion on the ground floor had an area open to the roof, with a balcony on the second floor. A stage was built in the corner, and several concerts were put on there. That's where Downing first met Crouch.

Not long after Downing met Crouch, Downing went on his own hitchhiking adventure. His plan was to go to Canada and hitchhike across Canada to Maine where a friend of his was working at the time in an amusement park. Downing planned to get a summer job there as well. He hitchhiked up to Boulder- which at that time hitchhiking was illegal in Colorado. Once Downing was in Boulder, he had to use a message board- a public bulletin board- to find a ride going west. He found some people that were headed west out of Boulder on a Sunday morning, so he headed to their house. He had been camping up in the hills in the mountains west of Boulder up until then. At about six o'clock that Sunday morning Downing was walking down the main north/south street of Boulder, when he saw a figure walking down the street towards him in a blue jean jacket with long hair. When they got about a hundred feet apart, Downing recognized the figure and said, "Crouch?" And Crouch responding, "Downing?"

"We were the only two people on the street in Boulder at six o'clock on a Sunday morning and happened to bump into each other. You know, those things have happened to me many times, running into people I know in the strangest places," recalled Downing. There are many stories like this one found in Red Dirt history- people coming across one another who just happened to be at the right place at the right time. There seemed to be synchronicity in the way the musicians and music scene came together.

In Their Own Words

Chuck Dunlap- I would say Red Dirt music is what we play on the back porch after we've finished with our gigs, and we still have a little fire in us and are not quite ready to go to bed yet. We've all been in different bands from jazz bands to acoustic acts and it doesn't matter, we all play what we can play. It's really what Red Dirt music is, right there. If you are able to take that and transfer it onto the stage, then you have hit something and that's really success in the Red Dirt music scene- I would think. If you can take that back porch feeling that doesn't sound polished but still sounds professional. Because it's made by professional musicians, and that's how they do it. There's no practice involved usually, it's just the way it comes out of us- that's Red Dirt music. The Red Dirt scene is a whole different thing, that is much broader and involves people who aren't musicians, who love the music or the rebellious lifestyle. They like that feeling of it, and they tend to lean towards that end instead of somewhere else.

Terry Ware - There's another great Oklahoma songwriter, Roger Tillson, he was a great songwriter. He and Steve (Ripley) were good friends. I actually met Roger whenever I was in college here. He was living in Norman at the time, just a great songwriter himself. I'm sure it's different now, but we really didn't learn about Woody Guthrie growing up in my era, out where I live. I really didn't start knowing about Woody Guthrie until Bob Dylan came along, you know? And I got into Bob Dylan in high school. Roger Tillson had an album that came out in 1971. It had *The Old Cracked Looking Glass* on it- a Woody Guthrie song. That's the first time I can remember hearing a Woody Guthrie song, recorded by somebody else. Roger kind of gets glossed over sometime or people don't know about him, you know, because he wasn't like a big, big star or anything. There are probably others. One of my main guitar influences of all times is Jesse Ed

Davis. He was from Norman. By the time I got here in 1969 he was already out with Taj Mahal. His playing on those Taj Mahal albums was just really- it formed the way I play a lot. I always try to get him in there as well.

Gene Collier - I was living in west Texas, and I was probably about in the first grade. This was back in a time- times were different- and you weren't afraid to do stupid things, ya know? Mom's only rule was to be home by dark. This must have been in about April or May because our feet hadn't toughened up yet. Mike Williams and I, one of my buddies, we decided to hitchhike. A Mexican guy picked us up, and we got in the back of his pickup. About 20 miles down the road we were thinking we better get out. We're getting a long ways from home, and it was about ten in the morning probably. It got real hot in that part of Texas, which is desert area. They had part of the Pecos River tributary. It was a canal that went for 80 miles or better and it was just 30 feet wide and three foot deep and just flowing fast and just cold water. About every five miles they had a little dam and lock like a little road where they could regulate how much water flowed, but they always had it wide open. We decided to skinny dip like all young little boys do and we got in the water and started swimming with the current and left our clothes in a pile. A flock of birds landed on the water, water birds. We as little boys, well what are you going to do? We was going to swim underwater and catch them by the legs, right? So, we chased those birds from about ten in the morning until two in the afternoon, doing about six miles an hour probably, down that current. We turned around and thought oh man, we gotta get back to our clothes. It was already really hot, and we started trying to swim against the current and we're thinking, oh we really screwed up. So, we started to try to run. Of course, two naked boys running- your feet get hot, and we would have to jump in the water. That part of Texas, in Pecos Valley, they grow cantaloupes. That was just the best in the world if you've ever had Pecos Valley cantaloupes. And the Mexican migrants would come in and work the field. In the morning when we got going, they were way out in the fields, and this was their watering hole. That was where they would bring a tin cup, and they would get a drink. When it started getting hot, they started working this side of the field, and this was about 12 miles of fields. So, we had to run back, trying to cover up as best we could- but you can't really run and cover up. We were running and we heard 'loco gringo ninos' about 80 times. We just had to run by them, because they were out there getting water, and we were just splashing on by. We were like sorry, but we gotta get back to our clothes. And they take a siesta about two or so, and during the siesta period a couple of the guys were playing guitars. They were just two guys playing Mexican music, and we had run by them. We got back to our clothes. We were at least 12 miles away from our clothes, and our feet were just burnt to a crisp. We got back about 30 minutes before dark, got our clothes on and hit the road. Got another ride, and they let us out just down the road from where we lived. I got in the house just before dark and mom says "what did you do today?" I says "oh me and Mike went for a walk and a swim". She said "well go in there and eat". The streaking mariachi band.

Coming Together

It didn't take very long before more people started filtering into the scene. Jeff Parker- someone who helped greatly further the Red Dirt scene for the next generation- started out in Norman, Oklahoma where he attended high school in the '70s. He spent much of his youth sneaking into clubs he wasn't old enough to get into, many times watching Randy Crouch and his band The Flying Horse, which he described as psychedelic country. "Randy is a great guitar player, and he had electronic effects that he would hook up to his fiddle. He would run a guitar wah-wah peddle on his fiddle with guitar effects and it's just this wild psychedelic fiddle sound. I've never heard anything like it. It was just really, psychedelic country. That's the only thing I could think of to describe it. It was like rock and roll and it was back during that whole, what we all called country rock. So, you had your Ozark Mountain Daredevils and New Riders of the Purple Sage and the Eagles, the Poco and all the southern California country movement that was going on. Randy would have fit in that whole deal, would have fit in the San Francisco music scene back then easily. It was real trippy and a lot of fun," said Parker.

Parker grew up with both his parents being musicians. His mother was a music teacher who started Parker out on piano at the age of five. His father was in a jazz trio in college that played gigs in various areas. His father also did barbershop quartets before getting into acting and music theater. While Parker was immersed in music his entire life, it wasn't until he was in middle school that his interest in music really grew. The family had moved from New Kirk, Oklahoma- where Parker was born- to Saint Louis, Missouri. Parker took lessons at Mel Bay Music with Mel's son Bill, and he was hooked on playing music ever since. Eventually the family returned to Oklahoma in the Norman area when his mom got a job teaching at Moore Schools. Parker started playing in bands while still in high school in Norman. Jim Downing met Parker in the early seventies when Parker was a roadie. Downing was in a band called Xebeck, which was a popular bar band around Oklahoma at the time. Parker started as a roadie and later joined the band. This would just be the start of Parker's career in the music scene.

Another musician that isn't necessarily lumped into the Red Dirt scene, but had a huge impact on it, is Kevin Welch. Welch was born in 1955 and was raised in Midwest City, Oklahoma. Welch joined Pat Long in the band New Rodeo in the first part of the '70s, and then they formed Blue Rose Café in about 1975. The founding members were Pat Long on vocals and guitar, Kevin Welch on vocals and guitar, Gary Johnson on bass, Steve Grunder on drums and Mike McCarty on guitar. Long was the primary songwriter for the band. Their mentor who was an art professor at OU, John Hadley, also wrote many songs for the band. This band was one of the first trailblazer Oklahoma bands in what was then called Progressive Country. In essence, they played a mixture of country, folk, rock, pop, swing, jazz and bluegrass to form a distinctive new layered sound. Mostly home based in Norman, they were wildly popular all over the state and more. While Welch would move to Nashville in 1978 to work as a songwriter and further his career in many other ways, both he and this band would be a huge influence on the musicians just starting out during this time as well as those in the future.

Steve Irby, still playing with Moses, started a company in 1973 called Stillwater Designs and Audio, building PA and pro sound systems for bands and venues. It began in an old house on South Main Street. "It was a pretty big music scene in Stillwater, and I think it was spawned in the sixties with all the bands and all the music creativity. It kind of really began to jump out in the sixties. The Beatles were probably one of the first ones to start it and were my favorite band and pretty much always have been. But then there was all the other ones; Crosby, Stills, Nash and Young and James Taylor and the Birds and the Yard Birds. We played a lot of stuff by The Band, by Creedence Clearwater. Steve (Ripley) kind of went through phases. He was really a music kid and so he would kind of latch on to a musician that he thought was really great, and so we would play all those songs. Johnny Rivers, we did a ton of Johnny Rivers stuff. He really liked Elvis, and we did a lot of Elvis stuff. Then there was the Bob Dylan era, that we played a ton of Bob Dylan stuff. Then later when he was out in California, he met Bob Dylan and was asked to tour. He did a world tour playing guitar for Bob Dylan. He was a big Bob Dylan fan back in high school, and we played a lot of Dylan stuff, so he knew all of it. And he was one of those guys that just could remember all the words and everything. Was really into the musicians and knowing everything about them, more than the rest of us. I think that was just always his dream to do that. Whereas the rest of us really just liked playing, but I don't think we thought we were gonna make a career out of it. Where I think Steve was always pretty much that way, either a career in that or as a recording studio," said Irby.

Ripley's recording studio Stillwater Sound is where Moses recorded their music, and it was how they recorded their album in 1974. It was the only album they put out. They hauled all of Ripley's recording equipment in a U-Haul to Enid where they had a gig booked at The Fillin' Station, and recorded the album live. "The guy that wrote our liner notes was a friend of my wife's brother and he was from Enid, his name was Mike Dougan. He basically coined the term Red Dirt first. I mean that was in 1974. It's on the liner notes of our album and he coined the term Red Dirt music. I think maybe that we were playing stuff that was a little more that way at that point in time, kind of Bob Dylan stuff and the Birds and just stuff that was not just really totally pop music. A little different, little more off the beaten path, you know," said Irby.

Irby's interests were in speakers and sound, and Ripley's was more guitars. Irby could be found building speakers for the band, and Ripley would modify guitars. "He eventually developed the Ripley guitar, the one that had a pick-up on every string. He was always experimenting with that. I remember, he made a paisley guitar that had like a paisley cloth that he laminated to the guitar and sanded it and everything and played that. He was into just doing different stuff with guitars and messing with pickups and all kinds of stuff. We were both kind of like tinkers, with sound equipment and guitars. We went kind of in different directions. But it's funny how things start and grow. It was an interesting period of time, and we had a lot of fun playing gigs. We were both really into music and equipment and it was really a lot of fun," said Irby.

While the sounds and style of this new genre were still being formed, many of the bands around Stillwater were playing mostly cover songs, but this began to change. "Well, there was a lot of musicians around and I think really what they call Red Dirt music, it's really a little more folky type music. It's not pop type music. We played quite a few cover songs and things because that's what people wanted to hear from the bands. Later on we started playing more of Steve's original stuff. But it's still kind of the same, people wanna sing along, at a dance or a concert. They wanna know the songs and sing along. I think that maybe what changed in the music scene with the Red Dirt scene, was more they're writing their own music rather than just playing covers and getting into that aspect of it. I think what we coined as Red Dirt on our album was maybe not really what it turned into, but it was kind of what it was at that point in time. I mean, that was just kind of earthy music, and if you think about a lot of the music that we played, it was more earthy or you might say bluesy. Creedence Clearwater stuff or you got Crosby, Stills, Nash and Young. Those groups and the Birds and some of these that were not really poppy type music, they're not just all hooks and popular stuff. There's a little more to it. I'm probably not the best person to define that, but that's what I noticed is that as the Red Dirt music progressed, it became more original music and took on a little bit more of a flavor of its own rather than playing cover songs that were kind of more I would say earthy. I guess if you call it Red Dirt is the earth, so maybe a little more earthy or folksy. I think it kind of evolved into that," said Irby.

Notably at this time Swing music was in high demand and brought people out to dance. There wasn't a lack of live music performances in various genres available every night somewhere in Stillwater. Another popular music at the time was disco, and the things that would pack the bars were deejays and line dancing. But there were still a handful of guys that were out, singing their own songs. Many of these early pioneers of the genre could be found playing music on the strip as the scene began developing. There were many venues on the strip during these years that offered live music and a place for the musicians to showcase their talent. These included The Golden Whaler, Lafferty's, The Other Place, Smiling Jack's, Pistol Patties, The Mason Jar, Willie's Wild West Saloon and the Jail Saloon just to name a few.

The still popular Willie's Saloon opened in 1974 on the west side of the strip and moved to its current location in 1985, which was once Acme Bar. Willie's was one of the most noted venues that played an important part for Red Dirt music and musicians, especially during the '70s and '80s. Just a little smokey dive bar with a tiny stage, it had cold beer, live music and locals gathered there regularly. Ned and Bill Bloodworth owned Willie's, and before moving, it was located next to Bill's Italian restaurant, owned by Bill and Karen Bloodworth. Both places hosted local musicians and gave them a place to forge their craft and earn some money.

Jeff Parker, who had moved from Norman to Perkins at this time, was a Junior at the high school. He quickly started getting connected to the Stillwater music scene simply because he was so enamored with playing music. "Bill had a restaurant called Bill's Italian restaurant, which was directly across the street from Willie's. And it was right there where Dupree Sports was, and practically everybody that worked there were musicians. Some of the names that I can remember are a guy named Hank Holly who was a bass player. Vernon Schubel who was a sax player, singer. There was a couple, Tank and his wife's name is Anne. They were kind of singer songwriter, musicians. So, it was all flourishing even then. I mean, we're talking mid-seventies. So that was my first experience with it. I was just like, wow, this is cool," said Parker.

While not the first on the scene, Bob Childers is widely known as the Godfather of Red Dirt music, which is a title well deserving. Spanning a three-decade career, Childers wrote more than 2000 songs. Most everyone who played music in the area would cover Childers' songs throughout the next several decades, and even to this day you usually can't be at any Red Dirt event without hearing his name mentioned. Childers was born on November 20th, 1946, in West Union, West Virginia, but moved to Ponca City at the age of seven. According to his brother Mark Childers, Bob received his first guitar, a Montgomery Ward Airline, as a Christmas gift from his parents when he was 16. He quickly learned how to play it. After graduating high school, Childers moved to California to study music. He returned to Oklahoma shortly thereafter, and found his way to Stillwater, where he soon found a community of like-minded musicians who were all trying to achieve the same thing.

Bob Childers. Photo provided by Sage Powell

"It was just kind of a fluke. I was hitch-hiking my way back to Ponca City, and these guys picked me up in Oklahoma City, and said they'd take me to Ponca, but that they had to stop off in Stillwater. When we did, I ran into a guy that I played music with in high school, and he told me about a party going on that weekend, and one thing or another happened, and I wound up going to hear a guy named Chuck Dunlap play. His music had something unique about it... it was kinda mystical (laugh), and I thought that's what I was lookin' for, and just a weird chain of events happened, and I wound up livin' down here. A few days after I moved here, Chuck moved in a couple doors down, and we got together, and I suddenly realized that it was like a magical place. The music was unlike that I hadn't encountered anywhere else," said Childers in an interview with the Texas Troubadours Website, archived on PayneCountyLine.com.

Chuck Dunlap said he met Bob Childers somewhere near 1975. Dunlap was walking on the OSU campus and spotted Bob from across the way. Childers was sitting under a tree with his guitar and a pad of paper, working away, and Dunlap thought- well that looks like a familiar sight. Dunlap walked up, sat down with Childers and started up a conversation and next thing you know they were sharing songs and quickly becoming good picking buddies. Quickly and easily that friendship blossomed over the shared love of making music. Childers' fast friendship with Dunlap helped create momentum for other local singer/songwriters as they watched these two forge ahead.

Almost everyone who shares their memories of Childers comments about how charismatic he was- how his laid-back personality and his easy-going philosophy of life earned him respect and loyalty from just about everyone he met. It's been said on more than one occasion that it was a good thing Childers never wanted to start a cult or steer people in nefarious ways, because he certainly would have been able to convince people to follow him just about anywhere.

Pam Potts, one of the first women to help form the Red Dirt movement, was from Stillwater and had established a music career around town at this time as well. She began playing folk music in the mid '70s, more as a cover artist. "When I was 21, I got a $50 guitar loaned to me with- well with promise to pay $50 I guess I should say. A guitar given to me with promise to pay and I never did of course which is typical for me back then. It was a real wide neck and kind of a classical guitar. It had a real wide neck and gut strings, and it was kind of hard to play and I would finger pick it and play a couple of songs. I met this guy one night who was quite accomplished at the guitar, and I acted like I knew what I was doing. I sang a song for him and then he picked it up and played you know, like *Classical Gas* or something really complicated. David Ely was his name, I was really embarrassed to death because of my inability to play but he recognized that I could sing and so we became a singing act. He taught me to play kind of a monkey see monkey do thing. I didn't have a clue what I was doing at all, but he would show me what to do, to mirror what he was doing. We would play these complicated songs and make quite a bit of money at first doing that. In fact, I think some my first gigs paid more than any of my gigs in my whole life," said Potts.

Pam Potts. Photo provided by Sage Powell.

At the same time, a friend from high school named David Shelton needed a partner for his gigs at the Holiday Inn and asked Potts to join him. "And somehow we merged together the three of us, me and the two David's. David Shelton, he wanted to sing like show tunes, real different kind of stuff. But I could sing that stuff, you know? I mean, why not? And David Ely could play it. And so, we would get through these crazy things out at the Holiday Inn, and they were paying us like $500 a week each. I mean it was in 1979; it was like huge man. I mean I was walking around like I was insanely rich. But it was great fun. I knew 13 songs to start with and we would just play those 13 songs over and over and hope that someone would leave after 12 songs or whatever. So that they don't have to suffer it twice," said Potts.

Soon Potts and Ely dropped off with Shelton and went more into a folk music direction. "We performed a lot of Joni Mitchell songs and Bonnie Raitt songs and things like this- really got my chops as far as learning how to have some stage presence. He was an accomplished musician and had a lot of experience. He was about seven years older than me. His parents were professional musicians. So, he knew what to do and taught me to know how to do things too. He taught me how to work a PA, and really everything that I needed to know to be on stage," said Potts.

By the time she met Bob Childers, she had already established herself in the area and had already been playing gigs regularly. "There were a bunch of us that were all musicians from Stillwater. You probably never heard these names but Ronnie Kershaw, Jimmy Drummond, me, Steve Collier. We all just grew up in Stillwater. But then we were all Red Dirt musicians too. Then Jimmy LaFave went to high school with us too, you know. I met Chuck Dunlap when I was 17 years old. I mean, this was before we went to bars. We did go to the Bar Ditch. It was where we would hang out. But we were 18. We were not supposed to be in there. We would run into the bathroom and stand up on the toilet, and that way they couldn't see our feet in there. Crouch down into the little things, from the cops that come in to look for the underage girls. Then they leave and we come back out of there," said Potts.

Jimmy LaFave was also one of the early pioneers who started playing music in Stillwater. LaFave was born in Willis Point, Texas in 1955, but moved to Stillwater while he was in high school. He played in the high school band at that time, but by the age of 15 he had switched over to playing guitar and started writing and singing his own songs. While he was in Stillwater during this time and had started to find his footing with his music, it would still be several years before he made a bigger name for himself in the area, coming into his own more in the late '70s. LaFave would become one of the most recognized and celebrated Red Dirt artists in years to come.

Jimmy LaFave. Photo provided by Sage Powell.

In just a few short years, from the start of the '70s until the mid-70s, things started coming together for the Stillwater music scene. While still a long way off from forming their own recognized genre, connections were being formed, new paths were being paved, and the musicians were finding new avenues both individually and collectively. This was the peak of the free love movement, when the average college kid would be scantily dressed and looking to have a good time. There were plenty of bars in the area that would feature music, giving musicians opportunities to hone their craft and find new fans. Music flowed in Stillwater- all kinds of music.

"It seemed like everybody knew how to play music for some reason. We all kind of clanned together. There were a lot of crossovers. You know, if you were in one band, you were probably in another. There were people that had rock bands in Stillwater, there were several of those. Then there were country bands, swing bands, and country swing. There was the Cimarron Swingsters, which were a great band, and they were fun. Then there were those of us who wanted to play acoustic instruments but not be country or not be rock. I kind of think that's kind of how this came about, it was a genre that encompassed blues and folk and a little light rock and you know, all this kind of stuff all kind of mixed together. We didn't even really know what it was back then," said Pam Potts.

In Their Own Words

Chuck Dunlap: I think Texas supports its music better than Oklahoma does. It treats it like a natural resource- like oil or cattle or anything else. They see it as such, and they pay for it. They treat it as a valid way to make a living, they treat it as an honorable way to make a living. Whereas in Oklahoma you are kind of on the fringes, kind of living in that underworld almost. That kind of second society that exists, and they have tried to bring it and it's coming up to that- where they are recognizing it as a part of our culture. Woody (Guthrie) had a lot to do with that. All the attention paid to Woody. He has a foundation in Tulsa, and so that's a huge difference. Along with that comes the ability or the natural evolution of people figuring out how to make money off of all that, to make themselves money when they aren't musicians or songwriters or have anything to do with it. They just have the ability to make money, and Texas has a lot of that. It's a real high business. There's a lot of money made in Texas with music. And that transfers from the music industry to the other enterprises as well. They have to deal a little more with the sharp edges of the music system, then being a musician and being a songwriter in Oklahoma does. So, people find a little refuge in Oklahoma. But to make a living at it they almost have to leave Oklahoma. Because you can't really make a living if you don't travel outside of Oklahoma, especially to Texas. That's where most of the groups from Oklahoma go when they want to make their mark - to Austin, to Dallas- because you can hit as many people in Dallas as you can in the whole state of Oklahoma. So, you're playing to larger audiences, you are reaching a larger fanbase and all of that. But along with that comes the trade, it comes with the people that – don't want to stab you in the back necessarily- but they don't mind hooking onto your coat, and coasting for the ride. It's not bad or good- it's what it is. I think that scene started when people like Jimmy Lafave and Kevin Welch took their music to Texas. They took the music from here in Oklahoma and took it to Texas. I think the same things happen in Georgia and Kentucky, and California, and everywhere there is, I think that music that's played in Oklahoma, gets played there and they like it. I don't think they have the opportunity to get together and LOVE it en masse as much as the people in Oklahoma do. And that has to do with the culture in Oklahoma; all the native influence, all the religious influence, all the gut it out, tough it out, just work at it a little longer and don't give up attitude.

Terry Ware - I like to say I'm a really lucky guy, and I am. That's a big part of any kind of career of any kind, you know- music or otherwise. Luck always plays a big part of it. Always. I have felt that I've always been geographic lucky. At the right place, right time kind of thing. Because, for instance if I hadn't moved to Red River with Ray when I got out of college- hadn't gone out there- I have no idea what would have happened. Just as Ray was getting ready to go out on his own, and just after he'd finished writing his Redneck Mother thing that kind of catapulted him at that time. Being part of that- that early thing in Texas- it was kind of coming out of Texas at that time that we got going. We moved back and everything, but that influenced a lot of what was going on up here, too. I know it did. There's a couple of groups from Oklahoma that really deserve recognition too from the seventies. One of them being Blue Rose Café, which was a band here in Norman, that included Kevin Welch in the band. And of course, Kevin is one of Oklahoma's great song writers. That was at the same time I was with Ray. I think they were a really important band. And they also did a song by a songwriter here in town by the name of John Hadley. John's, like, nine years older than I am. John, he's like a song writing mentor too. Kevin and John have actually cowritten a lot of songs together over the years. Blue Rose did a lot of his songs early on, and John was already an established songwriter by that time. He was actually an art professor at OU and then also a songwriter and he would spend the summers in Nashville just doing the song writing business. John and Bob (Childers) knew each other too, they got to know each other. But John, he's had songs over the years recorded from everybody from George Jones to the Dixie Chicks to George Burns, to Joe Cocker. I've learned as much or more about song writing from him than anybody. I've been lucky enough to write some with him and still do.

The Mid-Seventies

While the first half of the '70s seemed to be the genesis of the Red Dirt movement, it was really the second half of the '70s that picked up momentum. It was at this time there seemed to be the biggest influx of people onto the newly forming music scene, many arriving in Stillwater during this time to go to school. The bar scene was very popular with the college crowd and most people seemed to want to hear bands that had multiple instruments and harmonies. The solo songwriter thing wasn't quite as popular yet at this time, although musicians like Chuck Dunlap and Bob Childers were still carving it out along the way, making the rounds throughout town and continuing to forge a path for the single singer/songwriter acts. LaFave graduated high school and was playing around town and finding his foothold.

According to Eskimo Joe's Bio on their website, Eskimo Joe's opened in 1975, created by two OSU college graduates- Steve File and Stan Clark. File had the idea and name, and Clark knew of a two-story building to rent at 501 W. Elm St., and the two became partners. It started as just a bar at the time, but when the drinking age changed from 18 to 21 in 1984, they expanded into a restaurant as well. File came up with the name Eskimo

Joes because he wanted to let everyone know it would have the coldest beer in town. Bill Thompson, a freshman commercial art student, drew the logo and created the mascot. Eskimo Joe's would become another popular venue local musicians could play.

Even when they didn't have a paying gig, the local jammers were playing just to play. They got so much joy and satisfaction out of playing music, that was really all they wanted to do- whether they were getting paid to do it or not. Chuck Dunlap and Bob Childers formed a daily jam session together. They both were working construction as a day job and would meet up during their lunch break every day just to get the chance to play. "I would take my guitar in my car to work every day, and I would stop by there at lunch, and we would share songs. What we wrote the day before or the week before or whatever. We'd jam- that's one of my favorite memories with Bob. We spent a lot of time doing that- almost daily for a year – maybe longer. We'd pick songs out of the trash and rework them or give them to each other and say 'here, I couldn't do anything with this, do what you can do'. Then his friends or my friends would get together every once in a while, we would get together after work on porches and you know, just continue for hours. He was always willing to pick up his guitar and write a song, not just play one. He would say 'let's write a song'. I would go, 'wow I have to have inspiration and the time's gotta be right', and he would just go 'No, this is how you do it', and he'd pick up the pencil and paper and just started writing, you know, he taught me that," said Dunlap.

Pam Potts managed to find a way to barge into Childers and Dunlap's daily lunch jams. She would join the guys at Childers' apartment, which was located right behind The Barn off the strip on Washington St., on the second floor.

Pam Potts. Photo provided by Sage Powell.

They would get together and sing and play guitars during the lunch hour, Pam harmonizing with Dunlap. "It was a lot of fun and playing with Bob was always really challenging because he would just write a song every single day, maybe five or ten. They would all be good and all be different, and you'd have to learn them really quickly. He would just move at lightning speed on that stuff. It was a lot of fun," said Potts.

At this time Chuck Dunlap also had a band called Cimmaron with Randy Baxter and Jim Tilley, which gave him the hook to get a bigger sound, instead of just playing acoustic solo. "I've always stepped back to that even when I went to the acoustic thing for so long. The acoustic was a little easier to work for me. I started opening shows in about 75 for people like Emmy Lou Harris and Muddy Water and all of my idols. I did a total of like 34 shows out at Cain's Ballroom and Boomer Theater and Old Lady on Brady. There was this place in Oklahoma City called The Prairie Lady that was real good about that, and they would use me because I was inexpensive.

Chuck Dunlap Enid Concert 1978. Photo provided by Chuck Dunlap

I was a solo act, I could step on stage without any big set up. I really took advantage of that and worked it for what it was. I was really able to see that the high star musicians were just real people, like me and you. I got to talk to them backstage and I was able to take that with me. I was only 20 years old, 22-23. I always felt like I was able to be fortunate to have that experience when I was that young, that I had made it already. I never had that feeling like I needed to strive for anything more than my satisfaction for what I got out of the music in it all because I was able to stand in front of thousands of people and play music all by myself in my '20s. So, I felt that- and I was able to strip that down in a way from what music meant to me," said Dunlap.

Another important part of the founding music scene was Mike Hufford, a drummer who played in Steve Ripley's band Moses at this time. He moved to Stillwater in 1975, and opened Lamb Recording studio, which would come to play a huge role in allowing local artists to record and create albums. Located just east of Stillwater, Lamb Recordings was inside a little shed behind a mobile home out on East 51, which Hufford had converted into a little eight track recording analog studio.

Mike was married to Cheryl Hufford, who was a singer, and would perform with LaFave and other musicians from time to time, as well as sing in other bands. Lamb studios would soon prove to be very instrumental in propelling the careers of several local musicians, making studio recording available and affordable.

Lamb Studios. Photo provided by Craig Skinner.

During Labor Day weekend of 1975, there was a "48 Hours in Atoka" music festival that took place in Atoka, Oklahoma. According to Cindy Donovan-Wallis who wrote the article *48 Hours in Atoka* for The Chronicles of Oklahoma, this was Oklahoma's answer to Woodstock. The lineup included Waylon Jennings, Willie Nelson, Freddy Fender, David Allan Coe, Don Williamson, Larry Gatlin and more. The festival was widely promoted, and the crowd was estimated to be up to one hundred and fifty thousand people. The ticket price was ten dollars and included a t-shirt. Music historians consider this to be the beginning of the Outlaw Country movement. The full article about the event can be found on https://gateway.okhistory.org. While this festival had little to do with the Oklahoma artists forming this new scene, it does show the culture of the music atmosphere; that new genres were being formed, rules were being broken, and artists were more inclined to follow their hearts rather than cookie cutter rules set by the machine. The Red Dirt movement was born out of this atmosphere.

Bret Franzmann, who was born and raised in Stillwater, made his way to the Walnut Music Festival for the first time in 1975 at the age of 17. Franzmann had started playing violin in the fifth grade in school orchestra and then picked up the banjo when he was about 10 years old. Franzmann was a senior in high school in 1975, giving banjo and fiddle lessons to a couple of college students who had been to Winfield before and told him all about it. So, he and his friend Johnny Wright went to check it out that year. They proceeded to tell more people about it and the next year they brought a group of about six-eight people, and created the Stillwater Camp, which has been going on ever since. Franzmann would later join the music scene as a musician in several different bands.

Winfield Stillwater Camp. Photo provided by Sage Powell.

There was a coffee house on OSU campus at the time, created by Charlie Hill and Chuck Dow, called Aunt Molly's Rent-Free Music House. Aunt Molly's gave new aspiring musicians the opportunity to play in front of an audience, get a taste of performing and get audience feedback. It was a friendly place, a way to get connected with the music scene. It proved to be a good springboard for many of the musicians at that time. Raetta Gaybig, one of the early female musicians in this scene, came to Stillwater in the fall of '76 and started out playing at Aunt Molly's as well as a few other places on campus. She met many other players there that she would collaborate with over the years. Gaybig played in a trio with Richard Spears and Jeff Harris from '77 to '79 called Retta, Rich, & Jeff. They had a large following and played regularly at a few different places on the Strip. They also opened for John Prine and Michael Martin Murphy during that time. Gaybig would later add her vocals on Childers' first album.

Across from the OSU campus in Cowboy Mall there was what everyone just refers to as "The Music Store", owned by Ed Robinson. Robinson was a talented keyboard player and musician in his own right as well. Rick Peale, another local musician who played guitar, worked at the Music Store. John Buckner, who had lived in Stillwater his entire life, was just a young teenager in 1975 and would hang out at the Music Store all the time. It was how he got interested in playing bass. A couple of years later, he met Mike Shannon at the music store, another local musician. Shannon told him about a band, The Midnight Express led by Franelle LaFollete, who was looking for a bass player. "He told me that Franelle was looking for a bass player and she played all the time, played at good places. Made good money. I said, man, I can't play country, and he said I'll show you some licks. He was living in this little dump in Stillwater. It was caddy corner to where Daddy O's is now. It was literally one of those little efficiency rooms, apartments or whatever. I mean, you had a chair and a bed and a lamp. It was like Blues Brothers type stuff. And one of those toaster things that you could use a clothes hanger to toast bread on. But I went over there, he taught me some stuff and I went out and auditioned and I got the gig, and I owe that to him," said Buckner.

The band included Robert Parker, Rod Boutwell, Mike Shannon and Franelle LaFollete. The band was booked every single weekend, which meant Buckner didn't have to find any other employment- he could just play every weekend and have enough income as a teenager. This suited him just fine. While it was mostly just a cover band, it was in high demand at the time for parties, events and live music venues. "When we started playing, I was doing more pop rock. Then, Urban Cowboy the movie came out and we found that with country music, we were just booked when we switched to the country music genre. We were booked constantly. We played all the time. So, we were just a regular working band. Once we started playing country music, we played three sets of country music and then we had a complete set of old rock and roll," said LaFollete.

LaFollete and her husband were living in Stillwater, had a business called University Mobile Homes. Franelle's husband managed the band and ran sound. The band would stay successful for the next couple of decades, although they only put out two original singles during that time. It proved to be a great springboard for many of the local musicians to find their place in the Red Dirt scene. Mike Shannon left the band about six months later, deciding he wanted to do something else. "He just thought, man, I don't wanna be in a cover band even though the money is great. He wanted to do something on his own. And that's kind of when he went off and started the whole thought process of Daddy O's and everything. I think that started buzzing around his head then," said Buckner.

Mike Shannon attended a vocational music school called The Musicians Institute, which had a location in Hollywood, Austin and London. At the time it was a one-year music technical school, that would later branch out into graduate degrees where you could earn an associates, bachelor's or master's degree in music.

John Buckner and Mike Shannon. Photo provided by Sage Powell.

Shannon graduated from the Musician's Institute and returned to Stillwater to continue playing music.

Don Morris, who would officially enter the Red Dirt music scene much later, found his way to Tulsa in 1975- which would eventually lead to him becoming an integral part of the scene. Morris grew up in North Carolina and started playing music when he was a teenager, playing guitar and bass.

He joined up with his brothers to form The Morris Brothers band and toured out of Ohio at that point. "But we played all over the Midwest and California and Nevada and did a far East tour back in 1969. Then from there, played with a fellow by the name of John Schwab. We got in on the Steak and Ale circuit, which was a steak house- they were all over. But they had real cool bars for acoustic type venues. Played with him for two or three years and then I ended up coming out here to the Steak and Ale in Tulsa, in 1975, and ended up playing there for three years. So, we bought the house and never left," said Morris.

Morris' career would still take him on some twists and turns before fully settling into the Red Dirt scene properly, but this is where he entered the picture. Tulsa of course had their own established and thriving music scene which still hadn't fully connected to the newly forming Stillwater scene. But there were branches that led back and forth for both Stillwater and Tulsa musicians during this time and would continue to do so through the years. Of course, Tulsa Venues like The Cain's Ballroom and The Colony, among many others, would be important for Stillwater artists both at this time, and for many years to come. There is a great book about the history of Cain's called *Twentieth-Century Honky-Tonk* by John Wooley and Brett Bingham that is a deep dive into the history of the famous and well-loved venue. A definite read for any Oklahoma music fan.

Steve Ripley moved away from Stillwater to Nashville in 1976, but his influence and connections remained a big piece of the local music scene even while he was away. Ripley accomplished many amazing things during his time away from Oklahoma and was an inspiration to everyone back home. Moses found another lead player at that time and lasted a couple more years before disbanding. Ripley didn't stay in one place too long during this part of his career. He moved to Nashville to write songs and got a job as a sound engineer for Leon Russell. Following that musical adventure, he moved back to Oklahoma to work for the Jim Halsey Company as a record producer. Ripley jumped from there to Leon Russell's Paradise Records, as a studio engineer in Burbank, California.

A common theme of the musicians who laid the foundation for this genre to emerge is that to look at them, you wouldn't think of rock stars or flashy performances. Most of the musicians wore whatever clothes they happened to have on hand, never caring about their fashion choices. They didn't spend time cultivating their image or creating flashy personas. They were just being themselves. Their whole desire with their music was just to express who they were and to be true to themselves. This is what would become the philosophy and driving force of the entire Red Dirt music scene- what everything else was built around. These musicians didn't necessarily just choose the path of creating music, they were compelled by something inside of themselves- an instinct and necessity to create. It was a part of them. When they were creating music, they felt fulfilled, and when they weren't, they felt lost. They didn't want to follow rules or formulas. they didn't want to be forced into a certain style or sound. They wanted to explore until they found themselves in the music.

It's also why you rarely hear the same sounds and styles within the musicians that come out of Red Dirt, and yet they are all still considered Red Dirt music. Their whole aim was to express who they were as individuals, which meant each musician was creating the music that best expressed who they were and what they felt inside calling forth. Their goal was never perfection, or even finding fame, it was to share their creative expression and how they viewed the world. Their priorities started with being inspired and creating- they wanted to create music that fulfilled themselves. The audience actually came last as a priority. It wasn't about creating music to make an audience happy, but if the music they created connected with the audience- all the better. But that was never the goal, it was the icing on the cake.

"Seems like there's always a certain amount of people that no matter what you do, are either going to tell you they like it, and an equal amount of people no matter what you do, they're not gonna like it. So, you just really have to get where you trust your heart, you know, you trust your own instincts and discount... I mean it's good to hear people say they like the music, that's great. Not many people anymore tell me they don't, they probably think it, but they don't tell me anyway. But it still comes down to, if I write a song, I'm the only one that really knows if it's worthwhile doing it again or not," said Bob Childers in the documentary *North of Austin/West of Nashville: Red Dirt Music.*

In Their Own Words

Gene Collier on the Definition of red dirt - You know I really think it's Cimarron Valley. You go in and get in that water and try to go noodling or something, and your feet- your toenails- just stay red for 2 weeks. It's a nasty thing, but it's part of being red dirt. That red dirt in Cimarron Valley, it blows right over there through the Stillwater area, and to me that's what it's about. It's that river; Cimarron River. It's not the best-looking river. Probably the worst looking one, but it has spawned one good song after another. It's just made its own little genre. It's not the musicians doing it, it's the campfires. To me that's what it's about. It's about telling a story in your song, a little bit of your soul goes in there, and your love and admiration of somebody. It's an amazing thing I tell ya. It's down-home music.

Pam Potts - I used to ask Bob (Childers), you know, how do you write a song? And he said, man, you write about 100 songs, and you throw them away and then you write another one and then you are songwriter. In other words, do it, you know? I would force it. I would try so hard to force it and I wrote a song one night on cocktail napkins. It was a song about Bonnie Raitt. I'd seen her that night and then we had gone to a club afterwards. I just was in this passionate fit to write this song and I scribbled on cocktail napkins. God forbid if they got out of number, then I would be all lost in my song. Because I was just like a maniac that night. That was really the first song I felt like I had been inspired to write. I kind of laid that one down and that was a long, long time ago, But I brought it back, with my friend Kevin's help. Kevin Smith, that played fiddle with Bob.

John Buckner about Stillwater in the '70s- It was awesome. Of course, you know, everything was on the strip and then you had some places outside of the strip. But most of the music, it was a very vibrant live music scene. It was 18 to get into the bars and I wasn't 18 yet. I was 15 and I would go and sneak in. I would go to the Attic or Pistol Patties or, I guess there was a lot of places. Jimmy Lafave still lived in town, and he had just put out an album. I think Chuck Dunlap was playing around at that time- who is still playing. I consider him- he and Jimmy- the two biggest people for me that started Red Dirt. It was called singer-songwriters. They just loved to play. They were great. Jimmy, whatever he sang or played just was so full of emotion. He loved a good song, and he played with Chuck. And they were just musicians. I was just steeped in music. That's what I lived for. I didn't do anything else. That's all I ever wanted was just to be a professional musician. I had a lot of support from friends and family because I was just relentless with it. I was always playing, just going for the look; have the hair, trying to be a part of what you saw in magazines. There wasn't any social media or anything. It was all just what you saw every now and then on Friday nights on the Midnight Special. And in magazines, the rock magazines that were out. When I actually turned 18, I started legally going to the bars. I guess where Joe's print shop is now, there was a bar there called Whiskers. It was a dance and live music club, and they had regional touring groups. Same with Pistol Patties that was on the strip. I saw some really, really incredible regional acts that came through there. On the strip there, where I guess now it's called The Question Mark. There was a place behind it called Smiling Jacks. I played there regularly, frequently. Of course, there was Willie's, and Prophet L Rods, and Joe's- just a lot of places. There was the Sundowner south of town, Spavs north of town. There was a lot of places to play and if you weren't playing in the bars, people encouraged it. Everybody thought it was great that you played an instrument and that you would get up and play in front of people. They didn't really care if you were any good or not. They just thought it was great that you were trying. So, there was a lot of support from people that weren't musicians that enjoyed listening. If you played an instrument, you were golden, you know?

Terry Ware: Well, in the '70s, they were calling what was going on Progressive Country. Basically, what was happening then was a lot of people- and I'll use Ray and I as an example of that- Ray came from the folk music world and I came from the rock and roll music world. That was happening a lot. Lots in Austin in particular, people like Jerry Jeff. There were all these people from the folk music world starting to play with rock and roll people. I think what they're calling the Red Dirt scene- I think it was just a progression from that. I've been more identified as a part of, I guess of that scene here in Oklahoma. Playing with people like the Rangers and Jimmy and Bob. In Texas, whenever I played with Jimmy and Ray down there, the Red Dirt scene in Texas is different than it is in Oklahoma. The Texas Red Dirt Scene seemed to me, to be more like a party kind of thing. In just the kind of songs I heard come out of that. As opposed to, like, say something that Bob (Childers) would have written. Bob- I don't remember him ever writing a song about, you know, take your pickup truck to the lake and drink beer with your friends. That's kind of what I picture in the Texas Red Dirt scene. It's just more of a party.

Franelle LaFollett: I really felt like my band was a family. I was really close to all of them. I still keep in touch with all of them, you know, on Facebook and email. I really felt close to all of them, and we just had a good time. We got to open for George Strait, Johnny Paycheck, Earl Thomas Conley. Eddie Raven. We got to open for some pretty big crowds. That was at Norm's Ballroom in Ponca City that we got to open for all those performers. We really had some great opportunities and good times

Stillwater Expansion

Quickly the number of musicians gravitating to Stillwater expanded. Mark Lyon arrived in Stillwater in August of 1976, and on his first night in town he saw a flyer for a place called the Bar Ditch. The band playing that night was called Wallace Cotton. What tantalized him to go out was not the place or the band, neither of which he had ever heard of, it was the nickel drafts and 25 cent pitchers. Lyon was only 18, but at the time you could drink at 18. They called a vote in 1984 that changed it to 21. But on this night, Lyon got lucky and was there before that came about and by the time he was 21, they changed the drinking age back to 21.

Lyon went to the Bar Ditch that night to check out Wallace Cotton, which included Randy Crouch, Steve Pryor and Don London- who later went on to play with Becky Hobbs, a Nashville country artist. This experience blew Lyon away, going to this little bar and hearing so much talent from this band. Between Crouch playing fiddle and pedal steel and Steve Pryor doing his magic on guitar, it was more talent than one little stage could possibly hold. "They were playing music. I would call it country rock; would be the best way I could describe it. But they had this great jazz influence going on with it and a lot of western swing. I remember thinking-

I've seen big concerts. I've seen the big guys in Oklahoma City growing up, going to great concerts. But there at the Bar Ditch- I heard music that was as good as any music I've ever heard in my life- that first night in Stillwater. So, I proceeded to keep on going there and we'd hear acts like Alvin Crow and the Pleasant Valley Boys," said Lyon.

Steve Pryor, a talented blues guitar player, didn't come out of the Red Dirt scene. But he played within it and inspired many of the artists that did come out of the scene. Pryor grew up in Tulsa and began his career there. He would eventually move to California with a band in 1977, and then to New York in 1983. He toured with bands such as the Fabulous Thunderbirds, Joe Cocker and the Paul Butterfield Blues Band. He played extensively around the Tulsa area, recording his own music for decades and working with musicians throughout the region. Pryor shared the stage with Muddy Waters, B.B. King, Robert Cray, Bonnie Raitt, John Hammond, Coco Montoya, Steve Kimock, and Leon Russell. He was a legend, as well as a friend of many of the Red Dirt artists through the years.

Ben Holder, who owned the Bar Ditch, also owned Horse Thief Canyon, which was located out by Perkins on the Cimarron River. It was an actual horse thief canyon in history. It was where the Wild Bunch- also known as the Doolin-Dalton gang- and the Oklahombres, would steal horses and hide them there back in the late 1800's. Horse Thief Canyon was an outdoor music venue that would host several shows and festivals during the years.

After experiencing the live music scene in Stillwater, Mark Lyon started playing music around town a little bit. One of the first people that he came across was a guy by the name of Dub Cross. They didn't really play together at gigs but would get together and jam with one another. Dub Cross had an outlaw country thing going on as a solo performer, but a few years later he ended up being the singer for quite a time for a group called the New Cimarron Swingsters. This was a western swing band that formed in Stillwater around 1978 and quickly became one of the town's hottest acts to go see. Mike Shannon played pedal steel and guitar in it. "These guys were great, they played just killer Western swing music and that was part of that whole Stillwater sound at the time," said Lyon.

Craig Skinner and Mike Shannon. Photo provided by Craig Skinner.

Lyon started meeting some of the local musicians like Jimmy LaFave and Bob Childers. He also met Rod Boutwell at the Bar Ditch, who played guitar and pedal steel in a band called Old Trails Rode. They played the kind of country rock blend that was popular at the time. Billy Joe Cook played guitar, Rick Peale sang, Sherman Oaks played bass, and George Culture played the drums. "What I've noticed, it seems like college towns, in general, they're big mixing pots. Stillwater was. I won't say that it was unique. I'm sure that any other college town on the Prairie has the same kind of thing going on. But they kind of get a bubble over them and you get all this influence from all these people coming in, whether they're from foreign countries or other states. OSU had primarily been an Ag college. Oklahoma A&M is what it was called. So, a lot of the kids going there would have grown up in small towns and they would have heard a lot of country music. So, there was a big influence of that going on along with all the rock and roll and folk and other stuff. And it just seemed to be the right place at the right time for a lot of music to bloom. It was a really rich ground for that," said Lyon.

Danny Pierce, who wasn't a musician but was still an important part of this budding scene, got to Stillwater in the Fall of 1976, when he started school at OSU. Pierce had gone to high school and been friends with Mark Lyon before moving to Stillwater, which got him instantly connected to the music scene. "When Willie's was across the street- where Duprees was, the sporting goods place- it used to be on that side of the street before it moved across to the corner. Jimmy would be playing in there. Jimmy started playing with a high school friend of mine, Mark Lyons, as his lead guitar player. Small world, and I knew Mark from high school and so then we would go see Jimmy. Early on I remember him being pretty shy, he would often sing with his back to the crowd. He was learning his craft and all of that. I've often said if you listen to Red Dirt music- and I'm talking about Stillwater music here. I know that's a big term that gets thrown around a lot. But you know, it really is a recipe for how to live your life. I mean those songs have- there's a lot of meaning in there- at least for me," said Pierce.

In a few short years, Pierce would become one of the most well known and loved musical patrons that helped foster the Stillwater scene in a variety of ways. "A lot of good music came from Stillwater, it goes deeper than the Tractors and Steve Ripley. There were people in before that. Mason Williams used to hang out there, he wrote a song that was very popular called *Classical Gas*. An instrumental song you've heard probably before. But it really came into its own- the Red Dirt scene- with Bob and Chuck and Jimmy. That's my foundation really with those three guys and then the Skinners and everybody else that comes along," said Pierce.

Danny Pierce and Sage Powell. Photo provided by Sage Powell.

Bob Wiles found his way to Stillwater when he attended OSU at about this time as well. "When I first got to Stillwater in 1977, I got a job at the campus post office, and Jimmy LaFave worked at the campus post office. It was one of those fate type of a meetings. He was like, 'Hey, I don't know what you're doing this weekend, but my band is playing at this bar'. So, I went, and Bob Childers is warming up for him. So, the first band I saw- the first weekend I was in Stillwater- were two guys that would go on to be hugely important. I never would have dreamed at the time, but they both became dear friends," said Wiles.

While Tom Skinner had made his way to Stillwater in the early '70s- starting school there in 1972- after a year he ran out of money to pay for it and decided to go into the Air Force to help shape things up for him. He came back and re-enrolled into OSU in 1978, which is really when he began to make his mark in Stillwater. Skinner had just learned to play the guitar in the early '70s and played during his downtime in the military, teaching himself how to play. The first song he ever learned to play on the guitar was '*Down by the River*' by Neil Young. Tom Skinner was born in

San Francisco, California but moved to Bristow as a child. He grew up singing in the church choir, which led him to being in a rock band in high school called Tommy Delite and the Flames. While music wasn't his first love- that would have been baseball- it filled the gap once he realized he wasn't cutout for the big leagues. While at OSU he did a one-day walk-on try out for the team and experienced a fast ball that put him in his place, quickly realizing he didn't really have what it took. "I didn't really care about anything except baseball growing up, that was it. So, I had a big hole, and I just filled it with music. I had some friends that played, bought an old guitar and started learning John Prine and Neil Young songs and stuff like that," said Skinner in a 2014 video Interview with Red Dirt Nation (Youtube : *Tom Skinner Interview*, Red Dirt Nation).

Tom was the oldest of three boys, his brothers Mike and Craig all grew up singing together. From the church choir to riding around in the back of the family car- they learned about blood harmonies organically just through living life in a musical family.

The Skinner Brothers. Photo provided by Craig Skinner.

His brothers ended up following him to Stillwater where they formed The Skinner Brother's Band. "Tom was always in the picture, from a little bitty church kid getting up and singing a song. I was exposed to music through him. He turned me onto all of that. I love music too. We ended up playing music together, and I'm very grateful to that. I was probably 19-20 when we first started really playing music together. My father was a gospel singer. We had been around it all. We would see him get up and sing. We grew up playing music and watching music, and when we got old enough to get out there and do it- we went for it. I was grateful to play with my brother. He showed me a lot," said Mike Skinner.

Tom Skinner. Photo provided by Craig Skinner.

When Tom came back to Stillwater in 1978, he saw Bob Childers playing open mic nights around town. At an Earth Day celebration that year, he noticed Childers sitting in the crowd and remembered him from the shows he had seen around town. He went up and introduced himself to Childers, which led to yet another musical friendship.

Pam Potts met the Skinner Brother's not too long after following Dunlap and Childers to their lunch time jams. "There was a backyard in one of the bars called In the Beginning, that they played. But then they made it into Smiling Jacks as well, that a friend of mine owned. The Skinner Brothers would play back there and so I kind of met them. And oh my gosh- they were good looking. Those were crazy days. They had this one song they'd do, a cover song, Baby Drives a Mercury or something like that. I can't remember, but man I loved that song. Mike Skinner was super talented, and funny. Him and Tom would be so funny. I mean my god you'd just die laughing because they could just come up with crap, and they were just so quick and so funny about it. Just hilarious. Mike was so quick witted and so cute. Really curly hair, really blonde curly hair. I mean, my God, that's who we would chase," said Potts.

Mike Skinner had long, golden, curly hair and a thick blonde mustache. His baby blue eyes and barrel chest helped his good looks.

Kurt Nielsen, commonly known as Frenchie, was another one of the musicians that found his way to Stillwater during this time. He moved to Stillwater and met The Flat Mountain boys, which included Brett Howard and Bret Franzmann. "I moved up there, but I had known everybody all around. Brett Howard introduced me to Bret Franzmann from The Flat Mountain Boys. Then I met Chuck Dunlap and Bob and all those guys at the same time. Tom had just come back from being in the Navy [Air force]. So, they were trying to get him to be the guitar player in that band. So that's where I met Tom Skinner," said Nielsen.

Kurt Nielsen, Craig Skinner and Bret Franzmann. Photo provided by Sage Powell.

Bret Franzmann, who had started the Stillwater Camp in Winfield, had just started to play in bands during this time. He had played in a few bands while still in high school. Later he played with Chuck Dunlap and Matt Samples as a trio for about a year, before getting into the Flat Mountain Boys- which was a progressive bluegrass band. Franzmann credits the musical atmosphere of Stillwater during this time as the whole reason he even decided to pursue music. "There was a huge variety, I mean all different types of genres. It was a really happening scene. There was lots of clubs, lots of different bands playing throughout the week. Especially on the weekends, you could pretty much go from bar to bar and see different bands. Stillwater was just loaded with bands. There was a western swing band called Cimarron Swingsters, and there was all different kind of folk stuff going on. Chuck Dunlap, he was kinda almost jazzy stuff. A lot of different rock bands of different styles. There was something going on just all the time, and a lot of the camaraderie too, a lot of just jams amongst the different players around town. I was really fortunate to be a part of what was going on. If it wouldn't have been like that, I might not have pursued music like I did. I carried my instrument everywhere I went because I didn't wanna miss any opportunity. There used to be a Tom's Pant store down on the strip. It was an old house, couple doors down left from where Willie's is at. It had a big old front porch on it. We used to go down there and just play on that front porch in the evening on the strip- just break your instruments out and play. That's basically where I met Pam Potts was by doing that down on the strip. You want to have your instrument with you all the time because there was always gonna be something, you never knew when there was gonna be something coming up and you're ready to play," said Franzmann.

According to Kurt Nielsen, it was Childers, LaFave, and the Flat Mountain boys that were the hot stuff on the scene at this time. Dunlap was the first person to ever let Nielsen play on a stage in Stillwater, and Nielsen would become an integral part of the scene in time.

In Their Own Words

Mike Skinner - Our dad was a big booming singer- he didn't need a microphone. He probably sang at every funeral they had in those days. He had a gut for days and used every bit of it. He was a big boisterous fella, and I think we all sprung from that, we came about it naturally. He was a good man. We had started to put together our little two piece, and then when Craig got old enough and out of high school, he started playing with us. It became the Skinner Brothers, and everybody had a good time it seemed like. It was a pretty good time to be from that area. There were a lot of guys that wanted to be up there. We would get rowdy sometimes- it would get that way. We played a lot in Stillwater. Most people got along and everybody got up and played. You just got up and played. If you were somewhere hanging out, you were going to get up and play a song. Tom would always ask people "do you want to get up and play?" He always gave guys and gals the opportunity to get up and play, he enjoyed that. We all did.

Craig Skinner -My dad got me a harmonica, and that was back in 68, probably. We were on vacation. I took to that pretty quick, then by the time I was 12, I got my hands on a guitar. Which happened to be Tom's. I snuck it out and then would sneak it back in. I got my own pretty soon after that because mom and dad figured out what I was doing. So about 72 is when I started. I played trombone in high school band and had some piano lessons also. But I didn't really take to it and still haven't. Probably at about 14, we played at Western Heritage days, me and a banjo player friend of mine down here. We played dueling banjos. I was hooked. The first time I was ever in a bar was when I was 15 in 1975. They [Tom and Mike] talked me into coming and getting up there. The night before, the bass player got inebriated and fell off the stage. So, Saturday night they didn't have a bass player, and I was playing in church by then. They asked dad if they could haul me up to Tulsa and play the gig. Made 75 bucks, and I've been hooked since then. Tom was going into the Air Force at that time. And then I hooked up with Wayne Brown- rock and roll Brown. I got in good with him, and they played the Lake Country Ballroom, a big ballroom they played in Mannford. They had gotten into some kind of tiff with their bass player and needed a fill in. They needed the bass player and had heard about me. I took off over there. Stillwater was great. There were places to play and people who liked the music. The Skinner Brothers played for our own enjoyment; we didn't care if there was anybody there really. I mean we did, but we were playing what we liked to play. It wasn't like we were up there trying to put on some image like a country star today. It was about the music, and it was great. Up and down the strip- Jimmy Lafave, Bob Childers was around, they showed up out there, and the scene was just great.

Danny Pierce- Chuck was more just the singer-songwriter, usually just him and his guitar, maybe another guitar player with them. There was a guy named Leo Miller that played some banjo that was around. I used to work at a bar down on the strip called Molly Bloom's, back in the day. Those guys would come in and play there. Chuck's songwriting is just so fantastic. He had some songs about Stillwater you know, particularly. Writing about that, as did Jimmy on his early songs. They were really starting to craft songs about Stillwater and the music there in Stillwater. Chuck has one called The Estates. That was about where he lived, he lived out on the east side of town. But the farm kind of became The Estates, where people could go. He wrote another beautiful song called Sally. If you've ever heard his song about Sally, she was a girl at the bar. So, now they're writing songs about Stillwater and the people in Stillwater that they see going on around them. And that hits home when you're from there, you love that kind of stuff. Chuck's great. Very poignant with the song, right? You write those messages in those songs that teach you how to live your life and handle things and that's what makes it work for me.

Gene Collier - Getting to play with Tom Skinner, that was like magic happened, I tell ya. Holy Crap. The guy was just, it was just way too easy for him. For most of the rest of us guys, we would just beat our head on the wall trying to learn something or do something. But for Tom it was just like a duck to water for him. Amazing guy, I really miss him. I really do I tell ya. You know, my favorite Tom Skinner story- you probably wouldn't want to talk about it. But one night he came in about 2 in the morning and he was trying to be real quiet. He didn't turn any lights on because he didn't want to wake his little boy up. He said when he got in the house, he really needed to go poop real bad. So, he went and sat in the dark and pooped and when he flushed, something just didn't sound right. That was back in the cassette tape days. His little boy had thrown all his cassette tapes in the toilet and Tom had just come in and shit all over them. Man, that story about Tom was just one of the funniest things, and the way he would tell it, he was just a hoot.

Pam Potts - I remember one time Bob grabbed me in the middle of the night. That wasn't the first time I've ever been grabbed in the middle of the night to go record. I don't remember exactly what was going on or what number of his albums it was or anything at all. But he had me in someone's house in the bedroom somewhere with a recording machine, singing in this deal. Late at night or something and he gave me a couple shots at it and then I went home. I don't even remember much about that- except it kind of vaguely happened. Then one day I was listening to, I guess it was a cassette tape or something. But anyway, I got kind of mad. I thought my god, where did they get a Pam Potts imitator? You know, that's making me irritated because it just sounded like me, but it didn't sound like me. And then it was like, okay, that's someone using the kind of inflection I would do and how did they do that? You know, where do they find that person? And then it dawned on me. Oh, yeah, yeah. I did sing that. That is me and I realized it and then later it dawned me. Oh, yeah, that was that bedroom thing. You know, they dragged me in in the middle of the night to sing. I remember that. I've done a lot of recording.

Connections & Collaborations

Not all musicians starting their careers in Oklahoma were necessarily lumped into this forming scene, even though many eventually became a part of it in different ways. Mary Reynolds is one of those musicians. "I started singing very early and always wanted my parents to buy me instruments and do that. I was kind of shy about singing but I wanted to have a guitar, so I got a guitar at age 10. Mother got me lessons. I was in the band, went to OU music school. I thought I was gonna be a band director. I wasn't good at following rules and stuff like that, so I ended up being a performance major-but I didn't complete my degree. I learned a lot of people do music without that theoretical background. But I found it very helpful. Then of course I like all kinds of music so at school you get exposed to all kinds of things. Even more nowadays. In the '70s it was all kind of buttoned down and classical, and it's not that way anymore. I'm so glad for the people coming up these days that things are different. I kind of thought country music was so hokey and just a dumb thing that my parents liked. I couldn't get into it all. But the *Redheaded Stranger* came out, which showed me not just country music- but the traditional fiddle tunes, and blues and that kind of older underpinning sort of became available to me with that record. Also, my mother liked it, so we had a thing in common that was really cool," said Reynolds.

Reynolds began playing music for audiences in 1977. Though not from Stillwater, she played there occasionally. Reynolds performed in a band called Blue Herron to begin with, playing around Norman for several years. "In those days, bars were scary places and there weren't that many of them that had music and even fewer of them paid. I think The Library Bar where I got started was a relatively benign place to start. I think they paid $20 and then I got tips. Not exactly sure if I remember how much it paid really, but it was not much and it was hard. Then being a woman, you know was very different, was very much harder. Men wanted to run everything and although the guys that were in my band very much respected me, not so much club owners and people," said Reynolds.

Reynolds performed at Town Tavern in Norman, where the owners became patrons -steady supporters of her music. Reynolds recalls that these people, among others, would go out of their way to help and promote her. Musical fans and patrons would be just as much of a catalyst for these local musicians, as well as the newly forming scene, as anything else. Reynolds names Jim Tolbert as a person who went out of his way to promote local music during this time. The venue owners, promoters, and music supporters of this scene play just as big a part as the musicians do when it comes down to it. Many of the musicians credit not only each other for helping to find gigs and get their names out, but they also credit those who have a deep love of live music who continued to come to shows, tell their friends, and spread the word. The Red Dirt scene would continue to thrive because of the people and community of friends and fans that became family, as much as because of the music coming out of it.

Mary Reynolds moved to New York for a time and continued to have her own successful music career, returning to Oklahoma in 1985. While Reynolds was on the outskirts of the newly forming Red Dirt scene, she would come to play a part in securing a venue upon returning to Oklahoma, that would become a staple in the Red Dirt scene for years to come.

Another musician who didn't come from Stillwater roots was Stacey Sanders. Sanders grew up in L.A. but moved around a lot. He started playing guitar at the age of 11. He moved to Enid, Oklahoma in 1976 as a teenager and got involved in playing music with some of the older locals. "I used to play with a guy named Steve Bradley and Steve Flu. I was like 15 and they were 24-25 years old. They really inspired me as a teenager to dig into my roots of music and becoming a lyricist. All my guys from back in those days are long gone. They've been gone for many years. But I'd be remiss if I didn't mention them as inspirational in my writing," said Sanders.

Several years later, Sanders joined a blues band called Sweet Misery. "Then I really started enjoying my career in music. When I was probably 21, started writing some of my better songs, about in that time period, and started playing solo. And that's really what I've enjoyed for the last several years," said Sanders. Sweet Misery would play in Stillwater and on the strip a few times in the '80s, but it would be several years before Sanders would turn more towards the singer/songwriter aspect of his career. He would come more into his own later down the line and be more immersed in the Red Dirt singer/songwriter scene much later in his career.

Kevin Warren Smith, a member of the Cherokee Nation and a fiddle player, made his way to Stillwater at this time. Smith's great grandfather, William Spencer Smith- known as Black Billy- was a champion fiddler in Tennessee and Northern Alabama in the late 19th and early 20th centuries. His grandson- Smith's uncle Edsel- was a swing and folk fiddler. He was recorded by universities and in feature films, including a John Wayne film. "He played with Bob Wills when the band was in Oklahoma. Only my grandparents insisted that he not use his real name. They were concerned about the family's reputation and weren't completely crazy about his consorting with those particular professionals. He also made and repaired fiddles at The Chicago Store (Tucson, Arizona). He played in swing bands his entire life. Several other family members also played instruments at family reunions and other gatherings with a focus on western, Western swing, bluegrass and deep roots country music. My parents' musical heritage and abilities made a big impression on me," said Smith.

The only formal education on strings Smith ever received was when he took viola lessons in the fourth grade. The following year he took up percussion and began to play with neighborhood musicians in garage bands, which helped him get gigs. Smith was chosen to play drums in a regional TV commercial when he was in sixth grade. He completed graduate-level percussion before high school was over and he once filled in for the band Chicago's drummer who was unable to make a private gig in Oklahoma. Smith moved to Stillwater in 1977 to start college. But he quickly found himself focused on every opportunity to play music. The town was overflowing with great sounds, and Smith began playing more guitar and violin in support of local singer/songwriters. This experience exposed him to many new venues and musicians.

"Arriving in the college town of Stillwater in 1977 provided me with an abundance of opportunity for growth. I still played drums, guitar and violin. The music was varied. I got to play more rather than just continuing with bluegrass and western swing. My violin style in the '70s was based more on the violin sounds of David Lindley, cajun fiddlers, gypsy fiddle and players like Scarlet Rivera in her live Rolling Thunder Review days. I've always enjoyed being a side man more than a front man. And there were plenty of opportunities to do both. I have to point out the fact that Stillwater was a great place to be even if you were not a musician. It was great for artists and even poets. It was exciting for everyone who was open to a 'commune' kind of feeling. Romance was in the air; the town was buzzing with energy for all ages. Being a college town, it was youthful in spirit and the prairies were right past the city limits if you felt like keeping yourself grounded," said Smith.

Before Smith got to Stillwater, he had already learned how to be both a sideman and a front man in Tulsa and had gained enough experience to be accepted into the Stillwater scene naturally and easily. "All of my musical history had prepared me for supporting the songwriters I like with my fiddle and guitar. Sometimes drums. I also helped friends copyright and register their songs. I produced cassettes that featured local songwriters. I've got some rough tapes of my old songs too. Most of this stuff I've never shared with people," said Smith.

Smith said the real magic of the scene was based on musicians contributing to each other. The scene had been born out of a collective emphasis on collaboration and mutual support. The typical competitiveness of the music business just wasn't a part of this musical community. "Right away I came across plenty of musicians and singers who had different styles and moods. And whenever I found someone whose music excited and inspired me, I gravitated to marrying my music with theirs, even if just for one-night gigs. But no-one was monogamous musically. We all performed with each other off and on. In addition to Bob Childers, I loved performing and recording with Jimmy LaFave, Tom Skinner, music majors from the university, country musicians, musicians who could not be categorized, songwriters of all types and countless instrumentalists. And I do mean countless. The constant river of creativity brought people together. It reached a point where a whole week went by completely filled with gigs and practice, recording and jamming. Little time was given to our day jobs or mainstream education. A real community was established and most players always allowed guests on stage. It was ok if the guest was not a hotshot. Everyone just shared music. It came naturally and we were very aware of the magical nature of what developed. But luckily nobody tried to give it a label or take control of the magick, nor tried to setup definitions and boundaries. We weren't near a music business center, and we didn't think much about "making it big." We were just happy playing," said Smith.

Peter Nichols and Simon Miller Mundy- both British, both had worked with Leon Russell- settled in Tulsa and established Pilgrim Records. They put out two local albums in the late '70s: The Tulsa Sampler in 1977 and The Green Album in 1978. There is a great documentary about these two guys and the Tulsa Sampler album on YouTube, called *The Tulsa Sampler Story* by Rockvision which will give you much more background and information about it all.

The Green Album featured four songs by Randy Crouch. The Sampler also had three songs by the band El Roacho. El Roacho dissolved during this time and joined in with Crouch. Edd Lively was a talented singer and lead guitarist with El Roacho. The joined group became known as the Flying Horse band, as they were doing many of Lively's songs too. The members of El Roacho were Lively, Curtis Massey on saxes, John Hoff on drums and Chip Anderson on bass. El Roacho had previously recorded an album for Columbia Records, and Lively and Hoff had toured with

Freddie King as part of his band. The newly formed Flying Horse was a very diverse group musically, doing folk, country-rock, soul and even jazz and classical. For instance, they were doing a medley of *Lonesome Fiddle Blues* by Vassar Clements and *Impressions* by John Coltrane, as James Downing recalls.

Randy Crouch, Mike Brewer and Kevin Warren Smith. Photo provided by Kevin Warren Smith.

Randy Crouch and the Flying Horse Band were one of the top Tulsa bands at this time. They played all over the state; all the college towns, playing Tulsa, Oklahoma City, Lawton, Norman and Stillwater. There was a busy music scene going on over in the Fayetteville, Arkansas area at this time too. A lot of the bands that were from Tulsa were playing over in the Fayetteville market and then Joplin, and across the border in Kansas. Crouch and the band were making their rounds and drawing more and more people to their eclectic sound.

While the Stop Black Fox movement had been going on since 1973, it was still going strong at this time. According to the Laka Documentation and Research Center on Nuclear Energy website, a Claremore teacher from Inola named Carrie Dickerson became one of the people determined to stop the nuclear power reactors from being built near her town. It became her mission to educate the public and organize fundraisers to help the effort. A big part of that fundraising came from local musicians who performed at the many rallies and benefit concerts. In 1978 the movement recorded and released an album, called 'Black Fox Blues? For our Children'. One of the artists on this album was Randy Crouch and The Flying Horse Band, with the songs *Radioactivity* and *The Sun & The Wind*. The movement gained international press, and more nationwide acts such as Jackson Browne and Bonnie Raitt joined in to perform at a May 24th, 1978, concert at Mohawk Park in Tulsa to help the Stop Black Fox movement. "He (Crouch) recorded *Radioactivity* and *The Sun &The Wind* for the Stop Black Fox album. He was calling the band 'Randy Crouch & The Flying Horse Opera' which was also the name of a suite of songs he had written about cowboys and aliens. He had some fantastic musicians playing in that group, including Pat Murray on keys and Jim Strader on bass – they went on to have a be-bop trio later," said James Downing.

In 1978 The Sun Belt Alliance was going strong in Stillwater- which was one of the subgroups that organized to stop the building of Black Fox. They would set up many events during the summer months, which were held to allow people to register to vote as well as educate the public about the consequences of a local nuclear power plant. Sun Belt Alliance would also host events at Smiling Jack's on the strip and have musicians playing the event. Childers, Crouch and LaFave gravitated to the cause and could often be found playing at the Sun Belt Alliance events. "I would have seen these guys- you know kind of solo here or there, Up Your Alley or at Willy's- just here and there, and then with Sun Belt Alliance and those gatherings were kind of the tribe coming together if you will. The communal element as opposed to just going to the bar just to listen to a band kind of a thing," said Danny Pierce.

In just a few years Mark Lyon went from seeing his first show at the Bar Ditch, to playing in various musical formations around Stillwater. One of those was a band called Whitewater, which included Rod Boutwell on steel guitar and Charlie Hollis on bass.

Gene Williams and Mark Lyon. Photo provided by Sage Powell.

Lyon recalls a gig Whitewater had on the strip at Molly Murphy's, which was next to a little bar in the alley originally called Rathskeller, which LaFave was running and called Up Your Alley. One the same night as the Whitewater gig, some friends of Lyon's were playing next door at the Alley. "So, on break from playing with Whitewater, I would run over there and play 15 minutes with these other guys and then go back to Molly Murphy's. I did this like twice in one night and I was cracking up, you know, so they gave me the name Mark Sessions at that time," said Lyon.

Lyon joined LaFave in about 1978, starting at first as an acoustic thing, which eventually turned into an electric band and formed into The Night Tribe band. The band consisted of Ron Kershaw on bass, Dean Nixon on keyboard, Lyon on guitar and LaFave. While they went through several drummers at the time, the one that they settled on and played with the most was Ron Beckel. "That band was a really good little band. We did a lot of Jimmy's originals, but we also did just some classic rock and roll, some Chuck Berry, some Creedence Clearwater. I couldn't call it red dirt by any means, but at the same time, you know it was rock and roll- prairie rock- rock and roll out in the middle of nowhere. And there were certainly those influences. Jimmy's songs had kind of a James Taylor kind of a feel to them or folk type feel," said Lyon.

Charlie Hollis, who played in Whitewater with Lyon, was a local player in various arrangements, but he was also into sound engineering and recording. He opened a little studio in his attic in Stillwater at the end of the '70s, giving local musicians another easily affordable and accessible place to create recordings. Hollis recorded musicians like Lafave, Crouch and many others. This would just be the start of his recording career and would prove to be another springboard in allowing these musicians to get their music recorded.

Larry Wilson and Jimmy LaFave. Photo provided by Sage Powell.

Kevin Warren Smith was roommates with Bob Childers in various rented houses from 1978-1980. They wrote songs and played many gigs together during this time and continued to play together for years even when they no longer lived together. They played college bars, honky-tonk clubs, biker bars, and opened for visiting artists on bigger stages as well as house concerts. Sometimes they stood on the corners of town playing music, and sometimes they played in venues for better money. But they consistently played and wrote songs together. "We would occasionally get frustrated with each other over minor issues and ego problems, but we essentially worked and played together an awful lot- and we cared about each other no matter what. We both drew on each other's music quite a bit. It shaped both of us musically. For better or worse, to a greater or lesser degree," said Smith.

Kurt Nielsen said he and Smith met in about 1979, when Smith's car tires had been slashed by a bitter ex-girlfriend. Smith needed some cash to replace the tires and ended up selling Nielsen some musical gear. Nielsen says that they have been musical soul mates since then, that they see eye to eye musically far closer than anyone else Nielsen has picked with throughout his musical journey. Smith also spoke highly of Nielsen. "Kurt has always been a great musical compadre to travel with through all the musical journeys. Although he plays other instruments, he's mainly known for his mandolin playing. Being a sideman myself meant that Kurt and I were buddies on a lot of stages together. I respect his consistent desire to never miss an opportunity to play with people. Over the years he has surpassed me a long way in terms of numbers of performances. He is truly a natural musician. He plays for the love of it," said Smith.

Little did any of these guys know that they were forming the groundwork and philosophy of a whole new music scene. It was never the plan to form something entirely new, and it took many years for them to realize that's just what they did. They were just carving out a path for themselves, making up their own rules and playing the music that touched their souls- and in the process, it gave birth to something bigger than they realized. "We all knew without having to talk about it something special was happening with our music in those pre-red dirt days. When we were together on stage, we noticed more and more that some magical chemistry had come into our world. That magic began to attract attention of various kinds. But we never talked about it ourselves. It seemed almost too sacred," said Smith.

In Their Own Words

Mike Skinner - So many shows are just the same, exactly the same. But there are some that stick out- playing at Cain's or playing behind somebody that was going to make you nervous. There might have been a charge of feeling in the air. There's also a bunch of shows and you don't expect it to be good and something happens, and you get up there and bam-and it's like, I can play that. I can play that over my head, I'm out of my own league. Every once in a while, it would line up like that and it would be great. It goes all the way down to somebody just feeling better on the way to work listening to music. Everybody was just playing to be playing, it wasn't about earning a cut. Steve Ripley is a good guy. He's seen a lot. I had this postcard from him, he was hanging out at this music store, and he wrote 'just hanging out with George and the boys'. Him and George Harrison and Bob Dylan. He is rock, he is a rock star. He even made guitars so well. Chuck Dunlap was always fun to pick with. He's good.

Kevin Warren Smith- I've always been thankful to have grown up with Oklahoma music. It is wonderful and offered unique experiences. For instance, every now and then you'd hear a rumor about someone playing somewhere- not publicized. In high school I heard that Leon Russell was going to be practicing in a hay barn out in the country just south of Tulsa. About a 20-minute drive. I checked it out with a friend and sure enough, we pulled into the gravel parking lot and could hear the music. There were only a handful of cars. So, we got to enjoy the music of the Master while we sat on a bale of hay. Magic has always been here, even if the rest of the world didn't necessarily know.

Pam Potts – It's weird being a female in this deal because there's not very many. And then not only that I was always married to somebody else. So, it wasn't like I was freewheeling and sleeping with everybody in the band and all that kind of stuff like some women will. I mean, there are some, and I think when people see you on stage with a man- say I'm on stage with one man or any person- I'm doing that guy right now. That's the way that it is, it's a sexual thing. And it's absolutely not, and for me, it never was. I was always married. But that is what people assume. You have to almost make it stated. So that was really strange. There's always been that weird expectation of being a woman and it somehow turns into that, and I don't know other than it's just people's dirty minds or something. I don't know. But it's kind of a weird thing.

An Influx in Stillwater

The musicians continued to pour into Stillwater, most of them to attend school. Gene Williams arrived on the scene at this time. Williams had started playing music as a young child, his first instrument being the drums. He played in the school band all through high school. He started playing guitar at the age of 14 and started joining bands while still in high school. When he was a junior in College in Fort Smith in 1978, he was playing in a band with Danny Falkner, who had just graduated from OSU. Williams decided to transfer to OSU, where his sister was already attending school, to finish his degree. Falkner had told all his Stillwater pals to get in touch with Williams when he got there, which included names like Charlie Hollis, Ron Beckel and Phil Hyde. They were all older than Williams and had been playing in local bands for several years.

Williams quickly began playing solo shows around town as soon as he arrived, playing shows at Aunt Molly's in the student union. He made it one semester in school studying music before he decided to drop out to play music instead. He was having so much fun playing all the bars, he decided that was what he wanted to do with his life.

Gene Williams on stage. Photo provided by Sage Powell.

Williams was in a band called the West Street Band and Tom and Mike Skinner sat in with them. "That was probably in 79, and I just thought they were great. I made it a point to make friends with them. I was writing quite a bit of songs back then, and they started doing some of my songs. We didn't live very far apart, so I was going up to their house all the time, and we were playing a lot. They had two guitarists at the time with the Skinner Brothers Band- Mike Shannon and Mark Lyon," said Williams.

Mark Lyon, who was still playing with LaFave at the time, had started playing with Skinner as well. Lyon had gotten to know Gene Williams, who lived just down the street from him and Charlie Hollis and would frequently get together. It was typical of all the local musicians to convene at one of their houses and sit around and pick out songs. In fact, Williams moved in with Hollis and Lyon at some point.

Lyon went over to Skinner's apartment one day and they started playing together and seemed to click. That's when Lyon joined the Skinner Brothers band. "Rod Boutwell, he was the initial steel guitarist for the Skinner Brothers. That band would've consisted of all three of the Skinner Brothers; Tom, Mike, and Craig. Hearing those three guys sing together, my gosh, those blood harmonies that they could pull off was something else," said Lyon.

Jim Dodrill, Rod Boutwell, Charlie Hollis, and Mark Lyons. Photo provided by Stan Woodward.

Craig was still in high school at this time, still living in Bristow. Tom and Mike were living in Stillwater. Even though Craig was a good bass player, he couldn't always be at all the gigs they had booked so they also had a bass player by the name of Tim Smalley, and Tony Harrison played drums. At this time Boutwell had left the band, and Mike Shannon had stepped in. "So occasionally we'd play gigs, and everyone would be there, and Craig would get- I could tell he would get impatient. He'd be wanting to play bass, and Tim would be over there playing bass. So, he'd be sitting there with his arms folded, waiting for his vocal part to come up. But you know, he got to play bass a lot and Craig's done quite well for himself. But that was a really good period," said Lyon.

Randy Pease moved to Stillwater in the fall of 1978 to go to graduate school at OSU. Not long after Pease settled into Stillwater, he started walking around town. He walked down to the Washington Street Strip, with its array of clubs with all kinds of different music pouring out of the doors. There might be country here, bluegrass there, rockabilly there, and rock somewhere else. They all kind of bled out into the street. Pease believes all that music coming out of the clubs, kind of cross pollinated and eventually became Red Dirt music. "I think someone told me this when I first moved there, that Playboy or one of those magazines had named Stillwater the second most party college town in the United State. It was a partying place," said Pease.

Pease decided to check out one of those little bars where he stumbled upon Bob Childers playing. "He would just sing songs and tell stories. He was probably the one who got me to thinking that I could probably do this publicly. Bob's the guy who inspired me to start writing songs. And you know, he wasn't a great guitar player, but he was a good songwriter and a good storyteller. I just listened to him one night, maybe I'd been in Stillwater a couple of weeks, looking for something to do. Probably a weekend, I don't know. I don't even remember the name of the bar anymore. I'm sure it's defunct right now because they come and go. But I listened to him. The first time I ever met him in that club on the strip, he was just doing what he does. Sitting on a stool with a six string. I even wrote a song about my first encounter with Bob. It's called, '*I Can Do that*'. The hook line is, 'if I can do this, you can do that'," said Pease of his first encounter with Childers.

It wasn't long after that when Pease met the Skinner Brothers. "The first place I probably saw them was at the Stonewall, and they were good. They were really, really good. They had that brother harmony thing. Like the Everly Brothers or the Beach Boys or the Bee Gees. The kind of harmony only brothers can pull off. They were all really nice guys. Tom let me play with them. And later on, he recorded some of my songs and kept them alive after I moved back to the Midwest," said Pease. Pease had only been playing guitar about five years and never publicly at this time. So, about a year or two after he moved to Stillwater, he started going to try it out in public.

The first place he played was at Stonewall Tavern. Pease was an English Major at OSU and his office and most of his classes were in Moral Hall. Stonewall Tavern is right across the street from that building, so after class or work Pease would make his way over there. More often than not, the Skinner brothers or Gene Williams would be playing there. Eventually, Pease started playing between the Skinner Brother's sets. "Tom, he knew I played guitar a little bit. He lived a couple of blocks from me then. I'd go and visit him, and we'd pick sometimes, and he showed me some stuff. He started letting me play between the Skinner Brother's sets, and on a good night he might let me sit in with them on the second set. But that's kind of where I went public, you know, that's where I first started playing. Then that's where I had my first paid gig too. I hadn't been playing long in public, and I was kind of timid. It was one night somewhere where I did a set between somebody else's. Maybe I was liquored up a little bit. I don't know. I was really projecting- man I thought I hit a milestone. I was singing hard and from the heart. When I was all done, I went over to a table where Bob was. And he said, you'd do anything for attention. He'd always bust me. But I learned a lot from him. Sometimes I needed to get busted," said Pease.

Kurt Nielsen and Randy Pease. Photo provided by Sage Powell.

Greg Jacobs got to Stillwater in 1979. He graduated high school in 1972 and got into music directly after that. One of his best friends gave him an old guitar and he started learning how to play. Jacobs bought a Bob Dylan songbook that had all the chords, started learning with it. He then joined the military. Jacobs got out of the service in 1977, which was when he discovered John Prine and Guy Clark and really started trying to write songs. He went to school at OU for a couple of years, and then transferred to Stillwater to study forestry at OSU. When he arrived, Jacobs was working in the Veteran's office on campus in a work study program. He met a guy there and they got to talking music. Jacobs told the guy that he piddled around and wrote songs, but he didn't really play in public. Jacobs was still trying to get his confidence up enough where he could go play in front of people. The guy talked Jacobs into playing at the Stonewall Tavern. The guy knew the owner of the Stonewall and got Jacobs a gig.

Tom Skinner and Greg Jacobs. Photo provided by Sage Powell.

"I played a gig in there. It was either the first or second time I played in there when Gene Williams came in, and I met him and got to talking to him. Then I met the Skinner boys- Tom and his brothers Craig and Mike- which was just a great band. Those guys were just really good, and Gene played guitar with them. They had three-part harmonies that only three brothers could sing, it was just a matter of genetics the way it worked. So, I hung with those guys for a long time. I wasn't ever officially a member of the band, but I'd go to all the gigs, and I'd help them run the sound a bit. And in each set, I'd play two or three songs with them, just was running with them," said Jacobs.

Eventually Jacobs started playing some gigs of his own- Tom Skinner would play bass and Williams would play guitar- as a little three-piece band. From there Jacobs met Childers, and through Childers he met LaFave, and the rest of the music community in Stillwater at the time. "It was really a cool little music town. It wasn't a place where you could make any money playing in town, but there were a lot of places to play, and it was fun. The little music community were all good friends and close. When I look back on the good ol days, that was then- those early days. Now of course our lives were in constant turmoil, self-inflicted turmoil, but that seems to be the way you write songs. We reveled in that, that's what we did. But that's how I got to meet all those guys. Now Tom and Bob and I- we became really close friends. I just considered them as my brothers, we just were. We played around there until 84-85, sometime in there," said Jacobs.

Mark Mars made his way to Stillwater around this time. Mars had been exposed to music his entire life- his mom played guitar, and his dad played the fiddle. They moved from Oklahoma City, to California, then back to Oklahoma while he was growing up. He was building cabinets with his dad when they took a job in Stillwater in 1978. Mars had an old guitar that needed some repair work, so he took it to the music store on Sixth street called Breakaway Music, where he met Ricky Peale. Peale was in a band called Light Planet Band, which included Rod Boutwell, Charlie

Hollis, Dean Nixon and Cheryl and Mike Hufford. Soon Mars started running sound for the band. Not long after that, he joined Fornelle and the Midnight Express band. From there he joined the band Bittersweet with Mike and Cheryl Hufford and Charlie Kruger, which mostly performed original songs by Cheryl. Cheryl's sister Shelley married Gary LaFave, Jimmy's brother. Everyone seemed to be connected to everyone else in this close-knitted music community.

Lamb Studios was still going strong, and Hufford kept plenty busy with local musicians who wanted to record their music. Not all of them had full bands, so many of the local musicians would just be on hand or be called in to play to fill in the blanks for whoever needed it. Hufford, along with many others that recorded music for this scene, either didn't charge much or charged nothing at all at times when local musicians were strapped for cash but needed to get an album made. Many of the side musicians playing on other's albums would do so for free. It was never about making a bunch of money from their skills and talents; it was more for the joy of doing it and helping everyone succeed. Hufford would eventually move from the small shed into a larger studio, which was a little more south, but still east of Stillwater.

John Buckner was one of those musicians who would spend a lot of time at the studio, just waiting to play bass for whoever was recording that needed it. "If I wasn't playing or whatever, or wasn't asleep, I was out at the studio. I kind of just hung around there and people would come in and be like, hey, we need a bass part. Ok. I'll play. So, I was doing recording at that time and just bumming around Stillwater, just being a musician which I loved. Broke. I would get money from the weekend or whatever playing and would try to figure out how I was gonna make that last till the next gig. But it always worked out. I just remember those days, now that a lot of these people have passed or are no longer around. I just look back at that time. It was truly magical. It was just that bohemian lifestyle, where you just wanted to play. You wanted to perform and you didn't wanna be part of the nine to five shirt and tie. That you had something to say, and you had people tell you, 'I just love coming to watch you play', and that was their escape, and I enjoyed being part of that," said Buckner.

Mike Hufford also worked as an audio engineer and sound specialist at Steve Irby's company Stillwater Designs and Audio starting in 1979. Hufford's wife Cheryl sang in various bands during this time.

Brad Piccolo graduated high school in 1979 and started at OSU in the fall that year. Piccolo had received a guitar for his 15th birthday, so he took it along to college with him in his old Chevelle. It didn't take him long to start meeting others in the dorms and fraternities who had also brought guitars and instruments along with them. They would grab their instruments and get together on front porches and living rooms and play what they could. Bob Wiles met Piccolo when they were in the same fraternity. Their common bond at that time was neither of them were big fans of the fraternity. "I saw a guitar in his room, and he saw a guitar in my room, and we kind of gravitated together and ended up real quickly moving out of the fraternity house to getting a house, off campus. We became roommates and started trying to teach ourselves how to play guitar. We did a few on campus talent shows and things like that. Open mic nights, stuff like that. I always had fun picking together with our common musical interests. It's funny that one thing we all had in common was Jerry Garcia. Brad was a big Grateful Dead fan, and I really wasn't at the time. I was into bluegrass music, and Jerry Garcia was a banjo player. He had an album out called *Old and in the Way*. It was really influential, and it was one of my favorite records of all time. It was interesting because we all had a commonality with Jerry Garcia. But they were Jerry Garcia fans for the Grateful Dead, and I was a fan from *Old and in the Way*, which speaks to the diversity of the kind of music we liked. We liked all kinds of music. Rock and roll, and country, bluegrass and blues," said Wiles.

It didn't take Wiles and Piccolo long before they signed up and played at Aunt Molly's Amateur night, getting 30-minute slots to showcase their music. They would also invite another college friend they knew, John Cooper, who didn't play an instrument at this time, but would sing. It would be an early formation of what would later become the Red Dirt Rangers.

Brad Piccolo. Photo provided by Sage Powell

In Their Own Words

Mark Mars - Stillwater was the center of the earth. I'm sure you've heard that. I was younger so Bob was like some kind of shaman or something. Everybody loves him, you know? Bob, he does this when he played live. He might be going along then he would- what I would call break time. Just go left. Some people complained about that, that played with him, you know? But I viewed it as a challenge. Can I keep up with you? So, yeah, he was a lot of fun to play with.

Greg Jacobs about playing with the Skinner Brothers - It was rowdy, with the full band. It was fun, it was noisy. Stillwater had a good crowd, of course you had the college crowd. But we also had the older, late 20s early 30s- older than the college kids- and they were loyal, and they would pack every show that you played, and it was just fun. I would love to go back and relive a few of those nights, because it was just fun. You felt like a rock star, when you were playing. It was great, they were the good ol days. We didn't have cell phones, we don't have any video of that time. I would love to have some video of some of those gigs. None of us could afford a camera, much less carry it around all the time. There's not much documentation of that time. It was a good time. I don't know that Stillwater was any different than say, Austin, or any other college town of that era, that had its own music scene. The thing that was different about Stillwater was that it was our little music scene. Tom, Bob, LaFave, and Chuck Dunlap and Randy Crouch and all those guys were just so talented. They were just all such great musicians; it's just such a shame that not many of us had the gumption to do something with it. We just needed somebody to come in there with a checkbook that would help finance us, kick us in the ass, and tell us to get out on the road and get busy.

Bob Wiles -For me personally, not enough people talk about Greg Jacobs. Greg Jacobs is one of the great songwriters of our time. He's from Checotah, Oklahoma. He's not a huge self-promoter. He writes songs from the heart and for me- whenever I think of Red Dirt music and some of the greatest, sorta pioneers of music- I don't think enough people talk about Greg Jacobs. He is really something special. He's written a bunch of great songs. He was a history teacher, a high school history teacher. He writes a bunch of great songs telling the story of Oklahoma history. In fact, this came out horribly, but I told him one time- most great artists, whether it's a painter or a poet, during their lifetime, they're broke. And then when they die, someone discovers their catalogue of work, and they become legendary. We called him Lucky Breaks because he was not lucky at all. I told him I was listening to some of his songs about Oklahoma history. And I said, someday somebody is going to discover your body of work and it's gonna be like all of Oklahoma's History just right there in song. He said man, I wish they'd hurry up. I'm broke. I said, Oh, hell, you'll be long dead. None of the great artists get discovered until they are dead. It didn't really come out quite the way I intended it to. To me I was comparing him to Picasso. But it didn't come out like that.

Craig Skinner - Tom was a hell of a good songwriter, he was involved with himself, which was good. To be Tom Skinner was just where he needed to be. I tried to help when I could and tried not to mess anything up. I've done told you my pee story, didn't I? I was three-four years old. I was thirsty and we were on a vacation, in the back of a dodge station wagon. I woke up just crying that I was thirsty, and Tom said 'well here you are', and gave me this can of RC cola full of warm piss. I didn't even get it down my throat before I spit it all over him. That's when I realized that this is something in my life I need to deal with right here- brothers. I was supposed to be a girl, that didn't work out, they already had me named and everything. Little brother. Little brother came up tough.

Brad Piccolo - The Skinner Brothers were one of those bands that was already established by the time we started playing, so we kind of looked up to those guys along with guys like Lafave and Bob Childers. Those guys were already gigging, like Chuck Dunlap. But the Skinner Brothers, yeah, they were already rocking and rolling at that time. You could see those guys play at different places around town and we always looked up to those guys.

Because anybody that has already had a band, we were like, gee, we wanna do that too. Those guys really inspired us to do things like that and to get up on stage and play.

Kevin Warren Smith – We were less concerned about making big money or having dreams about entertainment status, and more concerned with satisfying our desire to stay in a positive flow of the music; emotionally, spiritually. But we didn't talk much about the magick because we didn't want to spoil it, because we just wanted to live it and respect it. And it's sometimes hard for musicians to turn away from their egos. This was a special time because of that rare gift of communal bliss. The seminal music from the 60's became more fully mature and amplified (no pun intended) in the 70's creating all kinds of sounds beyond definition. I mean I know you can go back and say here's the biggest hits from the 60's, here's the biggest hits from the 70's or the 50's. But that really doesn't elucidate the true, nor full spectrum, of what was happening then. Unknown and new species of music were being discovered all over the world every week and from inside our own hearts and minds as well. Stillwater in the seventies was blanketed with magic and mind-expanding creativity. The magic of the scene was based on musicians contributing to each other.

The First Three Albums

The first three pivotal albums for the Red Dirt movement came from Lamb Studios with Mike Hufford. Jimmy LaFave recorded and put out his first album, *Down Under*, in 1979. Bob Childers released his first album, *I Ain't No Jukebox*, in 1979 with the help of Jimmy LaFave. Chuck Dunlap put out his first album, *Daze Gone By*, in 1980, just a few months after Childers' album. These three albums, put out one right after another, had a tremendous impact on gathering more fans for their emerging scene, as well as showing others that it could be done.

While Kevin Warren Smith is widely commented to have helped produced both LaFave and Childers' first albums by many who were around at that time, he modestly says he just gave his thoughts about it all. "I was present during a lot of recording sessions, even when I wasn't playing parts. I know some people say I produced some recordings in those days. All I did was speak up about the way I felt a song was going. I liked arranging the music. And I would suggest additional instruments and harmonies be added by other singers and players. Every now and then I would add a part with instruments or harmonies, but more often I asked other people to play what I was hearing in my head. I think people just tolerated me and had respect for some of my ideas. Recording back then in small studios in the state was very intimate. There were periods when we were consistently there every day of the week. It was good for creativity. I played and recorded with Jimmy LaFave, Bob Childers, Pam Potts, Leo Miller, The Flat Mountain Boys and many others," said Smith.

When these three albums came out by these local guys, all one right after another, it created a momentum and a stronger viability for the Red Dirt movement. "Dunlap, he put out an album, and I remember Brad (Piccolo) and I were driving around one time listening to whatever the radio station was is Stillwater, and they played a song off of Chuck Dunlap's album. And, wow, all of a sudden, here's a guy on the radio that we knew. He made a record, and he had a song on the radio. And all of a sudden, that seemed attainable, you know? It seemed doable", said Bob Wiles.

While these three albums solidified many things for those in the budding scene, it would still be a long time before any of them realized they were creating something new that would be recognized as its own genre. The term Red Dirt to describe the music and the scene would still be over a decade away. However, this growing group of musicians were well on their way to creating it all through their desire to play music that fulfilled them.

Chuck Dunlap. Photo provided by Chuck Dunlap.

Bob Childers' first album did so well that he began touring nationwide after releasing it. He was even invited to perform at a no-nukes rally in Washington, DC in 1979 where he played to an estimated crowd of 200 thousand people. Childers had already aligned himself with many fundraisers and festivals for environmental groups, such as Sunbelt Alliance, and the Stop Black Fox movement. These same organizations worked with similar organizations across the nation, and a protest concert was organized for Washington. Kel Pickens was a local Stillwater Sun Belt Alliance organizer and helped get Childers on the Washington event. At this time Kevin Smith and Childers were still roommates, and Smith went with Childers to DC. "We were excited to go. Neither of us were hardcore protesters but we knew the cause well and were glad to help. Our songs were less in your face protests but rather were celebrations of nature, so we belonged with the travelers, and we were both excited about an adventure. So, in 1979 we boarded a bus that would take us from Tulsa to Washington. It was a special bus. It had an immaculate paint job featuring Native American spiritual designs. Not stereotyped or misappropriated symbols either. They were serious about true representation, and some were Native people. Many Native Americans were themselves involved with supporting environmentalists. I was told there was an effort to bring at least one bus from every state. Little did we know how massive the population of the crowd would be in Washington," said Smith.

The bus ride provided a lot of time for all the musicians to jam together during the trip. A few rows of seats in the back of the bus had been removed, giving them more space to play music, or to sleep. The passengers of the bus were musicians, protestors and people there just to support. One of those was a woman who made them food, usually peanut butter and sprout sandwiches. Smith recalls that there was at least one former Black Panther member on board. "I met musicians from across the region that I never had played with before. We stopped at a state park in Kentucky for the entire group to hold hands and 'OM' together. I was unschooled in Asian religion at that time. I would've felt like a hypocrite, so I stepped back. Bob then did the same. Luckily, it didn't ruffle any feathers," said Smith.

The bus arrived the day before the show, and they stayed at Georgetown on the grounds of a Buddhist Monastery in an estate manor. Smith recalled that it held great ambience and added even more magic to the experience. Childers and Smith broke off and went to different rooms, playing and singing for different people in the group. "That night, after I sang, I was asked why I didn't seem angry like the rest of the group. As in protest anger, I guess. I tried to explain that my faith in the abilities and sovereignties of nature over-ruled the fear and anger. It overwhelmed my fear of the stupidity of man. It was kind of a long-term view I admit. Interestingly, I found out later that Bob was asked the same question. We laughed about it," said Smith.

The next day, before the show, Childers, Smith and a couple of other Oklahoma musicians in the group stood outside the White House, on the outside of the gate, and Smith sang his favorite original song about the spiritual in nature. They were surrounded by a big crowd. Childers was behind Smith playing guitar while he sang. Childers started tapping Smith with his side of his guitar and when Smith turned around Childers motioned for him to look in the sky. "The sky was dark and cloudy and had been that way for hours, but right above where we were standing was a shiny sunlit opening and seven birds flying in a sunlit circle directly overhead, right on cue with the song I was singing. Birds featured in that song. And someone cried out that those birds were strangers to the DC area. Bob was very excited about this. Made me happy too. It's the kind of event we used to look for. Some of our gigs may not pay us much but we really didn't mind as long as we were in tune with the magic. Some say looking at things that way is too mystical. Maybe it's naive, superstition or even blasphemy. But we all happily shared that kind of worldview," said Smith.

A large stage was built across the Capitol steps. Far across the mall near the Washington Monument was a stage for the big rock bands. The smaller stage was more Americana, Folk and singer/songwriter in nature, with acts like Bonnie Raitt, Jackson Brown, Arlo Guthrie, Pete Seeger, and many more. "I heard later that an album was made indoors at Madison Square Garden that featured a repeat performance by the top-billed acts that played that day in DC. The mall and surrounding grounds were filled with people from end to end with 200,000 audience members. Over 400,000 according to other reports. It was the first time for us to play before a crowd that large," said Smith.

There was a large variety and diversity of people at the rally. From the famed Rainbow Family members to button-down businesspeople, and a lot of young people. Many people were still dressed like hippies of the '60s during this time period. "Mainly just a large mass of fellow humans who shared together through music. By the time it was all over I felt like we had accomplished something worthwhile for a larger community. The audience gave us a lot of energy and love. We hung out with the other musicians backstage and decided not to be bothered by the persistent drizzle. They hung huge plastic tarps over the stage area. It was nice. The monitor mix was good, and we felt comfortable playing. I thought I would be more nervous since there were many thousands of people in the audience, and we had never played in front of so many people. But I wasn't nervous when it was time to play. I don't know why," said Smith.

Childers and Smith decided not to go back with the bus. Childers had relatives in West Virginia- they planned to hitchhike out of DC and across Virginia. Eventually they ran out of rides, winding up on a country highway that didn't have much traffic, in the Blue Ridge Mountains. The gray clouds covered the sky. For hours they walked in the drizzling rain without seeing another soul. "Far behind us a long, old, dark car appeared slowly around the bend and came our way. My thumb didn't really want to invite it too close and fought against being raised. But the driver pulled over. I sat in the front and rested my feet between the empty liquor bottles on the floor. It was a wild ride on that curvy mountain road, but it gave us some much-needed miles. And we were grateful for the help," said Smith.

They soon found themselves in the rain again once that ride was over, and the sky was getting darker as the afternoon was at its end. It started to turn into night when Smith decided to go check out a side-road up ahead. Up the hill and later down that road, they found a small white country church. "I told Bob we were set for the night, and we hoped the church would be unlocked just in case humble travelers like us came along. We slept in the basement and woke early, grateful to whoever left the door unlocked. I think Bob wrote a tune about the church years later. We made it to his cousin's house and that night had a good meal and good sleep on actual beds," said Smith.

James Downing and Randy Crouch were working the coffee house circuit in Tulsa at this time, playing original acoustic songs. They became friends first, each playing music separately, but later Downing joined Crouch in the Flying Horse Band. "I didn't really play with Randy until about 1980, and I joined the Flying Horse, which was after the Green album. El Roacho had broken up and they sort of merged with what Crouch was doing. I called it El Groucho, but he had Curtis Massey, Ed lively and John Hoff from El Roacho, and he had Chip Anderson on bass. I joined up with them about the time of the Black Fox concerts, the stop Black Fox stuff. Then that band gradually mutated into the band that did the album, The Flying Horse album," said Downing.

Flying Horse was playing a benefit for Citizens Action for Safe Energy, yet another coalition formed to halt the Black Fox Nuclear power plant. The show was at Amber's Lounge, a biker hangout previously known as

The Keg, at 11th & Pittsburgh. Crouch asked Downing to play with him, as they didn't have a keyboard player. Downing jumped at the chance to play again in a band, having not been in a band for the previous eight years since playing in Xebec. "One of the songs Randy had written, which may not be recorded, was *Fuck You* – which lyrically was a convoluted rationalization for yelling 'fuck you' at an audience and having them yell it back. That day at Amber's, we did that song and Curtis played the sax solo on a Duck Call. It was outrageous and hilarious. Most of Tulsa's old hippies were there and Terry Stephenson mooned the audience," said Downing. In February of 1982, the Public Service Company of Oklahoma claimed the Black Fox Nuclear plant was no longer financially viable in Inola, and pulled out of the project, giving the activists their victory.

Randy and the Flying Horse Band played a very diversified selection of music, including a whole suite of fiddle jigs. They would play covers from artists like John Luke Ponti, Stefan Grappelli, Wilson Pickett, Orange blossom, the William Tell Overture, along with different rhythm and blues. The band would play at The Cains Ballroom in Tulsa about once a month, but traveled all around not only Oklahoma, but the surrounding states as well, keeping a busy schedule of gigs. "We played all over the region; Stillwater, Tahlequah, Miami, Cleveland, Mannford, Fayetteville, and Cain's about every 6 weeks. Little Wing was booking local bands in between major touring acts, and although we pulled large crowds, we didn't get paid very much. Cain's did advertise on the radio, so we got publicity from that, though KMOD was still calling us Randy Crouch and The Flying Horse Opera, much to Edd's displeasure," said Downing.

They pulled in a new bass player, an old friend and former bandmate of Downing, David Belford. Downing and Belford had a band together called The Contraband back in high school, and Belford had played in a popular band called Sweatband for several years as well. Downing remained a member of the Flying Horse band for a couple of years. After leaving the band, Downing joined LaFave and the Night Tribe Band. Mark Lyon was still playing with the Night Tribe band, and got Downing introduced into it as well. While Downing wasn't with them for very long, he recalls that they played Telluride at the Fly Me to the Moon Saloon, as well as some Tulsa and Stillwater gigs.

The '70s saw a large influx of musicians onto the newly forming scene, and the '80s rolled right in with even more musicians, connections and momentum. The first three albums from these pioneers carved out a whole new path for the rest of them, proving it was possible to write your own music and release it into the world. The scene was steadily filling out with musicians, studios, venues and fans, creating a steady foundation from which to grow.

In Their own Words

Mark Lyon - I'm gonna say it was 1981. I was about graduating from OSU. I skipped a semester or two because I was just burned out on school and I was playing so much music. I think it drove my folks crazy, you know they thought I was gonna drop out and never graduate. But I did graduate, not that I ever used it a whole lot, because I just wanted to be a musician. You know this probably has no bearing on much of anything. But I would be curious, there was a music teacher in Stillwater. His name was George Carney. I say a music teacher, he was more of an educator, but he had this class called the geography of music. And it was a fascinating class because it really talked about regional music all over the U.S. You know it went into country music, the roots of that where it was born, blues, rock and roll, jazz. And the only reason I'm mentioning him is, if he were still teaching that class then Red Dirt would be a part of that. This is very definitely a geographical type of a thing. George Carney, he was a real inspiration in my life and I'm kind of curious if any of the other Red Dirt people ever took any of his classes because he really spelled it out to me where music came from and how it came from and what influenced it.

Kevin Warren Smith - We didn't use the Red Dirt name back in those ancient days. Only because we just weren't thinking in those terms yet. Things would mature and the Red Dirt Movement would find its place. But in the early days we were just overwhelmed by the creative process of making the sounds and less thoughtful about defining or labeling or promoting. It's like in the visual arts. The process of painting (or playing) is the creative process we craved. Giving the painting a title, or label, buying a frame and putting a price on the piece are all after the fact. It's the same with music and other arts. The playing and singing are initially what it's all about. So maybe we were too naive to contribute much to the professional side of things. But thankfully, as time went by, the people on the Stillwater scene started taking responsibility for professionalizing the music and its presentation. The growth of Red Dirt Music movement has been a healthy and exciting thing for musicians and fans.

Pam Potts - There were a lot of players. I mean, it would be fun. We had a couple of times where everybody, I guess they threw a party of some sort. I don't remember if it was when they finished somebody's album or something, but I remember one time they threw a party out at Lamb studios. We all went out there and they had a stage set up, and people were just playing random- like random people were getting up together and playing. I played electric bass that night. First time I ever played and last time I've ever played. But someone taught me what to do. I was just having so much fun, it was a blast. I don't know what was going on out there. But it was just all of those people all out having a great time like that. I can remember just walking in the neighborhoods and you'd see people playing and you'd stop and play with them, sing with them or something, then move on down the road. I mean, it was just a real free thing. I often times will call myself the first Red Dirt girl because I do believe I am. Jimmy Lafave produced Bob's first album, and it was called *I ain't no jukebox*, and I sang on that album. Kind of as my debut of recording. I don't think I'd recorded anything before that. But then Bob and Kevin Warren Smith and I did Wednesday night shows at the Stonewall in Stillwater. Just week after week after week after week. Really did a lot of performing with Bob during that time. We did other things too, some Willie's gigs and stuff like that. Bob recorded a second album during that time as well and I performed on it too. But there were two women on Bob's first album besides me. There was one woman, and her name was Patsy Benson. She's older than me. She was on the first album. Then there was another girl, named Retta Gaybig. And her last name now is Yarbrough.

Danny Pierce - Mike Hufford was a drummer and played in different bands, but he had the first recording studio in Stillwater that I was aware of, and that's where Jimmy cut his first album. Bob made his first album out there. I think Chuck did his first album out there all with Mike Hufford, and so it was great to go out there. I'd go out there and set in on some sessions, you know, just to listen and spread the love kind of stuff. His wife was a songbird, she was the first kind of Red Dirt diva. Cheryl Hufford, boy, she could sing and would particularly with Chuck Dunlap. Mike made those first vinyls that that were pressed out there. I think that was important. Being able to make records in Stillwater, and all that good stuff.

Gene Williams - Well, it was great. There were lots of people there at the college and Washington Street. The strip was just a very lively place. There were 10 or so bars going at any given time, and there's a pretty wild place back then. Many of the clubs had live music, so we were playing a lot. I mean, I'd be playing an acoustic set with somebody on one night, and then I have a band gig on the next night. It was not uncommon to play three or four nights a week and never leave Stillwater. There was lots of light drugs around, you know? We were all in our early twenties. So, we're all experimenting with whatever was around, mushrooms and pot. Nothing really hard. Just, you know, it's just a real party atmosphere, and that was some of the best times playing I ever had, to be honest. I mean, the Skinner brothers were just wonderful singers and band mates, and it was just a paradise for the young guitar player like me. Tommy Harrison was on drums, great drummer. Tim Smalley on bass for the first period and then Craig Skinner, probably the last couple of years. Craig was the youngest, so he got out of high school. It was just, you know, literally sex, drugs and rock and roll. We weren't terribly business oriented. We weren't selling merch. Other than that one recording, that's really the only studio time we did. It was just all in the moment. We were playing clubs, and a lot of clubs in Tahlequah and Stillwater. We were just going back and forth, and occasionally we'd do private parties. Or gigs in Bristow where the Skinner Brothers were from, and it was just one big adventure. In the late seventies and early eighties, the Stillwater music thing was really vibrant. I was playing with different friends; we all were just kind of playing with each other and sitting in with each other. There was a band called Shiloh with Karen Rogers and Vickie that I sat in with a lot. And then Vickie and I worked together for several years on different projects in Stillwater and in Austin.

The Eighties Begin

Somewhere around 1980 Mark Lyon recalls a night playing music in Enid with LaFave and the Night Tribe band. Dean Nixon was from Enid, and Lyon assumes that was how they had ended up with the gig. It was a classic little country dive bar, filled with typical rowdy red necks. Lyon wasn't sure they were exactly the right fit for this particular place, but they did their thing all the same, playing originals mixed in with some covers they did. One of the covers they typically did at that time was *Suzie Q* by Creedance Clearwater. One time during practice, Lyon- joking around- closed off his nose to sing one of the parts of the song. LaFave thought it was the best thing in the world and decided that was how he was going to sing that part of the song from then on. So, during that verse that night at the gig, LaFave closes his nose and sings the verse nasally. A few minutes later a big, tough looking drunk guy walked up to LaFave and said something to him in his ear, and LaFave's face got a little pale. It was almost the end of the gig, and afterwards the guys asked LaFave what the man had said to him. He said the guy told him if he ever heard LaFave sing the song like that again, he would slit LaFave's throat. While that seemed like enough excitement for one night, they had more in store.

The band loaded up and got ready to head home. There were two vans, LaFave took his van, and Lyon, Beckel and Nixon took the other. Lyon recalls being on highway 51 on the way back to Stillwater, which has deep ditches on either side to help with flooding issues. Beckel was driving and Nixon was up front with him, while Lyon was laying down in the back with the equipment, dozing off. Suddenly, he felt the angle of the van change dramatically. Apparently, Beckel had dozed off while driving, just long enough to start going into one of those deep ditches on the side of the road. "He wakes up, over corrects, next thing you know we're over in the other bar ditch, and miraculously we get back on the road. He stops a minute, rubs his eyes, and goes, okay I'm awake, I'm awake. We go on, five minutes later it happens again. At that point we took him out of the driver's seat. I can't remember which of us drove home, but you know those two things that night, it was a bad moon rising, I guess. I don't know, but yeah that's one of the stories that I remember. I really enjoyed playing with Jimmy," said Lyon.

It was very common for all the musicians to play with various bands and change from one band to another through the years. Both Bob Childers and Randy Crouch are consistently quoted by others as frequently saying, "We're all in the same band, man." This fully encompasses how the Red Dirt music scene was formed. "By the summer of 81, Randy Crouch and Flying Horse had put out an album and their guitar player had left, they were looking for a guitarist. I had been just a huge fan of Randy's. I still am, his songwriting and fiddle playing and steel guitar playing are just beyond compare. I can't think of a better song writer than Randy. Just the sheer bulk of number of songs and the type of music, he can write any kind of music. I had a chance to join up with Randy and that kind of caused a little bit of a stir in the Skinner Brothers deal. But you know, musicians change bands and later on we all got along just fine. I moved to Tulsa at that point in 1981, I stayed there for two years playing with Randy and that band. As all bands do, it blew up. Randy moved. I still kept playing with him in various degrees of bands for several years, probably up until about 85. Charlie Hollis was Randy's bass player during that time," said Lyon.

Jim Suter met Bob Childers in about 1980 when he moved from Oklahoma City to Ponca City and started playing music with Steve Fields, who plays drums and percussion. They quickly formed a band called Zen Okies, Childers being one of the original members, along with Lele Stagner. "Bob was just kind of a guru, everybody kind of followed him. He was just such a great personality that everybody liked him. I don't think I ever heard anybody say an unkind word towards him. He just seemed to be a genuine, warm, friendly person. The first time I ever met him, I just felt like I'd known him forever," said Suter.

Lele Stagner would later open a bar and venue in Ponca city called Webb's World of Fun, which hosted many Red Dirt artists through the years. It was near the lake and the inside was decorated wall to wall with music memorabilia. Every band that came through would put their posters, stickers and flyers on the wall or sign the walls, creating the aesthetic that just expanded with time. Ponca City, and Webb's would become another popular place for local musicians to play, expanding their reach and introducing more people to their music.

Steve Irby transitioned from sound systems to car audio speaker design in 1980 when he developed Kicker speakers for trucks "Up until then, most of the pickups were two door pickups, they're not four door, or three and half door, whatever they are now. The music systems began to get better, and people were wanting better speakers. In a pickup truck, you can have speakers in the doors or the dash, but it's just kind of rattling around. The sounds rattling around in the door and they didn't put really subwoofers and bass speakers in there. And so the guys were getting to where they wanted some bass. A friend of mine had a music store and asked me to design a speaker to go behind the seat in a pickup truck that would make bass. So that was what I did for him and then he called me back and said it was a huge success and asked me if I knew what they called them. I go, no, what do they call it? He said, well, they call it the ass kicker because it kicks your butt right through the seat. I was like, well, that's right. I tried going out in my buddy's pick up after I designed it. We tested it, it really does. But it was super popular. I didn't think I would ever do anything in car audio except that. But he convinced me to try to market those to some other car stereo shops and we eventually did, and it just took off like wildfire," said Irby.

Stillwater Design and Audio would morph into Kicker Performance Audio, before eventually Irby decided to leave the pro sound engineering altogether and pursue only car audio products. Irby sold his sound shop to Mike Hufford, who was already managing the store, in the mid 80's. By 1986, Kicker had become the number one line of automotive speaker systems. Kicker is still run out of Stillwater by Steve Irby to this day. They design and engineer truck, car, marine, motorcycle, UTV and portable audio systems. Irby built a thriving, award winning international business from the ground up, based on his love of music and sound systems that started in high school. Their motto is "Live Loud", and Irby definitely has built a legacy on that.

Everyone still traveled to Winfield Kansas each year during the '80s for the Walnut Valley festival, making connections and getting time to play around campfires and tents, trying out music and fleshing it all out. "The Walnut Valley festival was a real, kind of a melting pot. You know, that's where a lot of us that didn't know each other before would camp out together and party together and jam at night. Everybody sat around campfires after the big shows had shut down and jammed all night to the wee hours. Of course, there were lots of mind-expanding drugs around at the time and that sort of thing, people would stay up all night and have a good time and write music and whatnot," said Jim Suter.

Winfield Campsite. Photo provided by Sage Powell.

Chuck Dunlap moved away in 1980, making treks through Seattle and Alaska as he continued his music career. LaFave continued to record new music and put out his second album *Broken Line* in 1981. Don Morris, still in Tulsa at this time, started playing with the fiddle player Jana Jay in the 80's, and would continue to do that for most of the decade.

Tumbleweed Dance Hall opened in Stillwater in 1981, about seven miles away from the campus. It was 18 to enter and gave the locals another place to go be entertained. The building was large and there was plenty of space to dance, which is what people liked to do. It became the prime place to go for youthful cowboys and cowgirls- all dressed in their ropers and pearl snaps- every weekend to hear some music and dance the night away. It would become another staple in the Red Dirt world. According to their website history, "The Tumbleweed Ballroom was a vision for Mr. and Mrs. Jack Hesser, R.A. Lospeich, and John and Linda Klinger in 1981. They purchased ten acres of land from Benny Bradley in the northwest part of Stillwater and started their creation. Tumbleweed Ballroom officially opened the doors for business in October 1981. (This is the same year the Billy Bob's of Texas in Ft. Worth opened their doors.) The next four years showed continued success and growth in dance hall business for their operation."

Steve Ripley happened to be at the right place at the right time for an opportunity to play for Bob Dylan in 1981. Jim Keltner, who was from Tulsa, was playing drums for Dylan at the time and helped get Ripley the gig. Ripley not only played in the band and went on a world tour but also played guitar on the album *Shot of Love*. During Ripley's time in California, he also created a new stereo guitar design and started the company Ripley Guitars in 1982. He collaborated on the design with legendary guitarist Eddie Van Halen, whom he had forged a friendship with that ended up lasting a lifetime. Ripley also created guitars for Jimmy Buffett, J.J Cale, John Hiatt, and many more. Ripley's mark on the music world was far reaching, and this only further inspired and motivated the musicians back home in Oklahoma, fueling the fire that it all could be done.

Tom Skinner entered a song writing contest in Tulsa in 1980 and won, the prize was a day of recording at Long Branch Studios in Tulsa. He gathered his band and some extra musicians, and they all headed down to Tulsa and spent a whole day recording a demo with nine songs on it. One of the songs they recorded was one Gene Williams had written. "We did one of my songs on it and I sang some harmony and played flute. It was a song called *Hard Driven Snow*. I was a big Jethro Tull fan in high school, and so I'd set in with them and play flute. I played flute on one of the songs," said Williams.

"That was- I think- all of our first time in a really good, big studio. So that was a real experience. We did those recordings and those were some pretty good things. That was a real high point for us," said Mark Lyon. Skinner spent a lot of time and effort sending off copies of that demo all around the country, in hopes of landing more gigs or publicity, but the effort didn't seem to pay off much at the time. The demo was never publicly released. However, a combination of an article Skinner wrote for a newspaper, a chance meeting with Marilyn Craig, and

Tom Skinner. Photo provided by Sage Powell.

that demo, would land them a gig opening for Pure Prairie League in Tahlequah in 1981.

Marilyn Craig, sister of multi-instrumentalist Benny Craig, lived in Tahlequah and was booking her brother's bands around this time. She had graduated from Northeastern University that spring and started working that fall in the student activities with the Northeastern Activities Board as the acting Director. During the spring of her senior year, she had read an article in the Northeastern newspaper someone had written about music, and she loved it so much she looked up the author. The author was Tom Skinner, who was writing some as he pursued journalism in college. Marilyn reached out and contacted Skinner to let him know how much she enjoyed the article, that Tahlequah was a great place for music, and he should come play sometime. Skinner told her he wished he would have met her sooner, as they had come to Tahlequah looking for gigs earlier that year and didn't have any luck.

Shortly after Skinner had recorded the demo, Marilyn came to Stillwater for an Activities Conference with her job, and spotted Tom in the hallway of the Student Union. They chatted and he mentioned that they had just recorded a demo, and he had it with him. She mentioned that she had her brother Benny's new demo in her purse as well. They decided to go to the student lounge and listen to them together. About a week later, Marilyn got the opportunity to bring Pure Prairie League to Northeastern. The band needed a pickup date and Tahlequah was in a nice location for it. Vince Gill was in the band during this time. Marilyn decided to call up Tom and offer them the opener spot.

"One of the highlights of that period before I was actually in the Skinner Brothers, we played a Pure Prairie League gig at the auditorium at Northeastern State University in Tahlequah, and they brought me out to play flute on the last song, which is kind of this, epic rock ballad thing. After a while, the membership changed, the two guitar players left and then I joined the band playing lead guitar, and I was with them probably two years," said Gene Williams.

Marilyn Craig would continue to be a presence in the music scene, and eventually her brother Benny would join the Red Dirt community later down the line. "They didn't meet Benny for a long time. I was telling all of them about Benny, and Tom said, you know, it's a good tape. I played theirs for Benny, but Benny had his own band, He was such a good multi-instrumentalist that if he wasn't playing at his own gig, he could play with anybody every weekend. Somebody would hire him just to come play with him. Dust and Gun Smoke, was the name of his band. He alternated between playing music with his band, he'd do that in the winter, and then in the summertime he quit and did rodeo. He rodeoed professionally too. So, I would get my heart broken every time. The band, I'd think we really had things rolling and the next thing I know he'd be quitting to go rodeo. So, I kept telling people about my brother, but people are like, well, where is he? I said he's playing music somewhere in Muskogee County, more than likely," said Craig.

Craig had graduated college in 1979, and right before graduation, she made her way to a bar east of Tahlequah called The Old Cherokee Warehouse, with a group of college friends. "I was with some college people, and they were good. They were fun people. But I'm sitting there with them, and I look over and I see a bunch of musicians and hippies sitting over there. I'm just thinking, I wanna go over there and sit. I love these people, but I want to go over there and sit. The very next week I was sitting over there on that side of the room. I always made sure and go back and talk to all my other friends. Randy Crouch was one of those people, they were some of Randy's friends and Marie Crouch. Her name's Wasson now, but she was the first person I really talked to out of that Tahlequah group. She invited me to a potluck and music thing at her house. So I go, and that's where I really meet Randy Crouch. Marie is a Choctaw, and she's a tall woman with long, dark hair. I told somebody, I said, I just can't see any resemblance in Randy and Marie. I said they just don't look like brother and sister. They said that's because they're not, they're exes- they were married. I have never been around exes that got along like that. I mean, I just thought, wow- they like each other. Randy, he was with Liz by then. It'd been several years since they split. But anyway, that's where I met Randy. And then I had the opportunity to book him," said Craig.

With Craig's job at NSU, she helped put together and book for the live music events. This would just be the start of her career with booking, marketing and public relations in the music industry. "But, man, Randy is a legend. I'll tell you what. The Epic song when he's sitting around the fire and the spaceship lands. I'm telling you right now. I've had him play that song where I felt like I got on the ship. He tore it up. Oh man. One time on Facebook there was somebody that put- they started it- and they were like what would America be if they didn't like Apple pie? What if? It started a chain, and it was actually songs and bands. My thing was what if Randy Crouch had not had time to party? I thought my gosh, yes, that would have changed the course of Tahlequah. He played music and he has basically represented Tahlequah for 50 years," said Craig.

In Their Own Words

Mark Lyon - One of the songs that Jimmy did, and this probably would have been closer to 80, or 81-82. I don't know how long we really played together- and with varying members of the Night Tribe- but one of his songs was about riding along on those red dirt roads at night. And that was the first time I really remember hearing red dirt brought up in music. I'm sure it has been brought up before, but I'll digress a little bit here. We just took red dirt for granted. It was in the neighborhood I grew up in. Oklahoma City had a lot of construction going on in it. So, every time it rained the streets would be flooded with red dirt. All the kids, you know, you go out in a white t shirt, and it always be stained red. So, it was just a way of life. We never really thought much about it. But that was the first place I can remember Jimmy talking about that- that song about riding around those red roads at night. And it's amazing how that term took off. But the Night Tribe thing was a whole lot of fun.

Jim Suter - Oklahoma didn't really do a whole lot of that kind of music at that time. We had some rock festivals, the KATT fest and all that kind of stuff going. But, as far as back when I first moved to Oklahoma City, it was hard to find a gig where you could play acoustic guitar and make any money. It was really kind of strange, but now there's all kinds of venues. Randy had little Dan Hostetter playing with him for years, which I've never seen him mentioned in any of the books I've read. So, you know, I think he kind of deserves a spot. Steve Fields is another one that's played and sang with just about anybody you can think of in that genre that I've yet to see mentioned in any books. I don't care about myself because I've always been a side man. I've always kind of backed people up and I've never really been the star of the show or the front man or anything like that. To me, it was just a really productive time when everybody seemed to be real creative. It was before the internet and there weren't boundaries like there are now. Everything wasn't a category. I mean, none of us walked around saying we're inventing new music or we're doing something totally different. We all loved electric guitars and acoustic guitars, and we like country music and rock n roll and blues and jazz and funk, and we just want to play everything all the time. It was a real fertile time. A lot of bands got started and really most of the bands of that era didn't have a huge amount of success, it was more bands after us that kind of took the torch and did things with it and had a little bit of business savvy about them. We were just having a good time mainly and it was like everybody could jam with everybody. Any night of the week you could find half a dozen guys just cramming in a bar somewhere playing together, just doing whatever you felt like. I don't know if you can ever re-achieve that or not, it's kind of one of those snapshots in time, it's a magical time that it's hard to recreate.

Marilyn Craig - I got to be friends with Guy (Clark). It was crazy, but I ended up being friends or working with a bunch of my heroes at Nashville and I didn't set out for that. It wasn't like I- I didn't write it down. I might have manifested it subconsciously. A lot of the concerts that we brought in at NSU- I mean, I liked them- but it was what we knew would sell. But my absolute favorites didn't necessarily play. We had Janie Frey was the attraction. She was the major and this guy named Johnny Duncan was supposed to open for her. And he had one hit that everybody knew, but he got laryngitis, and he was sick. We found out about a week or a few days before. So, I got to put who I wanted to in there. I put Guy Clark in. Guy came and opened for her, and he got there early. We had everything set and I worked with all volunteers, but the show was set ready to go. So when Guy came in, I took him down to Double D barbecue and introduced him to Bill Erickson. Pat Green cut one of his tunes. The *Wave on Wave* guy. I wanted to impress Guy. I wanted to give him a little local color. So, I took him down and Bill is such a great storyteller. He always was. And he knew how to make barbecue. So, they had barbecue and then Bill drove us out to the river. I was sitting in the back seat and Guy was up front with Bill. Bill gave him a little tour and we drove around and enjoyed about an hour before we had to go back to get ready for the show. So, after meeting him there, when I moved to Nashville, I was working for Jim Halsey. We were located on 17th Avenue. Just one block behind on 16th was the Tavern on the Road bar. So, I go in there, first week I'm there and who's sitting there? Guy. I was working by then. I was actually working on the Careers in Entertainment seminars. Guy and I talked about song writing and I had official business. I got to meet him down at the Tavern on the Road to talk about songwriting and drink beers and get paid for it. We were probably drinking wine. But, anyway, Guy was so good to me. I mean, he introduced me to people and gave me a big build up. It was incredible. And then Emmylou Harris, she's my favorite. The musicians that I've learned about through Emmy Lou and the songs and all that. I mean, it takes up so much of all the stuff I love. Rodney Crowell, Vince Gill, Albert Lee- Emmy, she is my hero.

Robert Parker - I was friends with Jimmy LaFave. When I first met him, he was a very good singer and a great guitar player, but he had the James Taylor style- he played James Taylor songs and sounded just like James Taylor. But then, in 1980 he had a conversion and started- I hate to almost say things because it might not be perfectly true because it goes back so far. But anyway, he began with his own style and had his own singing place. And had some bands. We were playing with a variety of people and that was for a little while. I was good friends with Bob Childers. I'd see him all the time and we'd talk. We'd play music, smoke weed and drink beer and stuff, which is what everybody was doing. He played acoustic guitar, and he wrote songs, you know. I don't recall him playing other people's songs necessarily. He was interested in being a songwriter. He liked being a songwriter and he wanted to perform his songs. One night, I think it was on the corner of Fourth in Washington. Directly across the street was the Acme Bar. It then became Willie's, but the original Willie's was more of a little shotgun bar. On the side of that was Bill's Italian restaurant and that was the first place that I played. I remember there was one night, Bob and I were sitting on the outside wall at Bill's Italian. Just drinking beer and playing guitars out there. Of course, back then there was this little window of time where you could drink beer and just walk around, drink beer going any place. It's not like that anymore. There would still be people up walking around but I'm talking about the middle of the night. When places are closed, it's probably some of the better, quote-unquote shows. Just jamming. Just talking, smoking cigarettes, drinking beer, playing guitar.

Red Dirt Finds a Home

A pivotal moment in the formation of the Red Dirt Scene was when it found a home base of sorts, at an old two-story house in Stillwater, on the outskirts of town, which was simply called "The Farm". Located off a dirt road called Sangre, the six-bedroom farmhouse was the kind of house you could once purchase from the big stores like Montgomery Wards. A large truck would deliver the unassembled house to your land, and you would put it together. The two-story farmhouse was simple, it didn't have air conditioning or anything fancy, but it had a lot of space. Sitting on about 160 acres of land, the rent was $100 divided six ways. It was perfect for a bunch of college kids. Danny Pierce became aware of the farm when a friend, and classmate, told him he was considering renting it out and needed roommates. "The guy that we moved out there with, we'd grown up in Oklahoma City together. He was a couple of years older than me, and we ended up in a statistics class together and he said he was moving into this farmhouse and was looking for roommates. I said, well sure. Went out, looked at it with John (Cooper) and he and I moved in for the summer of '79. David Underhill was the gentleman's name from Oklahoma City, that was able to get the place. He was only there for like a semester and then he graduated. Basically, left it to me to carry on at that point, which I did for the next 20 years," said Pierce.

John Cooper, someone that would later be a big part of the Red Dirt scene, was the one who went to check it out with Pierce, before he was even a musician. When he first moved to the farm, Cooper didn't even know how to play an instrument yet. He didn't begin playing music until the nights at The Farm turned from college parties into musical jamborees a few years later. "I moved into the farm in May 1979 with Danny Pierce, going to college at OSU and looking for a place to live. We drove down the driveway of this old farmhouse and we were like, man, we could live here. And basically, it was just a big party house for college kids, we were kings of the two-and-three-day parties. But as time went on and musicians found out about it, they would be drawn there because they had a place to play and people to play for," said Cooper.

Owned by the Schroeder family, it was still an active working farm when the guys moved into the farmhouse. The Schroeder family had leased it to the Arburg Mill Company in 1969 for 10 years but wanted the family to take it back over at that time. "Scott lived in Perry, married the (Shroeder) granddaughter. Scott's willing to farm it and all that, but don't want to live there. Him and David were actually in a fraternity together. So that's how David got into the house. So, when I moved in, the Arburg's had lived there. It was always sort of run down. It's not about the house- it's about the people. Scott started running the hay fields. They leased out the pastureland to another cattle guy and he was running cattle. Then I was sort of in charge of the house and mowing the grass. The family would come out from time to time and keep the front part of it nice. It really was like a small working farm. There was an oil well. There was cattle. There was hay being grown, and wheat- but it was kind of three different entities altogether. And so that was fine, it was really pretty quiet. John and I were pretty quiet kind of guys. We knew some people, but it took time to develop the relationships and all of that to where it kind of turned into a life of its own," said Pierce.

While the roommates would change from year to year - Pierce estimates about 150 in the 20 years he was there- one of the earliest ones was responsible for bringing in what would later become a farm tradition; croquet tournaments. Pierce had grown up with a guy named Robert Webb in Putnam City, where they went to high school together. Webb moved into the Farm in about 1980. There were many stories shared that talked about the croquet tournaments as being played in the nude at times. "Robert, he brought a bit more of a party element. Taco Bob is what he's referred to. Taco Bob had already been having parties, he had that network of friends that were doing that more. He had hosted a croquet party at a previous house that he had. So, he had already had the croquet party once or two times maybe. Then he comes to move at the farm and that's when the kind of the party element got kicked up a couple notches for sure. He also was working at the Hideaway. So now we got the Hideaway tied into the farm, and that elevated things. I became very good friends obviously with Marty and Richard Derber of the Hideaway and Hideaway cabin out of Lake Carl Blackwell. So now once we're in that, more people are coming out to the farm. More people are going out to Lake Carl Blackwell to the cabin and hanging out there and we kind of elevated things in that world," said Pierce.

"All you gotta do to throw a party is get the idea implanted into someone else's brain, and they'll run with it, and you can just sit back and enjoy. It was fun. Never a dull moment. The one rule at the farm was if you didn't know anyone, introduce yourself," said Robert Webb, aka Taco Bob.

Danny Pierce, Taco Bob Webb (hat), Kate Newcomer and Stan Wooward in The Farm kitchen. Photo provided by Stan Woodward.

Pierce and Cooper were big music fans, and they decided to start having bands come out and play on the front porch. The first band to ever officially play at the Farm was a Reggae Band from Tulsa called Local Hero. They set up and played on the porch and everyone danced around in the yard. While it started out just being a college party house for a few years, it evolved into a musical refuge for many local musicians throughout the '80s and '90s. It became a musical commune of sorts, eventually hosting more musicians in one sitting than any other place could offer. The Farm was a place where all these musicians could go and have camaraderie and a musical fellowship. They understood that the music they were creating didn't have to fit a certain mold, and they found freedom in that. It became an almost sacred breeding ground for music and talent. "It was basically the unofficial headquarters for Red Dirt music for twenty years. I think Stillwater allowed a setting- and the farm in particular- for this music to evolve. Red Dirt music would have happened whether the farm was there or not because there was just too much in the mix in Stillwater at the time. But the farm was an outlet that allowed all that to come together and I think it became stronger because of the farm. Because of that ability for people to come together out there. All of those different bands, all of those different sounds, weren't restricted by anything as far as, you gotta play this or that or whatever you played at all," said John Cooper.

It also provided a very laid-back way of life and living for them. According to an article titled *Remembering The Farm, the Oklahoma Commune where Red Dirt Music Was Formed* written by Rick O'Bannon in The Dallas Observer in 2014; they grew vegetables in a garden, they had cherry trees and pecan trees that they used for bartering and gifts. They made friends with an older woman who lived down the road and would trade cherries for her homemade pies. It was simple and easy. "We were pretty much the odd bunch of hippies in a farmhouse on the edge of town; part Woody Guthrie, part Jack Kerouac, part Bob Dylan. We were all out there, almost like the counter-counterculture just doing our thing out there in the farmhouse. It was just a magical era and time of creativity," said LaFave in the article.

Jimme LaFave (middle), Kurt Nielsen (far right) jamming at the Farm. Photo provided by Stan Woodward.

Seemingly more and more musicians soon found their way to the farmhouse, meeting other musicians and making connections. "Back then, when you get to college, there's so much more about your education than going to class, and these guys- they're exposing each other to music they brought from their hometown or their part of the state, their part of the country. It was a huge eye-opening experience, just everybody was in the process of broadening their horizons. Stillwater was much smaller back then. We lived there year-round. In the summertime when all the students went home, Stillwater turned into a real sleepy little farm town. And that was really our favorite time to live there. If that house had been in town, we probably wouldn't have gotten away with it, because we had a lot of late-night bonfires and all-night picking sessions. Basically, those older guys like LaFave, Tom Skinner and Chuck Dunlap, they would have a gig in town and after the gig, they'd all come to the farm, and they'd pick around the fire. And that was where we could watch their fingers, and figure out- Oh, Okay. That's how you make a D chord. It was a special time. We were really lucky to just be there at that point in time. Eventually the police found us, but they didn't really bother us too much because we weren't bothering anybody else. But they would let us know that they knew, they'd drive by. But we didn't really hurt anybody. No, it was a pretty darn special time," said Bob Wiles.

Jimmy Lafave wove lyrics about The Farm into a couple of his songs, on *Red Dirt Roads at Night* and *Ramblin' Sky*. The farm had made its mark on him and so many others.

This was a magical time in Stillwater, new musicians filtered in constantly, people played music all over town, and they had a home base at the Farm. The Farm would always be open and inviting with a revolving cast of characters. People moved in and out of the Farm constantly, and most everyone that found their way there was a music fan in some way. In fact, people would bring their own collection of albums to play during the times that a guitar wasn't in someone's hands. "We would take turns being

Jimmy LaFave playing at the Farm. Photo provided by Sage Powell

in charge of the turntable, and without meaning to, they exposed each other to all different kinds of music. There were some records that everybody liked. And there were some records they didn't. There was one guy that lived out there. He was a huge Billy Idol fan, you know, huge Prince fan. And before it was over with, we had come to appreciate Billy Idol and Prince. How could you not? They were just there," said Bob Wiles.

Stan Woodward (black shirt), a group inside the Farm house. Photo provided by Stan Woodward.

The drafty old farmhouse was hot in the summertime and cold in the winter, so people would prefer to live there in the spring and fall when the weather was milder. It seemed that as soon as the summer heat hit, some of the guys staying at the farm would find themselves a summertime girlfriend with a house with AC that they could crash at instead of the farm. The rent was cheap and could be split 6 ways with the 6 bedrooms, making it an idea place for struggling musicians or college students to afford. Danny Pierce would set out a jar for everyone to throw their portion in. "Used to be some great parties there, kind of a flophouse for musicians. Next to the house was a little shed which became the Gypsy Cafe. That's where people who on Friday and Saturday night might, you know, be rivals and trying to get their own crowd in to watch them. They'd get together and jam. That's probably how the music- different kinds of music- kind of spun into Red Dirt. That's my theory. Anyway," said Randy Pease.

On most any night you could drive out to the farm and find several people playing guitar around a fire, feeling out new songs, swapping ideas and trying out new material. The lyric ideas and tunes being thrown around, layered together piece by piece, with many different creative minds in the mix lent to the collaborative philosophy of the Red Dirt scene.

"For the guys that were going to school, you didn't mind living in a run-down old farmhouse that you didn't know if the water was gonna work or the electricity was gonna stay on. Or if the roof was gonna leak or if it was gonna blow away in a tornado. It was cheap, you could live there for next to nothing. And it was west of town. You could stay up all night and build a bonfire out in the backyard and have friends over and pick your guitars and that's how the whole thing started,' said John Buckner.

Jamming at the Farm. Photo provided by Sage Powell.

The farm also greatly fostered the collaborative nature that would be an integral part of how Red Dirt music was formed. The creative back and forth between musicians in the scene wasn't based on competition, no one was trying to outshine anyone else. Their collaborations were based on a mutual love for creating music and understanding the drive and need to do it. Competition serves the ego, and for the most part these musicians lacked that part of the equation. They wanted to support one another and have the highest possible outcome for everyone. Either consciously or unconsciously they knew they would get farther together than they ever would alone and so to support one another meant to support themselves. They were just as excited when one of their musical friends wrote a new song as they were when they wrote a new song. They would also be inspired by the songs being created by others, which fueled their own desire to write more songs. It was a creative whirlwind, a Red Dirt tornado that caught and held them in the vortex, but instead of being destructive, it fueled and fed their creative aspirations.

In Their Own Words

Gene Collier - Actually, the little road that went to the farm was named the Gene Collier Memorial highway at one time- had its own little sign. The road out there at that time, if you happen to pull into the farm, when you pull off the road, it used to slant just about 45 degrees, like 4 foot deep. So, if you went in and it was the least bit wet, you were over on the side stuck. So, I hauled a bunch of rock in there and did some backhoe work and fixed it for them. We used to play out there a lot, with Bob Childers and all of them guys. I was a little bit older than some of them, but it was just a fun wonderful life of Red Dirt music. I got to kinda just be in there and make a little of it myself and get to hear all my buddies, being proud of what they would do, ya know? But they were more serious than I was, it was just fun for me. A lot of those guys were trying to pursue it more than I did, but I'd always have fun with it for sure.

Mike Skinner - I just remember feeling this place full of musicians just playing and there wasn't any plan, it was just all of us doing it and playing and it seemed like a lot of fun back then. Some people were able to keep that fun part of it. And Tom would say, hell at least you are going to laugh. That was as good as it gets. I knew Crouch back in the old days. We had went to college back in Northeastern state, and there wasn't much music going on at that particular point. But Randy was around and every once in a while, we would run into him and you would be glad you did, you would be watching a miracle happen. He's also a funny guy. I have favorite Childers' stories but probably shouldn't tell them.

Randy Crouch – I was present for some really cool things that happened at the farm. They played croquet there. We had so many gigs there, going out to the bar, I just remember that place. The playing part has been spread out over a lot of places. I like playing the Cain's ballroom a lot. I love that place. The place has got a spirit, like Bob Wills. Granny's Attic was on the strip, downtown Tahlequah, was kinda like downtown Stillwater, it was real similar.

Bob Wiles - All those guys we got to know them so well and for so many years. I mean, you go to college and get a job and basically the first guy you met is Jimmy LaFave and then he says, hey, my band's playing this weekend. Come out and see us. And there's Bob Childers, that was a fate thing, you couldn't have even tried to plan that, you know? It was just dumb luck. To me we were in Stillwater at just the perfect time to be exposed to all these guys. You know, playing music and writing their own songs. Who were so accepting and supportive and, you know. Oh, I don't know. It sounds corny, but it was really borderline magical. One big melting pot, with all the right ingredients.

Pam Potts - It's very emotional. I was trying to tell somebody what it's like to be in a band and I thought, okay, I'll tell him what it's like. And here's the deal. You're on a stage and your hands are tied behind your back. And you can't speak either. Okay, and then you have to communicate with these guys. Well, so meaning you got your hands on an instrument and you're singing, so you can't speak, and you can't use your hands. So, you have to do it with your eyes or with your body. You can do it different ways. Usually, you do it with your eyes. You can do it with your feet, because you got your legs available. Say you're totally unfamiliar with the band, and you're playing the Science Project at the Colony. And you're just dragged up there for the night. You can do your thing, but you have to lead that band. They have to know what you're going to do before you do it, so you don't look like a fool or whatever. All you got left, is like your legs or your eyes or whatever. And so, a lot of people use their legs. And what you would do would be, you're getting ready to do your last thing or whatever you like, move your leg in some indicator of way to say, hey this is the end. And that's what you do. And then everybody knows, oh, I saw that leg thing. That's the end. You make some kind of body motion where they go oh, and then it gets everyone's attention and then they look for whatever you're going to do next, you know, but there's a trick to it. But when you're in a band with someone for more than a day, you learn to just kind of emote off each other, you kind of feel it. You kind of know, you get this thing going between you that's- it's worse than marriage. It's different. But it bonds you in a way forever, I mean, you have this thing.

Kevin Warren Smith: For a while I began to play more with just Jimmy and Bob and less with others. Jimmy could create more fantastic white-hot energy with a band more than anyone else I had played with. It could only be experienced live. Most music fans know that a recording often can't convey the spirit and power of live performance. I don't want to drop names of people Jimmy introduced me to except for one songwriter he took me to see in Austin in the '80s. I introduced myself to him and he handed me a cassette tape which said *"Hi! How are you?"* When Daniel handed me his tape, he also said to me "Hi! How are you?" It was great.

This was before he was famous. Visiting with Daniel Johnston was like being with an old friend you've been missing. Jimmy knew I would get into him. He was thoughtful that way. Daniel went on to write songs recorded by dozens of performers. Jimmy got me together with great musicians. He was really helpful, and his friendship was an inspiration. He was a great friend. He had a lot of influences that he thrived on to enrich his own compositions. And his performing, he made every song his own because he understood the songs he played. His writing and performing came from deep inside him. He didn't just study musical history and pass it along. He made sure what he did was genuine and honest. And that's how you do a cover song justice. You only pick it out if it moves you, but you don't try to copy the original singer/songwriter.

Chuck Dunlap - I just feel fortunate to be included in it, because I really came before that, and they let me step into it. I would come back, and they would wrap their arms around me. When I did come back for those three years, they included me as one of their own even though they had been working on it the entire time and I had just been stopping by and touching base with it and recharging my batteries. Didn't have anything to do with that day to day, ongoing, let's make this something. But all of those musicians in Oklahoma have something to do with it, and they are still doing it and keep doing it. It's like a brother or a cousin that goes off across the country and comes back 20 years later and you are like, hey let's play that song we used to play together. It's a hell of a story. And you hit the nail on the head when you called it an oral history. When you go back to any culture that was around before writing, it's not like they didn't have a history. It was just an oral history that was passed down pretty well from generation to generation, and that's what you are picking up on here. I consider people like Steve Pryor and Rocky Frisco, all those cats in Tulsa, the ones that have gone and the ones that are still here, those are all as big a part of the Red Dirt scene as Skinner or Childers or Lafave or anybody as well. They are just as important because that feeds that end of it. It's that side of the plate, that's the spicy gravy on it, you know. It's like a well-rounded meal, man. If you don't have it all and just have what you like, you probably are not going to be healthy after a while, musically.

Festivals & Fightin'

The '80s continued to bring in new people while everyone was still finding their place in it all. While Tim Terral moved to Stillwater in 1975 to attend OSU, it was several years before he joined a band. Terral started playing music in the fourth grade taking lessons at the Guitar House of Tulsa. When he was in high school, he bought a 12-string guitar and never put it down after that. While he lived in Tulsa before college, he made his way to Stillwater occasionally to check things out before moving there. "I remember driving from Tulsa to Stillwater one time and the Pistol Patty had a live remote and Jimmy LaFave was playing, I'd never heard of Jimmy LaFave. I thought, man, this guy's got a really good voice, and I really like his songs. Obviously, he did some original stuff as well. So that was my kind of first experience to Jimmy, but I never did see him live. But, in terms of the scene- I think for as small as it was- there was a lot of really good music going on," said Terral.

Terral played more folky music during that time but fell into bluegrass after he moved to Stillwater. He befriended musician Gary Sampson and played with him often. Terral made his way to the Walnut Valley Festival in Winfield in 1979 and watched New Grass Revival there. "I had heard about New Grass Revival. The New Grass is probably our Touchstone for lack of a better term because we just love their stuff. We really did, and I saw them first in Winfield in '79. I think it was then I was turned on to them. So, it must have been with some of the Flat Mountain Boys - Johnny Wright, Bret Franzmann, and Gary. Johnny and Bret, I think, knew about all this stuff more than I did for sure. I think that's kind of probably where I first learned about New Grass and some of this bluegrass stuff- which I never thought I'd get into frankly. But really enjoyed it once I did. Once we went to Winfield in '79, I kept going for years after that. I left for a year, after the spring of '81. I was off that summer and fall, having to come back in the spring of '82 to pick up some classes from my architecture degree. And that's when we kind of got together and decided to form the band," said Terral.

The band that they formed was the Red Valley Barnstormers with original members Kurt Nielsen, Tim Terral, Gary Sampson, Kevin Richmond and Buddy Watson. While this progressive bluegrass band was a short run project - starting in 1982 and playing their last show in 1986 at Willie's Saloon- they seemed to effectively bring in several musicians that hadn't been there before as well as make their mark on the scene. Many different people played as honorary members of the band during the four years, including Jim Harris, Kenny Cornell, Shelby Eicher, Rick Morton, Cliff Parrett, Dale Pierce, Bret Franzmann, Johnny Wright, and Tom and Mike Skinner. "Originally, I don't know who came up with the Barnstormer part. We were kind of brainstorming and stuff and then I think it was Kurt Nielsen that came up with the red part because of the red clay soil that we had around there in the Cimarron River. And so, it's just a nod to the area. So that's where the red of the Red Valley Barnstormers kind of came from. I did a little logo of a Barn who we called Barney, the barnstormer. But, there's a picture of like a World War one fighting guy, but he wasn't really fighting. He just had the paraphernalia in the bi-plane and stuff and, we just kind of took that and ran with that a little bit. But that's kind of how the name came about and kind of where we came up with it," said Terral.

The Red Valley Barnstormers gave their very first performance in 1982, during a break for the Skinner Brothers Band at Hogg's Breath Inn. But they eventually played all around; Willie's, Stonewall Tavern, Couchman's Inn, and Spav's to name a few. "We knew Tom and Mike Skinner. Mike was a fiddle player. And Craig of course. They were playing the Hogg's Breath Inn and Tom said, come on down and play one of our breaks, and this is like 15 or 20 minutes. So, we worked up four or five songs. I remember sitting before that first gig, at Kevin's house. He was on Duck St., where his house was. We're all getting ready to go over there. We're all kind of nervous because we never really played out as a band, probably played out that much, period. I hadn't for sure. We went over the Hogg's Breath and I'm not sure what time we started. I'm guessing it was around 10 or 10:30pm. But Tom was so nice, and those guys are so nice to let us play their break. That was our first quote-unquote gig, or live performance, it wasn't really our gig," said Terral.

It would become an integral part of the Red Dirt philosophy and culture for the established musicians to give new musicians chances to get up and play during their gigs. While all of them did this, Tom Skinner is especially known for his graciousness in getting other musicians up on stage. While some joke that it was just because Tom didn't want to have to play as long, and happily gave up his own set time to take longer breaks, it certainly helped set the tone of the culture and became part of just how things were done. Mentorship plays a huge role in the entire philosophy of the Red Dirt scene, and it would trickle down and continue to be that way all throughout the next generations.

The Flat Mountain Boys and Red Valley Barnstormers were both progressive bluegrass bands, but they were all friends and didn't see themselves as competitors. "They weren't really direct competition. They did more country rock than we did. The Flat Mountain Boys did the same kind of stuff we did. But we were all friends. There was not competition. There's plenty of places to play and go around and there's certainly no bad feelings with anyone. Those guys were all really nice guys and a lot of fun to hang out with and they were the only ones I can really think of that played the kind of music that we played. That wasn't a real popular genre at the time. It was really kind of odd in a smaller town like that to have two bands who did the same kind of stuff. Although we didn't do a lot of the same songs. There wasn't a lot of overlap that I recall in the songs that we did and the songs that they did, but still the same type of stuff," said Terral.

In fact, Terral and Kevin Richmond had a mutual friend from high school, Chris Walker, that they attempted to talk into joining the band. They convinced Walker to come up to Stillwater in the hopes of joining up with them and then ended up losing him to The Flat Mountain Boys. "He came up, he was in our band for like five minutes. We did a radio show, an OSU radio show. We had a live interview and had recorded some songs for them to play and stuff. And Chris was there. We just had said come on, just join the band, come on and hang out with us and we'll talk on the radio, which he did. Then he quit about a week later and joined the Flat Mountain Boys," said Terral.

Jim Blair showed up on the music scene at about the age of 19, in the early '80s when he came to attend OSU, playing banjo with The Red Valley Barnstormers. Jim Blair joined them on banjo in 1983, and Mark Stephens joined in 1984 on mandolin. "We played a lot of *Old and In the Way* (a bluegrass group featuring Jerry Harcie, David Grisman, Peter Rowan and John Kahn). We also did a lot of Hot Rize, New Grass Revival, Leon Russel, Jimmy Hendrix, the Beatles and Van Morrison," wrote Jim Blair, in a press release he wrote for the reunion of the band 31 years later.

Blair was born in Texas but raised in Oklahoma. He was a singer and multi-instrumentalist who came from a musical family. His father was a Grand Ole Opry performer who had been a member of Bob Wills' Texas Playboys. Blair would come to play a big role in the Red Dirt music scene in many different ways in time. "Jim was there for the whole duration after that. He was a doer. He got stuff done. He's a behind the scenes wizard, man. He had it all going," said Kurt Nielsen.

"We were good friends. We were both banjo players so kind of knew each other through that. He played with Kurt in the competing bluegrass band. I was in Flat Mountain Boys. I'd say we were two bands that were kind of similar, played similar style of music. But me and Jim were always really good friends though. I really liked Jim a lot, very interesting guy. I was really impressed with what he was doing musically," said Bret Franzmann.

A gig came up for the Red Valley Barnstormers in the early '80s, to open up for New Grass Revival at Horse Thief Canyon. But a few of them weren't sure they were up to that, thinking their music was nowhere near the caliber of New Grass Revival, and one by one they started to lose the nerve to follow through.

"We went to Winfield, in the Walnut Valley festival and had an open stage at Winfield. We had the Barnstormers up there and we just didn't do very well. At least we didn't think we did, we were nervous. Probably were a little bit because Winfield was a big deal to us. It was an open stage. It wasn't a big stage by any means. I think it was in a barn somewhere which is now where they sell T-shirts, but it was a thing. What actually happened- this is very embarrassing, but this is the truth. I was the coach of my company softball team. This is the excuse that I came up with on why we couldn't do it. Rick Morton and me, he didn't really wanna do it either. We're both nervous and we're kind of concerned because of that bad experience at Winfield, it probably wasn't nearly as bad as we thought it was. But, being a musician, you're your own worst critic. I came up with the idea. I'll just tell them I did a head slide into second base and jammed my finger and that was the story. So that was it. That's why we didn't do it. Of course, obviously, I kicked myself since then. It had been a great gig to do. I'm sure we'd have been nervous as heck. But that's how it happened that day," said Terral.

Not everyone lost the nerve to play - the bass player Kevin Richmond was not going to give up the gig. He was a John Cowen fan, who was in New Grass Revival. Cowen was one of his heroes, and Richmond wanted to open for them. Richmond and Blair both knew Garth Brooks- a relatively newcomer to the music scene at that time- and they asked him and Dale Pierce to fill in for the gig, Garth would sing. This was one of Brooks' first big shows, but just by being at the right place at the right time, he ended up making connections that would help him down the line.

"I was at that gig at Horse Thief Canyon. When The Red Valley Barn Stormers played. I was at that gig, but I was with the folks. They had a barbecue stand and I was over there with them. We were there to see New Grass. We knew those people in the band, and we were thinking that they'd stay and hang around and party. But Leon Russell was playing in Tulsa at Cain's, and they wanted to get back to Tulsa to play the last set with Leon. Just so happened that Randy Crouch was playing in Stillwater that night and we went down there," said Marilyn Craig.

According to the book *Garth Brooks: The Road Out of Santa Fe* by Matt O'Meilia- which will be discussed more later- Dale Pierce and Garth Brooks knew one another through school and track, and had a band called Dakota Blue with Jim Kelley during the early '80s. They played Aunt Molly's Amateur Night on Fridays in the Student Union. It was on these amateur songwriter's nights that Tom Skinner met Brooks, as he was also there performing regularly. Unfortunately, Kelly perished in a plane crash in January 1982, and that was the end of their band. Brooks, who worked at Dupree Sports, would also take a job as a bouncer at Tumbleweeds in 1983.

Tom Skinner, who got the nickname Tiny somewhere along the way, graduated from OSU in 1982 with a Public Relations degree. Craig Skinner said he can't tell the story of how Tom got the nickname Tiny, but that it involved him as well. We'll just have to use our imagination on that one. Tom married Jeri Alexander in August of 1983, thus becoming Tom & Jeri, which probably invoked a chuckle or two through the years. Tom got a job at the post office, along with his brother Mike. This was also when he landed his steady gig at Willie's saloon.

Rob Boutwell and Tom Skinner. Photo provided by Sage Powell.

Tom didn't even have a telephone in his house, which made booking gigs harder to do. Willies on the strip had quickly become the Red Dirt headquarters. Greg Jacobs played every Wednesday night there for about three years with Gene Williams. Thursday night Tom played with whoever he wanted to put together for his night, often circulating through different friends. Friday and Saturday the Skinner Brother's band would play. Many of the musicians basically lived in Willies, that was the spot to be.

The Skinner brothers were well known for their blood harmonies but also were known for their fighting. The three could be found fighting amongst one another, or with others, on any given night. One night playing a gig at the Sheraton Hotel east of Stillwater, a drunk patron kept giving Craig money to play the same cover song over and over. They played it a couple of times, and Mike started getting annoyed and told Craig to knock it off. By the end of the night, the three brothers were rolling on the floor in a big tussle, knocking each other around.

Rod Boutwell, Jed Lindsey, Tom Skinner, Mike Skinner (back turned), Craig Skinner, Ron Beckel on drums. Photo Provided by Stan Woodward.

"They were notorious for getting in fights, usually it was something Craig started, but he and Mike were notorious for getting in fights with each other. I remember Tom telling me a story about Mike one time because Mike always had cool vehicles. They're both living in Bristol, and Mike had this motorcycle. He left one day, and Tom wanted to ride it. So, he gets on there, starts driving it and the thing stops, and he didn't know what was going on. He had just ridden it for a few minutes. Of course, he didn't realize how some people turned off the gas tank, keeps the gas from going in the carburetor. Mike did that and Tom didn't know anything about that. So, he thought he hurt the motorcycle at first. He walks it back to the house. Puts it back on the porch. Mike comes back there and flips it off the kickstand, starts getting ready to start. And Tom is watching and thinking oh man he's going to be mad at me if it doesn't work. He flips the gas tank and kicked at it one time and it starts. And Tom goes, DAMN, I didn't know that. I thought that was funny. Those are the kind of Tom stories; he'd tell you stuff like that. It just cracked you up. Tom was one of my heroes, man," said Kurt Neilson.

One evening the Skinner Brothers Band was playing at a place called Club 21 out on Perkins Road. It was an apartment complex that had a bar in it, which was common back in those days. The bar was located upstairs. "One winter night after our gig, Craig Skinner, who almost won the state wrestling competition in high school. Good cat. We were standing down at the bottom of the stairs and this couple came down the stairs and the girl said to us, hey, we really liked the band. We said, thank you. Appreciate that. And then they were walking outside, the guy made the mistake of turning to his girlfriend and saying they really sucked. And at that point Craig kind of went on automatic. And he had the guy down on the snow, and he was beating him up pretty bad. And the girl was biting his leg, and I remember getting my arms around Craig and saying, hey, man, it's Gene. I'm the good guy, don't hurt me. I kind of pulled him off the guy. That was one experience," said Gene Williams.

While Craig was known for his fighting skills, he was also known for his pranks. "Craig is just such a cut up. For a little while he was real bad about hiding in the dark and just coming at you like a big bear, and you know that'll really scare you. When he first done it to me, I had taught taekwondo for 20 years and I had fought world champion fighters. I was really keyed up, and the first time he did that to me, I just missed his head with a kick, and I would have just absolutely had him on the ground. But it's just like being attacked by a big ol' bear you know, in your mind," said Gene Collier.

Another story that widely circulated, mostly by Tom himself, was the time he went to Cain's Ballroom to see the Nitty Gritty Dirt band. Skinner might have had one too many drinks that night when he couldn't help himself from jumping onstage with the band and grabbing an electric guitar and strapping it on. He didn't have time to play it before security hauled him off and threw him out the backdoors of the venue. No real harm was done, to the show or to his person, but it made for a great story to tell his friends. Tom was known for his sense of humor, his love of jokes and pranks and his distinctive laugh. Tom's voice had a soft cadence and an inflection all his own, there's few that can sound the way he did. His laid-back persona and mischievous grin made him an easily likeable friend to so many.

Craig Skinner had been living in Bristow up until this point and moved to Stillwater in 1984 to try to further his music career. He hauled his trailer house on the side of town, about a mile from the farm, where he lived for about four-five years. "I lived about a mile away from the farm, and there was always somebody with a guitar out. Somebody put it in your hand, and everyone would help with songs- just clean them up, polish them. We made music and I'd go home and then start it all again the next day, but always a good place to be and lots of people hanging out," said Craig Skinner.

Terry Ware was still playing in his band The Sensational Shoes in Norman at this time, which was in place from 1979-1986. The Norman based band performed originals as well as a batch of eclectic cover tunes. There were 11 different lineups over the years, but according to Ware the longest lasting and best of those was Johnny Hughes, Rita Longhofer, Marlin Butcher, Stacy Harris, Steve Crossett and Ware himself. In 1983, Ray Wylie called Ware up and asked them to be his backing band at an outdoor concert for the Veteran's Association in Dallas with Delbert McClinton, Table of Thunderbirds, Bos Henderson and BW Stephenson. Ware was happy to oblige. He would continue to get the occasional call to come play with Hubbard until 1986, when Hubbard asked Ware if he would consider coming back full time with him. Ware felt like his band in Norman had run its course at that time and agreed to join Hubbard once again. He stayed with Hubbard for 12 years this time.

Charlie Hollis moved to Tahlequah for a while at this time, moving his studio there, and recording Crouch and others in that area. He continued recording for LaFave and Childers, and all his other musician friends as well. This would be just one more stop before Hollis planted his studio in a bigger area with much further reach.

Lamb Recordings was still going strong and was involved with many different projects. One of these included recording for the K.I.D.S Radio show, which premiered on September 19th, 1981, on KSPI FM radio station broadcasting out of Stillwater. The weekly radio show aired on Saturday mornings at 11am and was created by a Stillwater music teacher named Carolyn Meyer and an account rep for the radio station named Kel Pickens. A new theme song for the show, *Happy Gnu Year*, first aired on January 2nd, 1982, and featured several local musicians. Ricky Peale played lead guitar, Mike Hufford on drums, Carolyn Meyer on piano and vocals, and Donnie Mitchell on bass. The sound engineering for the theme song was provided by Hufford at Lamb recording studio. Local musicians would lend their help with character voices for the show as well, and on that particular episode, Randy Pease played the voice of Walter the Rooster. The original episodes of the K.I.D.S radio show can be found on YouTube, as well as on podcast platforms such as Spotify, Apple and iHeart radio.

Childers' second album, *Singing Trees, Dancing Waters*, was released in 1983 and was recorded at Lamb Recordings.

In Their own Words

Greg Jacobs -The early days, in the '80s, that was the good ol' days. That was so much fun. We were such close friends, I'm sad that they are gone. I still think about them, I think about Bob and Tom most every day, one of the two of them will pop in my head about something, and I just miss those guys. I really do. They both had a distinct advantage on me in that they were both very personable guys, very extroverted guys. I've always been kind of an introvert- kind of shy- and that's the kiss of death in the music business. I'm not a guy that can sit around and brag on himself, it just doesn't work for me. And it didn't bother Bob in the least. Bob was one of a kind. Bob was the original snake oil salesman. I've seen Bob Childers in Willies, just have that rowdy crowd at closing time in the palm of his hand. He was just that kind of a guy, very personable guy, just a great guy. He could work a room. If he got a room that was just right, he could really work the room. He was almost Ray Wilie Hubbard, he could almost do a set and just play two songs and talk the whole rest of it and people loved it. That was Ray's trademark. Me, I always was more kind of quiet and stand in the background kind of guy. I just speak through my music, ya know? In the music business, you've got to sell yourself. There's 10,000 people like me out there, I was just never really good at that.

Rick McCord- It was real folk based. It was real farm based. Chuck Dunlap and of course Bob Childers and Tom Skinner and all the Skinner Brothers. They all just kind of had a big footprint on what was going on in

Stillwater. It's kinda funny because, fast forward 10 years, not a whole lot changed except for the fact that it just started getting some momentum. It seemed like the music really never changed, it just got some attention. It just got attention and started getting some money thrown behind it quite honestly.

Gene Williams – I was friends with Bob Childers, and I played on several of his albums back then. This was over a seven-year period of time when I lived there. Greg Jacobs and I played every Wednesday night at Willie's for about three years. I was in the student entertainer's rock band, called The Risk. With Diane Fisher and Zig Ziggler who now lives in Tulsa, works at a music store. I got to know Jimmy LaFave pretty well. Jimmy introduced me to Bob. Bob had moved back to Stillwater in the eighties, early eighties, and we were at Eskimo Joe's one night and he introduced us. Bob was a really prolific songwriter. Really a serious songwriter. And a real personality kind of cat. He really had an interesting persona. I didn't do many live shows with him. I did a few, but he liked my playing, and he asked me to play on several of his records over the years.

Growth & Expansion

Many of the budding new musicians got their first chance to play music in front of an audience at the Farm and were encouraged by the elder tribesmen of the music scene to get out there and play. "Jimmy eventually noticed that I was coming to a lot of the gigs. One night after one of the gigs, everybody went out to the farm, of course it was the usual thing. People would show up at the farm and there would be a jam out on the porch. I was there one night. Jimmy had seen me a bunch and I've met him, and he knew that I kind of was really starting to play. So, he just kind of put me on the spot and he goes- play us one. It was a bunch of people there and I think there was a guitar there at the farm. It had like four or five strings on it, it was a beat-up old guitar. So, I sit there and played one and he said, hey, that's not bad, man. He was one of the first guys that sort of nudged me to play something in public and I'll always acknowledge him for that. He was very nurturing, and he would give credence to anybody, even a beginner. He would take time to mentor them, talk to them and encourage them. Stillwater was just full of people like that, that just were very encouraging and nurturing. That's the reason I think the scene grew out of that kind of feeling and sort of a sense of camaraderie," said Brad Piccolo.

Brad Piccolo at the Farm. Photo provided by Sage Powell

It was also about this time that Bob Wiles and Brad Piccolo got disillusioned about living in the restrictive fraternity and moved into a house together on Sherwood Street, which they dubbed the Sherwood House. Piccolo had met a guy named Stan Woodward in one of his classes at OSU and pulled him into the mix of musicians as well. Woodward graduated from Edison High School in Tulsa in 1979 and came to Stillwater to go to college. "I showed up to Stillwater. I'm a jazz drummer. I was playing jazz in high school. But I played rock and roll with just jamming around, but mainly just was playing jazz. I didn't play drums every weekend, but I had a drum kit. I brought it over with me on a later trip. When I first came over to school though, I didn't have any room. I just had my dorm room. So, all I brought over was my guitar and my amplifier. The first week of school through some weird serendipity, I end up sitting with or near Brad Piccolo in one of the engineering classes. I don't know how we connected, but it was pretty obvious early on, that we played music. So, he came over to the dorm room and saw my guitar and then I went to his place. I think he was living in a fraternity house or something. But next thing I know, I'm over at this house. I think it's on Sherwood and he and Bob Wiles are living together at this house. Bob Wiles, being the funny guy he is, he goes - hey, Woody, you got a drum set, just bring it up here. I said, where am I gonna store it? He said, just put it here. So I bring my kit up, I set it up at the house there and my full intention was just to go by every once in a while, play it or whatever. Funny story on that is that Bob started playing my drum kit. When I showed up in my first little jam session over there at their house, Bob had been playing my drum kit and basically gotten pretty good. Taught himself how to play drums on my drum set," said Woodward.

"A menagerie of different musicians would crash out over there. We had drums set up, Stan Woodward – Woody - he set his drums up over there. Bob had a guitar. I had a guitar. We would sit there and jam, endless hours, day and night over there. It's a funny story on that place. We moved in because we had a friend that said they had a rent house, that Sherwood house, and they were moving out. They said, well, if you guys wanna move in, we got some openings. So, we moved in there and the funny thing was we never even met the landlord. For like three years, we never even paid rent. We moved into this house. The landlord, all we knew was his first name was Reggie, but he never showed up. He never came. We just lived there free for like three years. We finally got paranoid, like he's gonna show up and collect money. So, we moved to another place. which also ended up filled with musicians. Everywhere I moved in Stillwater, became a musical house basically," said Piccolo.

At this time Piccolo was mostly playing solo shows as he learned his craft more but eventually started playing in bands. "Before long, in places like Willie's and The Lighthouse and all that, I started playing solo gigs and this and that. It was just a very good scene, if you could play guitar and had some songs, it was pretty easy to get a gig. I was just there at a lucky time that was very open to having performers and stuff. I kind of feel lucky that was the time that I was there," said Piccolo.

Brad Piccolo. Photo provided by Sage Powell.

Brad James found his way to Stillwater in 1984 when he was 17 years old. He hadn't started playing the guitar yet, he was just starting to get interested in it. The afternoon he was moving into his dorm room, he heard a guy playing guitar and it proceeded to wreck his college career. "I started going down to Washington Street and I would have met guys that were in Brad Piccolo's band. Brad, Greg Morris, David Dyer, and Bret Absher used to play a lot with him too. David Dyer was much more of a Tulsa guy than a Stillwater guy. I remember seeing them in a street dance on Washington Street where they literally blocked off right in front of Coney Island. There was a stage, and the street was blocked off, and I remember thinking- I've got to meet these guys. The lead guitar was so far above my head. I remember watching Kevin Pharris, the lead guitar player, just watching him real close. Later he said- I saw you watching, I was trying to make those chords real big for you. And so, I fell into this group of guys that were a lot older than me. Seemingly at the time. When you are 17-18, people that are 27-28 seem way older. They just kind of took me under their wing and showed me the ropes," said James. The band that Brad Piccolo was in at this time was called Los Guys. They didn't really have a band name, and Brad Absher jokingly threw out Los Guys- referencing a Cheech and Chong movie, and the name stuck. This band would have a blues and rock vibe to it. Eventually the name transformed into Low Skies.

Greg Morris, known around town as a talented electric guitar player, was a student and teaching assistant at OSU and would eventually become a professor there as well. Morris had been influenced by the blues and rock- Eric Clapton and Stevie Ray Vaughan being huge influences on him. Slightly older than Piccolo, he taught Piccolo a lot about playing guitar. Morris also played in a band called Side Street with Gene Williams.

Greg Morris, John Maldonado singing, Terry Piersen, Dave Dyer. Photo provided by Stan Woodward.

"Greg was an excellent guitar player, electric guitar. He played I would say blues-based guitar. He always had a nice house. It was always sort of outside of town in the country and we'd go over there and rehearse. He was kind of a big reason why I got started. He took me under his wing. Also, Brad James when he was just a little kid at the time, probably about 16 or 17. He would follow us around and Greg showed him too. So, we kind of gave him a little shot to get on stage with us here and there. It was a very nurturing scene," said Piccolo.

James was allowed to sit in for a few songs with Los Guys if he would wind cables and carry gear and learn how to run sound for them. "I learned live sound engineering from some real experts, David Dyer and Greg Morris and Piccolo. They were all very encouraging. But Piccolo was just like, oh man you oughta get a band. So, they introduced me to what we now call the Red Dirt Music scene, but it was just the guys. It didn't have a name. Jimmy LaFave had just moved away, Bob Childers had just moved away, but you would hear about them in these conversations with these guys," said James. Of course, James quickly made his way to the Farm upon making all of these musician connections. "People would hang out, play croquet, just hang out at the Farm. Then drive out to Willie's and do the electric rock full set. Which was amazing because they would have untold amount of people on that tiny little stage that is about as big as two twin beds. Then everybody would head out to the farm. But I remember that was a lot of education right there, a lot of history. I was just a kid. Sometimes Bill Bloodworth and Dolly would let me into Willie's, but sometimes they wouldn't. So, I would be standing there just looking in the windows. But they saw me fix an amplifier for Brad Piccolo one time. Something broke, and I had to solder a speaker cable back in to get it to work, right there on stage while the band was playing. They thought- he must need to be here. It was very informative, and I didn't know what I wanted to do with my life, but that made me really hungry for music. I wanted to be a professional guitar player, but I didn't know how to play yet," said James.

Tom Skinner was the first person to let James get up on stage to play and sing a song, at Stonewall Taven during a songwriter swap with Greg Jacobs. "They were just sitting there doing their thing, and it was still when you could come in through the front door off of the street of Stonewall. Brandon Keith had a night class, and he comes in with his bookbag, sets down his book bag and those guys take a set break. They go, hey get up and do something. So, three incredibly amazing musicians, and I'm just getting started and had never been on stage before. But I walk up to Tom and said, hey you let guys get up and play? He said absolutely. I remember how weird it was to sing into a microphone and think, oh shit. I played about two songs; one was an original by my friend Mark Ballou. Not the Mark Ballou from Big Smith, but the exact same spelling, different guy.

That really set the hook. It was so exciting. I was like, I think I'm going to do that," said James.

Brad James. Photo provided by Sage Powell.

James would eventually move in with Greg Morris on Duck Street, who were both leaning into the blues. "We both really had the blues when we first met because I was dropping out of college and had a baby with a lady that I didn't really know. And his best gal for many years had just run off with his best drummer of many years and moved to Austin. So, he taught me how to live the blues and why the music was important to everything. He was a great guy. It would have been Greg that turned me on to JJ Cale and Jimmy LaFave. Piccolo was more my introduction to Bob Childers. But Greg definitely kind of turned me on to the whole scene. Because I was working for him with sound crew, it was easy for me basically to just sneak in and be in nightclubs when I wasn't allowed. When I wasn't supposed to be in there. He was kind of instrumental. I mean, he showed me how to dial up a tube amp and get a tone, how to run your tube screamer, how to drive your Stratocaster. He was just very helpful and insightful. My life would be very different if he hadn't taken me under his wing. He gave me my first Jack Kerouac book. So, yeah, it brought about a lot of changes," said James.

Many of the musicians were kind of like gypsies, moving here and there. Childers was no exception, he seemed to be living in various places at various times, and the exact times of each place are not always clear. He traveled from place to place, sometimes living with his wife Robin and his two young sons, and sometimes not. Sometime in the mid '80s he made his way to Tahlequah and lived there for a short time with Robin and the boys. Tahlequah started to have their own little music scene come more alive at this time. While Randy Crouch was a legend in that area and lived there, he frequently was on the road with his band and not playing there much. But at this time more and more places became available to play in that area. Bobby Martin lived in Tahlequah. His parents had bought him a guitar when he was about 11-12 years old, but he didn't get really interested in it until he was about 16. At that time, he saved up some money and bought an electric guitar. He started playing in bands around town by about the age of 18 after graduating high school in 1975. He continued to play for the next several years, semi-professionally at first and then more full time. In 1984 Martin and a friend convinced a bank loan officer, who happened to be the dad of a high school friend, to give them a small business loan of five thousand dollars to open a recording studio. They purchased some recording equipment, including an eight-track reel to reel recorder and a mixing board. They found a space in downtown Tahlequah with cheap rent and started the Master Tracks Recording Studio. They had a little basement office area which used to be a bank. The bank had been upstairs and down below was the office area and a bank vault. They used the bank vault for a vocal booth.

"Well, the Master Track studio- when we started it- we were doing little demos for bands like Randy Crouch. He was our first client, him and his band came in and that was an interesting time," said Martin. Martin's friend lost interest after the first year and sold his shares of the studio to a former radio DJ named Glenn Stepp, who became partners with Martin. About this time Kevin Warren Smith decided to move his family to Tahlequah, having family in that area. "Kevin was really the one, he showed up at the studio. He had been hanging around and writing with all these guys and were performing with them in Stillwater. When he got to Tahlequah, he found me, and we started writing together and recording together. We collaborated a ton and then he started inviting his Stillwater guys to come to the studio. Because this was a place that they could record that was pretty cheap, and musicians around that could play. I wanna say, it was maybe a year or two after Kevin got there when Bob moved there. But I can't tell you the exact date that Bob was in town. He and his wife at the time and his two boys who were little, they were probably four and six or something like that. They had a little bitty rent house. I don't know if they moved to Tahlequah for any specific reason or he just moved there because Kevin was there. But he was at the studio a lot and we wrote a song or two together. They never saw the light of day, but it was cool to hang out with him," said Martin.

During this time, more venues were opening, and regular music festivals were happening on the river, making it a much more active music scene. A new bar called Ned's opened at this time. Martin had played in bands with Ned's son before, and Ned's goal was to open a bar that had a live music focus as a venue. Martin credits Ned's with helping to kick start the live music scene in Tahlequah. Marilyn Craig was still in Tahlequah and found herself connected to many of the musicians in the scene. Many of them had her write bios for them as she booked them gigs. "Kevin Smith, I wrote his bio. I said- Kevin Smith is a man whose many talents are constantly competing for his time. He was a multi-instrumentalist. He was a songwriter. He had all that music going. He played fiddle, violin, but also he was a painter, an artist, a visual artist. Glenn Stepp had that studio. He was the co-owner of the studio, but Bob Martin ran it, and Kevin Smith was down there a lot, and this guy named BJ Foreman, and Angie Bliss," said Craig.

Martin was doing much more as a musician than he was at the studio. He played in a band called Saint Anthony's with Kevin Smith, Bob Childers, Angie Bliss and BJ Foreman. "The studio was great, but it wasn't keeping me that busy as far as making a living at it. So, I was playing music probably more than I was recording. We just happened to have the studio there that people could come and hang out and record during the day. During the days, a lot of the time it just became a hangout. We'd have three or four, or six or eight or more people just come in and they would just be in a corner over there jamming or writing a song. So, we'd get something, a good idea. We'd start recording something. And it was really more of a demo studio. We weren't really set up to do really full armed productions. Like now I can do way more production on my laptop than I could in the mid to late eighties with that reel-to-reel tape. Although we got some pretty nice recordings out of it. I've still got a lot of the songs. I've tried to keep track of a lot of them. I've got a lot of that still at least somewhere. It might just be on a cassette tape. But it still exists somewhere. I've got quite a bit of it," said Martin.

Marilyn Craig also wrote a bio for the Saint Anthony's band and for Bob Childers as well. "When people are like, have you been to the farm? I said when they were putting the seeds in the ground I was there. I started going to the farm in about 1981, and I had some friends that were singers, Connie McQuay and Angie Bliss. So, we'd go up there. We went there a lot for jam sessions and stuff like that. Coop and them were living there and I wrote a bio for Bob Childers, for the Godfather before he was the Godfather of Red Dirt. I wrote a bio on him. There was a band put together out of that studio. It was Bob and it was Bobby Martin who ran the studio and played drums or bass, and this guy named BJ Foreman and Angie Bliss. And they were all songwriters. I'm writing a little bio for them then because I'm gonna book them some places. They were mainly writing great songs in the studio and playing on those. That's what started this. I write a bio about them and I'm like, everybody's songwriters. How many songs has everybody written? And among this band, they have 2100 song titles. Angie was kind of running the band at the time and she was calling practices and Bob wasn't showing up for them. She was mad because she wanted them to be polished and play. So, she decides, she just tells him- if you don't show up, you don't get to be in the band. Well, kicking the father of Red Dirt music out of the band! The funny part of it was when we had to take the number of songs that he'd written out, all of a sudden, the number of songs the band had written went from 2100 to 100. We lost 2000 songs when Bob dropped out of the party," said Craig.

Another Tahlequah musician of note was a guy named Sparky Fisher. Sparky was a guitarist in town known for his exceptional skills. "He was kind of one of those savant guitarists that just everybody knows about because he's such a good guitar player. He wasn't really a songwriter or singer, but he was just known to be an amazing guitar player," said Martin.

The mid-80s would be when Red Dirt moved outwards and into new areas, Tahlequah being just one of those break away communities.

In Their Own Words

Craig Skinner -I wouldn't trade it for nothing. I wish we would have been a little bit more savvy, to try to make it a business thing. We don't have a lot of recorded music from those days. Sure got a lot of memories. It was kinda tough being the younger brother with the job in the Skinner Brothers. It cost a lot, but there's a lot of memories. I remember one of the few times I saw Tom get inebriated, at Wild Willies. I saw Tom slide across the floor on his knees, singing "HELLO DOLLY! I SAID HELLO DOLLY!" Onstage Tom would play the musician, he could remember words to songs. Tom was really an artist. I almost have to have an iPad to scroll the words. He could remember the melodies and things like that, he knew all the lyrics. Even a brand-new song he just heard on the radio, he could pick it apart and knew how the steel guitar and fiddle and keyboards all go together. The lyrics are just the melody line to me until I learn the song. People like Bob, the simplicity of the lyrics is a part of Red Dirt too. I can listen to somebody telling me straight up and simply, instead of beating around the bush like some of that Nashville pop. It's straightforward and don't have to play too many notes. It's nice to have something to look back on like it mattered. It is. It really is. Enjoyed the hell out of it. Except for the dying. A couple of things weren't so fun about being a part of it. It was all about the song. The song being played, the song being written. It was really cool to be around all of it and be a part of it for sure. Sometimes it was really trying and demanding. It didn't kick my ass too bad I guess. I had a lot of fun.

Brad James -Catalyst stuff; there was Willie's, there was the Farm, there was the whole Washington street culture, what became the Wormy Dog, there was the big joint at the end that was many different things. Willie's was seemingly one of the most long lived. But Washington Street was really a magnet, like a 6th street in Austin or something. There were music joints up and down there. Some of them you could sneak into and some of them you could use a fake ID, and it would work, and some of them it wouldn't. But there was rock and roll going on down there full time. I even remember one of my very first weekends in Stillwater, over at OSU, walking underneath the student union little portico overhang thing. Guys who I later realized was Bret Franzmann and probably Frenchie, they were under there because it sounded good and they were just playing acoustic bluegrass, folk music. I remember Stillwater being musical from the time I got there, so it really set the hook for me.

Stan Woodward – Piccolo and those guys moved out to, I think, 32nd street south of town. It was hilarious. We had jams out there in the living room under a chandelier. We'd have 75 people crammed into the living room and just people in the yard. Ecstasy hit in like 1984-85. That was when you'd walk into a bar, and it was still legal. Nobody knew what it was. There'd just be a bowl full of ecstasy pills. People were doing mushrooms, people were doing ecstasy. People were drinking beer. I don't remember a whole lot of hard liquor, but it was just a lot of people were tripping like all the time. And so you had to go rescue people. You'd be at one of these jams and then somebody would be out under a streetlamp- 300 yards out in the middle of nowhere- tripping and you had to get him out of the field or just go rescue. My memory was that there were a lot of rescues of people that were seeing things and having experiences. We had to get them back to safety. There was a lot of just little psychedelics going on around the edges.

Moving Out of Oklahoma

LaFave was one of the first musicians to successfully transplant his Red Dirt music outside of the state, when he moved to Austin in about 1985. While many artists had been touring and gigging in other areas, this was the beginning of the music having a strong hold and a base outside of Oklahoma. This would give it a much wider audience and a chance to flourish beyond what they had done so far. LaFave is the one who made it easier for the next generation to find a foothold in Texas, blazing the trail that they would follow over a decade later. While he was the first, others quickly followed suit in the '80s, trying their hands at moving into other areas and states to progress their music.

Gene Williams moved to Nashville in 1985 for just a little while but never felt like he fit in there. So, when one of his sisters passed away, he moved back to Stillwater within the same year. However, also that same year Williams' friend David Wheelie asked him to move to Austin with him, so they packed up and left. "So, in the winter of 85 we went to Austin, and I started playing with Jimmy LaFave. Jimmy was the host of an open mic at a place called Chicago House, near Sixth street. So, every Wednesday night we played there for several years, and we got a really good following.

You know, that was better to move to some place where we could get noticed and get on the map. I played with Jimmy for five years, and it was a really great time," said Williams.

The scene in Austin kind of revolved around a couple of bars, the Chicago house and the Outhouse. The Outhouse was famous for Townes Van Zandt, Rich Minus, Jubal Clark and songwriters from a little earlier era. The Chicago house was where all the young players were going. "I was 27 when I moved there, and we were playing a lot of the early South by Southwests, which were just wonderful shows. And Jimmy and I- we really had our act together. Jimmy was such a wonderful singer songwriter to play off of. I remember one night, playing the South by Southwest at Chicago House, and it was just absolutely packed to the rafters. It was just way too many people in that place. And it was just one of the funnest gigs I ever played. You know, I guess it was at our apex, because the first five years that I was with Jimmy, we just performed as a duo. We played lots of shows and hardly any out of Austin. It was all just focused on playing right in Austin. I think that's what made him famous. We just kept hitting it, and we had the best spot at the open mic. Every Wednesday night at Chicago House at nine o'clock, we would play a 30-minute set, and that would be when the crowd was at its apex. We had several really good write ups in the Austin Chronicle. One year, I think I was voted the sixth best acoustic guitar player in Austin. They have these contests, and so that's a little claim to fame," said Williams.

LaFave seemed to flourish with his move to Austin, opening more opportunities for him and his music than he had in Oklahoma. "Jimmy had this real wry sense of humor. It was just fun to listen to him talk, and fun to watch him talk to fans and other people. He just wrapped people around his finger somehow. And of course, there were always all kinds of women following him around. He was just a very charismatic guy. I think he had a stalker at one time. I don't know what happened. I remember him telling me that, that he had a stalker," said Williams.

Back in Tahlequah, recording and playing live became a constant way of life for Kevin Warren Smith. Bobby Martin and Smith stayed busy recording themselves and others at Master Tracks studio. After moving to Austin, LaFave brought Tom and Paul Zografi to record in Tahlequah. After that it became common for people to come from distant places to record there. There was a constant stream of local Oklahoma musicians as well. Martin and Smith became experienced as studio musicians as well as engineers. "Tahlequah was sort of home base for Kevin, and I guess, Bob for a little while. And then they drew in some other musicians like Jimmy LaFave that already moved to Austin about that time. He brought some people up that he had run across in Austin because he was sort of, kind of wanting to be a producer. He got a group called the Zografi Brothers. They were not really Red Dirt, but they were in that orbit, I guess. And then he brought a guy up from Austin, his name was Hank Sinatra. And we recorded kind of an EP, I guess, with Hank. Jimmy came up and he was sort of like the producer and orchestrated everything and it was interesting. He was sort of, I don't know, sort of cowboy punk, I guess. Which at the time, I don't know if there's a name for that then. But anyway, it was a really interesting time," said Martin.

Marilyn Craig continued booking bands and booked LaFave while he was in Tahlequah recording. "Jimmy Lafave came in and recorded there during that time and I met Frenchie, Kurt Nielsen, down there and the Gray brothers from Austin. Jimmy recorded quite a few things. I worked at the college, but I also booked bands and one summer I booked Granny's attic. Every week I booked the band. I worked the door because they were working for the door. So, we wanted to make sure we got every dime that came through there. And I booked Jimmy there. He got to Austin. He was very welcoming and very helpful to all these other people coming behind him. He was so gracious," said Craig.

Smith and Martin continued to collaborate, writing together and putting together publishing companies. They had a focus on promoting songwriting and songwriters. They would record compilation albums with various musicians that made their way to the studio. "It was just kind of a little community that was created, and it really didn't start until Kevin showed up. He's the one that kind of started it. Really when we started writing together and recording together, I think at that point we realized- hey, we could put some of these folks you already know together and then we'll just start recording some things. It was never a business that made much money. It was about just being able to hang out with a community of songwriters and musicians. I mean, I was hoping I eventually made enough money. We barely made enough money to cover the rent most of the time. But it became sort of just a known place to go hang out and be able to collaborate with other songwriters. Just sort of a little collective of creatives that were just hanging out. I didn't think of it as anything to do with Red Dirt because I don't even know if that term had even been knocked around at that point," said Martin.

Childers recorded his album *Four Horsemen* at the Master Tracks Studio during this time. "Probably, the first one of the most memorable Bob memories: Bob had this this big old Chevy panel truck from the early sixties, which he'd hand painted white, and had named it the White Buffalo. I remember one day, he loaded up in the white buffalo with his wife at the time, Robin, and the kids and we drove down to Tahlequah to Bobby Martin's recording studio. I put my parts down on an album he made called Four Horsemen, which I think was only released in cassette. I think that was the first album I ever played on his," said Gene Williams.

Musicians that had started their journeys in Stillwater, being raised on the collaboration and mentoring culture that was born out of that, began to take that philosophy and style out into other areas, spreading and cultivating an even larger community. "When I look at this Tahlequah thing with the studio, it became this little spin off of sorts, of what at least was going on in Stillwater. And that's really because of Kevin, he sort of moved that little satellite away from Stillwater and kind of planted it in Tahlequah for a period of time. And so a lot of the same people came in and recorded. Some of those same folks, especially that Kevin knew. Bob ended up coming to my little studio and recording and I guess that's how that little satellite community kind of created," said Martin.

Kevin Warren Smith, Hank Sinatra, Kurt Nielsen. Photo provided by Stan Woodward.

The musicians were discovering they could create their own musical communities even if it wasn't centered around Willie's and the Farm any longer. They could take that magic and recreate it in a sense and draw in musicians in other areas. "I think that there was just a special group of people that they just had so much fun, and it was the stuff that poured out of them. It happens all over the place but there was something very specific happened in that sort of Stillwater orbit. They had to do that, and I think that when certain types of people or certain people get together, they feed off each other. That sort of collaboration and feeding each other becomes contagious in ways that you don't think about making any money off of it. You're just having too much fun just in the moment doing it. And I think that's why you see so many of these sorts of rotating bands that play, because there's not one or two or three that are driving it all, it just really is a sort of a big collaborative effort. It's pretty rare to find those kinds of things," said Martin.

There didn't seem to be any big plans being made, they didn't have their sights set on major recording contracts and record labels. They were creating music for the sake of creating music. They fed off each other's creativity and encouragement, cocooning themselves in a community of like-minded people who all seemed to be happy exactly where they were, doing what they were doing. "And I think that little slice of time at that studio in Tahlequah, that was a real joyful time for that reason. None of us had money, we're all just on food stamps. Probably some of them, kind of just getting by. But we had no lack of joy. Just being able to sit down together and write songs and occasionally play those songs, there's something very satisfying and joyful about that. I still don't know that we were doing anything that special other than people saying that it was, because at the time obviously we didn't say we were doing that. We were just hanging out and trying to see what was coming out of our minds. Like the big get-togethers they had at the farm. I think there was a realization. Yeah, this was fun. But I don't know if there's any realization that it was gonna be important 40 years later- or two years later for that matter. But I think in the middle of that, you just get so excited about it. It's like, wow, what is this really? Something exciting is happening here, that doesn't usually happen," said Martin.

At some point during this time, Bob Childers, Kurt Nielsen and Kevin Smith were considering a move to Austin and decided to make a trip to check it all out. They all piled into Childers' White Buffalo to make the trip. "Bob's white Buffalo was notorious because if you sat in the back seat, you're gonna get poisoned. Because he had an exhaust leak that went up through the floor. We definitely found that out on the big road trip, I got pretty sick from it. Kevin started to get sick from it," said Nielsen. Smith and Nielsen complained about the exhaust and commented that they were feeling sick, but Childers wasn't very receptive to the complaints, so soon they dropped it and just tried to hang in there.

The group set out for Austin late in the evening. At about midnight - Childers driving, Nielsen up front and Smith in the back seat- they were driving through a small town in Oklahoma. They pulled into the only gas station they saw with lights on, which may have been the only gas station in town. Childers and Nielsen went into the store, and Smith stayed outside to pump the gas. "When we went in there- Bob in front of me- at the time he looked as Rastafarian as he ever did. I walked in behind him, and behind the counter I see this little lady with a CB radio. And she's kind of clicking it with her hands, you know, just hitting the talk button. I didn't think anything about it. I went and bought a couple of beers, he bought some other stuff, and we went out to the car. By the time we get to the car, at this point, Kevin had change places with Bob. He was gonna drive, and I was in the back seat. So, we all get placed in the seats. Two cops come out of nowhere. No car, nothing. They came out from behind the building. Guns drawn. They said, we have reason to believe there's an open container in this car and pulled us out of the car," said Nielsen.

"I stayed with the truck and pumped gas. Then I climbed up to the driver's seat because it was my turn to drive. I watched them go into the store and suddenly got a dark feeling. We looked like hippie hillbilly musicians that folks there probably haven't seen much of. One of my buddies, I won't say who, was particularly well lit. I felt a little paranoid as headlights appeared from behind the store and a car came out to the side of the building. It was a local cop car. The two human shadows just sat there in the car until Bob and Kurt came back out. Then they got out of the black and white and walked towards us. I was told to step out of the truck. And our hands went flat against the vehicle," said Smith.

The cops had the guys with their hands on the hood as they glanced around the inside of the White Buffalo. They went through a grocery sack of smashed cans and said it was an open container. They were all frisked and a pipe was found on Childers. The cops said the guys could go ahead and tell them where the pot was, or they would tear apart the truck and find it. Smith and Nielsen's recollections start to differ a little here. Nielsen recalls that Childers told the cops that it was in an International Coffee can on the dash. Smith recalls that it was in a small metal mint container. Either way, the pot was found where Childers told them it was. Since Smith was in the driver's seat when the cops arrived, and was closest to the evidence, he was the one they were going to charge for it. "My buddies both spoke up for me. They explained the box was not mine and I wasn't even a user of the substance at that time. It didn't matter. The older cop pulled out a pink pad of tickets. He explained that we could be arrested and stay behind bars until we could see a judge. He then quickly said, but there is another option. If you guys admitted you were in the wrong, we could sign the pink papers, pay a fee of $100 each in cash and then leave town and there would be no record of the event. I felt as if we were on a stagecoach that was being held up in the 1800s," said Smith.

Smith's money was in the back of the truck in his fiddle case. The younger officer unsnapped his holster as Smith climbed in the back to get the fiddle case. As he opened the case, the officer suddenly put his hand on his firearm and cautioned Smith to open it slowly, as if Smith were a 1930's gangster getting ready to pull a Tommy Gun out of the fiddle case. Instead, Smith pulled out all the money he had for the entire trip - and they weren't even out of Oklahoma yet. They all three handed over their fee. Afterwards, as they all climbed back into the White Buffalo and prepared to head off, an older gentleman approached the officers still standing there with the guys and proceeded to chastise the cops for harassing what were clearly out of towners. "When he started chastising the cops, we thought - whoa. This guy must be the mayor or some type of official with the city. He starts going, people are not going to do business in this town if you're going to do this to people. Then the two cops looked at us, kind of waved their hands and said see ya boys. But they weren't going after this guy. The guy had enough clout that they weren't going after him, but they just wanted to get us out of there before we were totally clued in on their thievery thing. The band Big Smith, I think it was Big Smith. They were going through that town, and the same thing happened to them. They wrote a song about it. Eventually that town got busted, for the same type of deal, for speed traps and just harassing people," said Nielsen.

The guys carefully left the gas station and proceeded to dig into the chips and salsa that Nielsen had purchased at the store. By the time they made it to Austin, Nielsen and Smith had to immediately lie down because they both had exhaust poison headaches and upset stomachs. "We complained to Bob and expected he might now see we had exhaust poisoning. But no, he was sure it was the salsa from the gas station. I'm sure he would stand by his position even today," said Smith.

Nielsen and Childers didn't decide to move to Austin during that adventure, and a few weeks later they all loaded back up and took a trip to Nashville just to scope it all out. Nielsen decided to move there soon after. He moved to Nashville and realized Childers had followed him there. "When I moved to Nashville, I was there one day. Didn't tell Bob Childers where I lived, but he's knocking on my door the next day. So, he moved in with me for six months after that," said Nielsen. Nielsen got a job within a day of arriving, which kept him pretty busy. He didn't end up playing as much music as he hoped during his time there, but he did get to sample the Nashville music scene up close and personal. The first week they were there, they went to a local songwriter's night and met a guy from Connecticut, named Jason Hunt. They found Hunt to be a great songwriter and quickly formed a friendship.

Kevin Warren Smith also moved to Tennessee around this time, but not Nashville. "Although I often sang and played frontman solo and with bands, what I've always enjoyed most is being a sideman for someone whose music I love and care about. We played on a lot of stages together. But I became burned out of playing with so many people that I needed to go someplace where I could concentrate on the songs for a while. I didn't want to go to Nashville, but I did want to go someplace as rich and musically nourishing. So, my wife and I moved to Memphis with our kids. I loved being in Memphis in the last part of the '80s. It was powerful and I had great experiences. I even got a couple of my songs played on WEVL. There may not be as much music business activity there compared to Nashville, but the music of Memphis itself was truly wonderful and sometimes enlightening," said Smith.

Mary Reynolds moved back to Oklahoma from New York in 1985 and started the Sisters of Swing with Mary Free and Kim Turk. "It was just kind of nuts. I don't know why I did this, perhaps a lack of focus. But I was planning to move with my partner at the time, we were planning to move to San Francisco to join the band of Tuffy Eldridge. He was a songwriter around here and then moved there. But for some reason I called Mary and some other friends of mine that sang, and an old friend of mine that I met in college and had a five-piece vocal group. Now there's a lot of problems with that, you have to come up with five notes for people to sing, and that was the challenge. There's a model and we did a lot of swing stuff. I was also in love with do-wop music and the model there is a bass, three harmony parts and a lead, so there's your five. Mary could sing very low, and her two sisters eventually ended up in the group and they all could sing very low, so we had that advantage. The Arts Council got behind it in a big way. Shortly before the Sisters of Swing got started, the outdoor concerts really started. The Arts Festival was going on but then their Twilight Concerts in the park and the downtown things started. This was about 1985. The Sisters of Swing had some falling outs and getting back together, but we were together over a period of 32 years. We had a lot of fun. We didn't travel to many places. That was another thing that somehow didn't quite translate out of our native habitat," said Reynolds.

Upon moving back Reynolds rented out a house on 2805 N McKinley Ave. in Oklahoma City, and would occasionally host listening parties, which was just a precursor to what this establishment would come to be in the next decade. This was the beginning of the Blue Door listening room, which would become yet another Red Dirt staple along the way.

In Their Own Words

Kurt Nielsen- We recorded about, I'd say half a dozen to 10 tunes with Jimmy LaFave at Lamb Studios. They were all acoustic, right before Jimmy moved to Austin. Including *Minstrel boy*, *Only One Angel*, and a bunch of other ones. And it was just great stuff. I wish I had some of that stuff still on tape. Especially *Minstrel Boy*, I think my favorite mandolin part I ever put down was on that song right there.

Bobby Martin - Yeah, it's weird too. Like, I mean, of course you got a person like Garth Brooks who is right in the middle of all that. But he's sort of an outlier - the way his career path took, even though his genesis, his start was the same as those other guys. In fact, he played a lot with those same guys. But all those amazing musicians and songwriters and just that creative atmosphere and the farm and all that - just that whole creative community really set a foundation, or at least sort of a reference point. Where all these other folks kind of just learn from that and saw that happening and it was like, oh, we could do that. That is cool. So, I think that the little thing in Tahlequah was just sort of a little spin off, maybe a little satellite, that came out of that Stillwater scene. But even that expanded into other folks too,

Gene Williams - Jimmy and I had a lot of wonderful gigs. We were roommates for about a year, and it really was difficult losing him. It's been very hard to lose all these guys. Because, you know, when you play with somebody- just one on one like that for a long time- it's a big piece of your soul. When Jimmy came back to Oklahoma and did those final concerts, it was so good to see him again and get to talk to him. The church in Perkins Oklahoma, Monica Taylor puts on shows. Jimmy had a concert there, and I got up and played with his band for a few songs. I will always admire him for the way he went out. I mean, he played every gig he possibly could, until the night before he died. That was just an amazing show of strength, and you know, it's incredible.

Musician Reunion & Santa Fe

The second half of the '80s brought even more musicians and events that would give the forming scene stronger roots and stability. Eric Hansen moved from Shawnee to Stillwater in 1985 to go to High School. Hansen started playing music at the age of 11 and had played in various bands throughout high school. As a young teenager just roaming around town, he would look through windows and try to peer into the doors to watch bands playing. Hansen was playing in a little three-piece cover band called Steamroller, which played classic rock. They played the Teen Club in Stillwater, and on the OSU Campus. Eskimo Joe's had bands playing regularly and was one of the first bars Hansen ever played in, even when he was underage. Hansen would go on to help create the next generation of Red Dirt artists, but this was when he landed onto the scene.

Eric Hansen playing drums for Tom Skinner. Photo provided by Craig Skinner.

Eskimo Joes was celebrating 10 years as of 1985. According to their website bio, "As Joe's popularity grew, so did their annual birthday bash. To celebrate the 10th anniversary in 1985, the party spilled onto Elm Street, marking the beginning of the Eskimo Joe's street party that would become the largest single attraction to Stillwater, except for OSU football". Eskimo Joe's annual parties and festivals would become a staple in the Red Dirt scene for generations to come, building into big name acts and larger stages.

The Farm was hopping, and it didn't take too long before Danny Pierce realized he didn't even have to go into town to see music any longer. He was working on his Doctoral degree and teaching classes, which left him little downtime as it was. "I just learned I could just sit at home and everyone's there. It got to the point where guys were like – damn, I gotta go into town and play for a few hours. I'll be right back. Just tell everybody I'll be coming back, everybody stay - don't leave. Well hell, I'm just gonna take a nap while you guys go play and then come back. It got to be where I wasn't going into town as much and just enjoying all the things going on and I'd cook a meal for everybody when they were done," said Pierce.

By 1985 John Buckner had returned to Stillwater after moving to both Dallas and Florida to try his hand in different rock groups and blues bands. Garth Brooks had been playing around town for a few years and had just started playing Willie's every Wednesday night. "Garth was starting to play around town. Playing Willie's, just kind of doing happy hour. I had a friend that told me you need to go see this guy play. He walks around the bar with a ball cap on and he works across the street at Duprees and if you tip him five bucks, he'll play whatever song you want. That was his thing. He connected with people where other musicians at the time, they were just kind of like on the stage and people sat in the audience and you really didn't talk to them or whatever. You just kind of sat and watched and drank and partied and danced and whatever. Garth man, he went out, he engaged people, and people responded to it. I didn't think he was really the best guitar player or singer that I'd ever seen. I thought Jimmy and Chuck were tons better. But I loved the way he interacted and engaged people, and I knew at that point that he was probably gonna go somewhere. I didn't know or expected he'd be as big as he got," said Buckner.

Willie's was actually one of the places where Garth Brooks found his footing in the scene, attending open mics nights there until he secured his own every Wednesday night spot. Many of the musicians said during Garth's time at Willie's, the crowd changed a bit. His crowd tended to be a lot of the younger college crowd, and they packed the place out during his nights there, pushing the older crowd away. Although many don't think of Brooks as a part of the Red Dirt scene, he was a product of that environment and credits Red Dirt for where he is. While most agree that Brooks was an anomaly of the scene, with a penchant more for the performer philosophy of music that wasn't a part of the Red Dirt culture, he did form his roots on the budding Red Dirt scene. "I wouldn't have a career without Stillwater. It is the birth of my music...red dirt music. From the earth...what you do with it after that is up to you...but Stillwater gave me everything I needed to know about music. My music is what it is on the outside, but I believe with all my heart that Red Dirt music is the backbone of my body of music," Brooks said in a 2010 interview with

Aaron N. Moore for his college thesis *Playing in the Dirt: Stillwater and the Emergence of Red Dirt Music*.

In fact, it was in 1985 when Brooks made his first trip out to Nashville. He didn't get the reaction he expected there and quickly returned home to regroup. After returning home he started the Santa Fe band in 1986, and married his longtime girlfriend, Sandy. The band started out with Brooks, Tom Skinner on bass, Jed Linsey on guitar, and Matt O'Meilia on drums. Matt O'Meilia would later write a book detailing how the Santa Fe band got started and how Garth Brooks' career evolved, titled *Garth Brooks: The Road out of Santa Fe*, published in 1997 by the University of Oklahoma Press. His book, along with an interview with O'Melilia, were used as a reference and resource for this book. It's a great book for deeper insight into this band and Brooks' beginnings.

Tom was 32 at this time and had just had his son Jeremy in the fall of 1985. He had made a trip to Nashville in 1986 to be on the "You Can Be a Star" TV program, singing his song *She Gave Away Her Heart*. "I had gone to Nashville with Glenn Stepp from Tahlequah, that used to own Stepp's mobile homes there and had a studio. Glenn had heard some of my songs that I recorded there and took me to Nashville to try to get me on 'You Can Be a Star'. God love him he was trying. I didn't really want to be on 'You can be a star', but I wanted to see Nashville. So, I took the trip, came back home and talked to my wife and told her that's what we need to do. As soon as you graduate, let's go to Nashville, and she was kind enough to give into my wishes and desires. And so, in the meantime, waiting for her to graduate, Garth had come to me after my band - me and my brothers had sorta taken a break – and he comes, and he wants to start a house band. And I had just had a son, so I had a little baby at home, and he wants to start a house band where we won't have to travel and joined up with him," said Tom in a 2014 YouTube interview with Red Dirt Nation. (Youtube : *Tom Skinner Interview*, Red Dirt Nation).

Skinner's You Can Be a Star letter. Provided by Craig Skinner.

Santa Fe's first gig was at a bar and dance hall called Bink's, where they would make a connection that would serve them well. Bink's had a large dance floor and plenty of room. The band would play there every Friday, Saturday and Monday night. Tuesday night the band, minus Brooks, would be the house band for the local talent showcase, which then turned into lingerie shows and wet t-shirt contests, as the owners found creative ways to bring in more people. Not long after Santa Fe was established and playing regular gigs, Tom brought his brother Mike into the band on fiddle and harmonies. The connection to Bink's allowed them to be asked to open for the nationwide acts coming through town that summer, including Dwight Yoakam, Johnny Paycheck, New Grass Revival, Steve Earle and more.

Sante Fe recording inside Lamb Studios. Photo provided by Craig Skinner.

The inaugural Jimmy LaFave Musician Reunion festival took place in 1986. Jeff Parker, who was going to college in Oklahoma City at this time, had been playing regularly at Eskimo Joe's and Willie's in Stillwater with a couple of bands from Norman. "It was at that time, as far as Red Dirt goes, Jimmy LaFave was really kind of our poster boy, so to speak. He had moved to Austin, and it was just really creating national interest in what he was doing. He would come back every summer and do a Stillwater music reunion at Willie's and it was just crazy," said Parker.

Kurt Nielsen and his new songwriting buddy Jason Hunt drove from Nashville to Stillwater for the first Musician's Reunion, held on April 25-26, 1986. As soon as they got there, a photographer from the Stillwater News Press snapped a photo of Hunt, who ended up being the first performer of the event, even though he wasn't from the area. The musical community was loose and inviting, they were happy to hear anyone get up and sing their songs. The poster advertising the event listed dozens of names, and ended with "Etc, Etc, Etc! And last but not least, their friends! & All other music lovers!!!"

It was definitely an open invitation event. LaFave brought people with him from Austin, and other people from out of town made the trek to see LaFave come home. Many of these people ended up at The Farm, sleeping in cars and tents.

After they closed down the bar at Willie's, everyone made their way to the Farm to keep the festivities going. It would be just the first of an on-going annual event that everyone looked forward to.

A few weeks after the event, back home in Nashville, Nielsen got a call from Randy Pease saying he was coming

Rod Boutwell, Gene Williams, Jimmy LaFave, Bobby Spencer, Ron Beckel. Photo provided by Stan Woodward.

over and had something to give to Nielsen. "Tom, I think he was working at News Press or he just got done not working there anymore. But Randy brought the paper, and he said, 'Hey, sorry. I had to stop because I went fishing in Tahlequah and didn't have anything to wrap the fish up with'. So, he took this newspaper and wrapped the fish up in it, but he let it dry and gave it to us. And Jason was on the front page of the newspaper. Never had been to Stillwater before in his life," said Nielsen.

Nielsen had met a woman from Oklahoma in Nashville by the name of Patsy Benson, who had a little three-piece band. Benson also was running a popular songwriter night in a shopping mall in West Nashville. Benson already knew Childers, as she had come into Lamb studio to sing backups on his first album recorded there. Nielsen and Childers met a lot of the local songwriters at these songwriter nights, including a songwriter by the name of Stephanie Davis, who had moved there from Muscle Shoals. Davis had a little four track studio set up, where Nielsen and Childers did some recordings with her. Childers and Davis also wrote a few songs together. Davis had learned the ins and outs of how to make connections in the Nashville music scene. "She knew who the people were in the music industry. We'd go to the songwriter nights with her, and she goes, That's so and so over there. She had money, so she'd check to see what they were drinking. Then she'd buy him a drink and send it over there," said Nielsen.

Childers released his album *King David's Lament* around this time.

It was in the spring of 1987 when Brooks planned to move with his band Santa Fe to Nashville, to try again at making it in that world. O'Meilia, the drummer, didn't want to make the move to Nashville and left the band. Troy Jones replaced O'Meilia before the move. It was already Tom Skinner's plan to move to Nashville, so this just made sense to him that they could pool their resources, get a place together and possibly have more luck than doing it alone. Tom had asked Childers- who lived down the street from Music Row at this time- if Brooks and Jed Lindsey could come stay with him for a bit and if Bob could drive them around town to find a place to live before they moved there. Childers introduced Brooks to a woman name Stephanie Brown at this time, and she invited Brooks to record a demo at her home studio. They decided on the song *Luck of the Draw*, written by Childers and Greg Jacobs. During the visit they found an old five-bedroom, three-bathroom house in Hendersonville, 20 miles North of Nashville and decided it would work for the band. They signed a 6-month lease, and all promptly moved there.

"The way things shifted and changed in Stillwater was one reason it was easy for me to up and leave. People were leaving, like Bob, and they went somewhere and were fitting where they were fitting. It seemed like people were looking to get out at that time. We had been there a while, and we had talked about going and doing this and that and ran into Garth. It just started out that he wanted the college money that was around there, we played pretty well together. We hit up all the cowboy places, even though we did play more rock and roll type music and not cowboy music. But it all just fell in, and we played around Stillwater for as long as we could. We got to the point where if we were going to make any money at music we had to go try to do it," said Mike Skinner.

All the band members and their families lived in the one house together in the very beginning, working during the day and playing gigs at night. Tom's son Jeremy was about 18 months old when they moved there. Jeremy says his first memory ever is from that house, just a picture in his head, of blue carpet and a bay window in his room. The group all promptly found jobs to be able to pay the rent. Tom got a job at a convenience store, his wife Jeri got a job at Wal-Mart. Mike found employment at an office furniture store, and Troy as a maintenance man at an apartment complex. No one is quite sure what Jed did. He left during the day and came back and had money for rent. Brooks landed the manager position at Boot Town down the street from where they lived, and he got his wife Sandy a job there as well. The Oklahoma guys found themselves in a whole new world in Nashville.

"We looked around and was like, damn where are we at? Garth was where he belonged, which isn't saying anything bad, he just was. But the rest of us was like what the hell is happening? It destroyed me, because somebody comes to tell you what to expect - best case scenario you get a record deal, worst case you come back to Oklahoma. And this lady came to tell us we had to pay our dues. She was hooked up with some big star, and she was trying to tell us. She told us you will pay your dues and play every night at these little dives, and it doesn't even pay for your ticket out of there. Tom looked at her and said well, is there any way around that? It's a strange place. We worked during the day and played at night. We all met ourselves coming and going. It took its toll. It was like six families in one house," said Mike.

Marilyn Craig made her way to Nashville at this time, as she continued to pursue her career in the music industry. "I did the concerts at Northeastern. We did about four major country shows a year. After I'd done that for eight years, I was wanting to go to Austin. I really wanted to go to Austin because I love Texas music. But there wasn't any mid-level management in Austin then for music. I mean, I had to have a job to leave my job. So, I thought I'm gonna have to go to Nashville. I had worked with the Jim Halsey company. My friend Max Boydston, who's involved with the Oklahoma Music Hall of Fame, he helped start that. He set me up a couple of appointments in Nashville. I was just going out there on a scouting mission and I just wanted to see, basically how I could use the skills I had and get a job out there," said Craig.

Max Boydston got Craig an appointment at RCA Records and at Network Inc which was a PR firm. Craig made her way to Nashville for those meetings. She found herself with some time in between the meetings and decided to go check out the new Jim Halsey branch that had recently been opened in Nashville. "I thought, well, I'm gonna run up there and see them while I'm here. And it just so happened that they had a company that was called Pro Tours. The Judd's owned it, and they were getting ready to hire a marketing person, a marketing manager for it. I ended up going back out there and interviewing for the job about two weeks later and I got it. The first week in town I go get an entertainment magazine, the Nashville scene. I'm flipping through it. It says Suler Café, Skinner Brothers Thursday night. I'm like, oh my God. I went down there and of course, I went and visited with Tom and Jeri. Jeremy was a baby, and Garth and Sandy, all these people lived together. Then the single guys, Mike, and a couple other guys lived in the basement, and they had this big house that they lived in. I think I've told people before, I know the people that taught Garth how to play. So, I met Garth but really, I couldn't wait for him to leave the room so

Tom and I could visit and smoke a joint. Garth wasn't up for that. Garth did great things. He really did. He was a different animal. Garth, he's an entertainer and his goal was to be either a superhero or a super something, a super entertainer, idol type person," said Marilyn Craig.

In Their Own Words

Danny Pierce - But Stillwater, what a great music town. I mean I'm sure you've heard, more albums have been stolen out of Stillwater than out of Austin, Texas, right? And that's what Jimmy would say, and people look at you funny. Then of course you just have to mention one name, right? It's like, well, Garth Brooks. Garth was great but he played Willie's every Wednesday night for free, and we'd be like, oh hell we don't wanna go to Willie's tonight just to hear Garth playing down there. No disrespect to Garth. But he's playing, *Please Come to Boston*, right? Cover songs and stuff like that. And okay that's great. But over here these people are writing their own songs and playing songs with messages and that's much more what we were into for sure in that regard.

Matt O'Meilia - Bob Childers, he let me quote a whole verse of one of his songs, *Luck of the Draw* and that was perfectly appropriate for the book because it had to do with how some people go out there to Nashville and make it big and they're maybe not as talented as somebody else. Somebody super, super talented doesn't make it. And so that's what Bob's song was about, it ain't all in the luck of the draw and he was super kind. He's just like, yeah, use it. So, they call him the Godfather of Red Dirt and all those little terms and categories and titles came along later on, but it was just a bunch of guys hanging out playing music and nobody knew. Everybody kind of knew something special was going on back there in the Stillwater days. But when you're on the inside. you can't really see it, you can't really see it until things start happening.

Stan Woodward — Matt O'Meilia's dad and my dad were both artists. My dad was a weather man in Tulsa named Lee Woodward and Matt's dad was a guy named Jay Amelia who was a really well-known artist in Tulsa. Matt and I didn't even know it, but we were both drummers and both kind of playing in different universes up in Stillwater. Kind of slightly different times. But we would walk by and see Garth at Aunt Molly's Rent-Free Music House, which is the student union and people just walk by. He's in there playing lone guitar, maybe 5-6 people hanging out. But the farm was the after-hours party on the weekends, and it would go all weekend. It might start in the day and be croquet and crazy stuff and then it would go all night, Saturday night and you'd go out there Sunday and pick up your gear. I'd go home and I just leave my drum kit out there and show up Sunday and see what was left out there.

Kurt Nielsen - I remember, actually, Randy Pease. You know, he's a writer, number one, and he's writing short stories. He wrote a short story about me because I was the first one to get to Nashville. They called me the Path Finder because I was the first one to move down there and I had a little Nissan truck. So, he wrote a short story about me driving around on music row because there's a building over there. I forget the name of the record company. But it was the one that Garth was with early on. They put like, sashes - like a Miss America sashes– along the building. Giant ones that lay over one side. I remember one week goes by there and it would say, Garth goes gold. Couple weeks later - Garth goes platinum. Anyways,

Randy Pease wrote a short story about all that time. Randy's got some good stories for sure.

Eric Hansen- As a little teenager roaming the streets, I'd go ogle through the front door and look through the windows and stuff. But I never got to take part really. Willie's was already, and was always, kind of a steady venue. Eskimo Joes, in the beginning the guy opened that bar, Stan, was kind of a musician. He played saxophone and he kind of played with some bands, way back in the '70s and stuff around Stillwater before he started his bar. They didn't end up being what I would consider in any way a music venue. But here and there, you know, he'd still have some bands. So, Joe's was going and they did have some bands play it. One of the first bars I ever played, my high school band, was on the deck outside of Eskimo Joes. Back when it was just a rock building, and they built a deck next to it. There was some booths out there and a little stage, so the bands played there at that point in the mid to late '80s. And there were some bars, like even Murphy's, that's still there. Now, JR Murphy's had a stage and had bands playing. Been a long time since that's been anything other than the college dance bar, you know, in the modern era or whatever. But way back, there'd be bands rocking in the backyard and even playing the stage inside, back when I first moved. Otherwise, once I got older in high school, the first bar I could go anywhere near was Joe's. I think Murphy's was 18 and up, some of that era, but I didn't really go there. Tumbleweeds was 18 and up. I never remember considering it any sort of, form or fashion, a music venue back then. It was the heyday of country, the prime country dance place, where people wanted to put on their rockies and their wranglers and scoot the circle to a loud PA screaming out the top 40 country.

Nashville Adventures

It wasn't long before playing cover tunes and paying their Nashville dues would get to be too much for the Skinner Brothers, who wanted to create and play their own music. Just a few months into their six-month lease, they decided to leave the band. They continued to live in the house until the lease was up, but they decided to pursue their own music instead of playing with the Santa Fe band. Tom Skinner then got a job at Gibson Guitars. Tom would rebuild and tune Epiphone Guitars and make all the final adjustments to the instruments. He worked alongside Joe Diffee, who was from the Sand Springs area of Oklahoma. Jed Lindsey would soon join them as well.

While many had moved to Nashville, Greg Jacobs had moved to Kentucky. His wife had majored in Animal Husbandry at OSU and loved horses. They moved to work with thoroughbreds. While Jacobs lived there, he would drive to Nashville every weekend to hang out with Childers and Tom, writing songs and jamming. "Bob and I used to write together some, but Bob and I were both very stubborn. We could not write a song together in the same room. We did our best work together when I lived in Kentucky, and he lived in Nashville. I would send him an idea on a cassette, and record what I had. I would mail it to him, and about a week later he would mail something back of what he added to it, and we would slowly put a song together. We would argue over a word. I'm pretty picky. Every word is there for a purpose, and if he wanted to change a word I wrote- nah, I'm not giving up that word Bob," said Jacobs.

They wrote the song *Luck of the Draw* that way, Jacobs sent Childers the first verse and the chorus, and Childers sent it back and he had written a verse. Jacobs had laid it on his desk and hadn't done anything with it, when he received it back again from Childers, who had taken it to

Greg Jacobs. Photo provided by Sage Powell.

Garth and Garth proceeded to write a third verse for it. "If you asked my opinion, I don't think it's a real good little song, but I do have a demo of Garth Brooks singing that song that I have a co-write on. Bob put it on one of his records, I think it was the *Nothing more Natural* record. I asked him, I said Bob, you took this little song, and you took all the publishing, which is cool with me. I don't really care. But what if Garth comes and sues you? And he said I hope he does come and sue me; I could use the publicity. I wish he would," said Jacobs.

According to Matt O'Meilia's book, Stephanie Brown took the demo she recorded of Brooks singing *Luck of the Draw* to Bob Doyle, who was the head of ASCAP at the time. Doyle was losing interest in that position and wanted to instead make the move to managing artists and get into the music publishing business. Brown convinced Doyle to come check out Brooks singing at the Blue Bird Café songwriter night. Tom Skinner played the same night, directly after Brooks. "Bob Doyle just fell in love with Garth and quit ASCAP and became his manager. Of course, Bob Doyle eventually got fired from Garth. But Bob Doyle was one of those prolific stage-show guys. He got Garth flying around on a rope and all that stuff, you know. But Bob Doyle is the one who made Garth a millionaire for sure," said Nielsen. From there of course Brooks' career skyrocketed, and his time connected to the Red Dirt scene ended.

One evening, the Skinner brothers were playing a gig downtown and spotted Childers in the bathroom. This particular evening, the Skinner brothers had eaten some magical mushrooms and mentioned this to Childers, who replied that he had never had them. They asked if he wanted some, and he said yes.

Bob Childers and Kurt Nielsen. Photo provided by Sage Powell.

"I loaded him down with enough for him to see the light and so he was walking down the alley following the light. If you listen to that one line, for reasons that don't matter I was walking down the alley..., his lyrics came from tripping on mushrooms. Bob was a natural too, he was real good. He was a gentle spirit, he really was. He was a different kind of guy, Bob was," said Mike Skinner.

Greg Jacobs eventually moved into a house with Tom, Jeri and Mike on Madison on the east side of Nashville while going through a divorce. The Okie friends were all providing support to one another far from home. "We had a little four track tape player. I was working as a carpenter because I finally got tired of starving. Tom would stay home all day and he would play with that four track. I got home one evening and we'd been working on this little song, and he said- hey I finished that song *Jamie and Billy*. He played it for me, and it was great. Well neither of us ever did the song, as time went on. I forgot all about it," said Jacobs. Jacobs would stumble upon this recording decades later and put it on an album, called *Encore*.

Gene Williams, Greg Jacobs and Kurt Nielsen. Photo provided by Stan Woodward.

"When we went to Nashville. I never dreamed of being a performer, that wasn't my deal. I didn't want to be Garth. What I wanted to do is write two or three songs a year for Garth. And let him do all the work and go on the road and I could just kick back and do whatever I wanted. I wanted to be Donny Schlitz- he wrote *The Gambler* for Kenny Rogers. Donny could retire off of that one song. That's who I wanted to be, just write a hit song a year. Back in the '80s- I don't know how it is now- but back then you could call the producers out there and you could schedule an appointment. You could come in and play your songs for them. Bring in a little cassette with three songs on them, and they would listen because they don't know- you might be the next Donny Schlitz. Every time I would do that, just like clockwork, they would hit that start button and listen to the first 30 seconds of the song. You got that Nashville format; you got to hit those chords within 30 seconds and get the hook. They all told me as a rule, they would look at me and say, you are a pretty good songwriter, but you aren't a commercial songwriter. Go home, listen to your radio, and bring me something like that. I tried. Country music was very popish in the '80s. I just couldn't do it. I was more of a John Prine and Guy Clark disciple. I was a storyteller, and I didn't have the ambition to sell out the BOK. I just wanted to write songs for people who did. I never achieved that goal, but I still have my little catalog," said Jacobs.

Jacobs was known as Lucky, and Bob was called Bob-a-ra, Tom was Tiny. If you peruse these guys' catalog of songs, you'll notice they sing about one another in their lyrics, using nicknames along the way.

Steve Ripley moved his wife and two kids back to Tulsa in 1987, at which time he took ownership of The Church Studio, which Leon Russell had owned in the '70s. His studio and expertise became vital to the growing scene during this time, as he continued to work on music and help others record and produce albums. The '80s was a thriving time for the musicians in this scene.

Towards the end of the '80s, a group of Tahlequah and other Oklahoma musicians made a trip to Nashville, including Kevin Warren Smith, who was living in Memphis at this time. The trip had been arranged with a few musicians and promoters in Nashville, who were expecting them. The highlight for Smith was going to the Cannery, a well-respected venue with successful acts. "Vince Gill was playing that night and was giving another great show on guitar and voice. At one point I was standing at the bar, and he came up to introduce himself. I had been a big fan for years. He was very gracious and offered to listen to any recordings of songs that I may have brought with me. I thanked him but left no tapes with him. I told him I was taking my family from Memphis back to Oklahoma and was going to turn my back on music for a while. He was surprised and I was surprised but he seemed to understand," said Smith.

Not long after that Smith and his family did move back to Oklahoma and Smith made a drastic change to focus on the visual arts. "I kicked myself later of course, for not returning Vince's kindness. You'd have to understand my state of mind at the time. It was traumatic to leave music, and I couldn't do it just part way. I knew my family should be back in Oklahoma. And although it was exciting to make contacts with people in Memphis and Nashville, I began to get depressed thinking of my kids growing up in another state with no grandparents or uncles or aunts and cousins. I got to grow up enjoying my extended family in Oklahoma and didn't want them to miss that. I'm glad we came back when we did," said Smith. But before completely stepping back from music, Smith decided to do a little summer and fall tour in 1988. While there were no home computers to search out information for in those days, Smith knew from experience that Oklahoma was full of a lot of great small towns with events happening, and festivals meant potential gigs. Smith grabbed an Oklahoma map and started circling the towns he wanted to play. He went to the library, where each Oklahoma town had its own little phone book. Smith started figuring out who to call in each town where he wanted to play and started booking festivals and other opportunities all over the state. "A few I did alone but I had various bandmembers with me at other bookings. It all depended on what town and who was available. And just like that I was set to play at the Okeene Rattlesnake roundup, Glenpool Black Gold Days, Mayfest in Tulsa and many other great gigs that helped me heal a little bit and eased the transformation into the visual arts," said Smith.

It was also in about 1988 that Kurt Nielsen met John Prine while living in Nashville. At this point he had been living there for a few years and had made a strong connection to the Songwriter Night that Patsy Benson hosted. Nielsen and Jason Hunt regularly attended and played the event, and Nielsen said it was the second-best Songwriter Night in Nashville at the time, with the Blue Bird being in the top spot. One night, John Prine walked in the door. Benson motioned for Prine to come up on stage and play, which he did. Prine got his choice of guitars available on stage that night. "Jason at the time had a guitar like Ben Hahn, it was a pen guitar made in Japan. He had one of the tuners broke off. I want to say the B string tuner was busted off, and then he had his name written in electric tape on the front- Jason Hunt. Anyway, so Prine naturally goes straight for that guitar, picks it up, looks at it and says- got a bust off tuner, I guess I can deal with that. Everything's gonna have to tune from that one string", said Nielsen.

Prine proceeded to play a few tunes. Hunt, about 21 years old at the time, had never heard of Prine, but instantly fell in love with his music. After the show, Hunt went back to his apartment, locked the door for two weeks and learned every John Prine tune he could. When he came back out into the world, he had written a song called *John Prine Ain't Got Nothing on Me*. "Of course it goes 'John Prine ain't got nothing on me. Just a dozen more years, and 100 more songs, and a good sense of reality. But I bet we would get along'. So that was the chorus, basically. He recorded it. Then somewhere a week or two down the line, we were over there at the songwriter's night," said Nielsen.

Nielsen was standing at the bar with Childers. Hunt was on stage about to play his new song when the guy had who recorded it for him walked up to Nielsen and let them know that Prine was there and about to hear the song, and Hunt had no idea. "I look across the bar and there he is, he's got a paper in front of him. He's reading it. And so, me and Bob just got to sit back and start watching this whole thing happen, you know? Jason's up there and he starts singing this song. He's just going through the first verse. We look at Prine, he kinda stares up from his glasses while he's reading his paper and pays attention for a second. Then of course, John Prine gets up. So we were watching to see what Prine would do," said Nielsen.

Prine stood up, walked all the way around the bar and then beyond the stage, and snuck around the back end of Hunt. There was another microphone over there that he walked up to. The song comes to the second chorus and Prine started singing it with Hunt. "Jason does one of those, looks at him and looks back and forth, you know, like, what the heck? He thought it was me at first because me and John are about the same size, both little bitty. But he did that double take, and then John gets off the stage, and he's just grinning ear to ear. He comes over there and he goes- Man, I love that. My mother will love that. Nobody's ever written a song about me. He was just all happy as all get out. He started talking to me and Bob, and Bob doesn't waste any time. He says, hey, my name is Bob Childers. Prine goes, my mom lives in Childers, Texas. We just had a great time," said Nielsen.

The guys sat and talked to Prine all evening, and at the end of the night Prine wanted to show them his car outside. "He's got this, like, 52 Ford Coup and he goes- I want to show you guys this because, man, this is what I did this morning. He'd taken a drill and drilled holes through the taillights, put those blue dots to get the purple lights that they put on Harleys. He was so proud of that. He said, watch this- just watch my break lights. He had to show us his break lights and everything, but it was pretty cool. I like the heck out of that guy, he's the real deal, real people," said Nielsen.

It wasn't long after that night Childers decided to move to Austin to be closer to his children, before ending up returning to Stillwater soon after that. Tom Skinner followed suit about six months later and moved back to Bristow, Oklahoma. Nielsen and Mike Skinner stuck around a couple more years before heading back to Oklahoma. "So, we all moved into that house and started our education on how the business works out there. Eventually, to make a long story short, I kinda- after I don't know- six months a year or something like that, I didn't see anything happening with us. It was just a struggle with me and working and my kid. Talked it over with my wife and we decided to come home. I think we stayed another six months, maybe a year, before we saved enough money to come home. And that's what I did, and it was within minutes of that Garth hits the big time. But I made the right choice in coming home, you know, my son got to know his grandma and grandpa, and I got to play music with some great people all my life around here. So I made the right choice coming home, for me. I was just kinda burned out on in it out there, the struggle was too much," said Tom in a 2014 video interview with Red Dirt Nation (Youtube : *Tom Skinner Interview*, Red Dirt Nation).

While many of the Red Dirt artists didn't find exactly what they were looking for during their Nashville adventures, Marilyn Craig did find success in her career while there. "I worked for the Jim Halsey company. After the pro tours gig, Jim Halsey owned a part of that company. And when he decided that he was going to sell his interest to the Judd's, I talked him into hiring me and I stayed with him. At the time he had 40 country music acts on his roster. I represented the college market for him. I also did seminars called Careers in Entertainment. Billboard Magazine was the sponsor of that program. I did that for a couple of years and then Jim sold his company. So, I had a job at Net Network. I ended up getting a job at networking. I had the Marlboro Music tour. I did a lot of traveling with that one. We did talent round up around in major cities. It was to sell cigarettes. But of course, that wasn't why I was going. I just want to see all that good music," said Craig.

For the Marlboro Music Tour, they would bring in people who worked in the record industry in Nashville to judge the contests. There would be eight bands that performed for three nights in a row, competing to be in the top three out of each night. Those top three would advance to the following week to the finals. "So, I might do three nights in Houston, and then I would fly to Dallas to do the first three nights of that next leg. And then on Thursday, I would go back to Houston and do the finals. That was what I did with them. I worked with a woman also that her name was Tricia Walker. She had Trisha Walker International, and she booked country music festivals in Europe. She was an English woman. I worked with her part time for three years. Got to go to Switzerland a couple of times, with Rodney Krell and Roseanne Cash. They played the Fruit in Switzerland festival. Then we went to London from there because they did a couple of TV tapings. So, I got to do that, and that was pretty cool. Well, it was good except they didn't pay. You didn't make very much money because there were too many people wanting in the business," said Craig.

In Their Own Words

Mike Skinner on Nashville - Just fantastic musicians out there. Every night playing in a club, there were great players. Everyone just jamming. That's an interesting scenario watching these studio players- the best of the best- just out playing with each other. You gotta do something to impress everyone, everyone trying to impress everyone. I spent three years there. It was a good experience, I'm grateful I got to do it. I got to see some interesting things and play some good music. I'll always be thankful for that. Old age is something else, you just lose so much, that's just part of it.

Bob Wiles - Greg Jacobs was in Stillwater playing the local bars at the same time as Tom Skinner and Childers, and LaFave. Then, at some point- now they all didn't ride in the same car- but a lot of those guys moved to Nashville. Tom went to Nashville as a member with Garth Brooks band, and Childers went to Nashville. You know, if you were a songwriter, that was where you felt like you needed to be. And Greg Jacobs went to

Nashville. Jacobs had grown up on a Farm. Really a ranch. I believe he got a job working at a thoroughbred horse farm working with racehorses. Childers, I never was quite sure what Childers did. I think there was some sort of issue with the statute of limitations, and he didn't want to talk about exactly what he did. Tom Skinner worked at the Gibson Guitar factory, and at some point, they all came back. We had been fans of theirs in Stillwater, we knew of them, knew their songs. But when they moved back from Nashville, is about the same time the Rangers were getting going. And then we had the opportunity to become friends and really get to know them. If they had made it big in Nashville, things would have been completely different for the Red Dirt Rangers. They all went to Nashville, LaFave went to Austin. Austin was really a budding music scene at the time. LaFave found his place in Austin, and I think eventually the rest of them felt like, you know, rather than Nashville, we probably should have gone to Austin like LaFave did. But if you're a songwriter, you feel like you need to do that.

Greg Jacobs - We had stars in our eyes that we wanted to be stars, but we didn't know how to go about it, and we weren't really willing to work that hard to go about it. Now we worked hard at our craft, don't get me wrong. We worked hard at writing. Bob and I in particular, between the two of us, we had a little competition. Bob and I were always trying to out write each other. It was very friendly, and it made us both better writers. Bob would always accuse me of stealing lines, and I would accuse him of stealing lines, and it was all in jest- all in brotherly love. As I look back on it, it made us both better songwriters. I still to this day can't believe those guys are gone. Time goes on.

Chuck Dunlap - I've got Tom's picture in front of me right now, I keep an 8x10 of him giving me a big old hug and he's laughing and I'm just hugging him right back. My wife is in the background just looking over at us. Me, Tom and Randy played together that night. We would have faced a brick wall and played together, we just loved playing together. Skinner was like Bob, only more so. He took Bob and distilled it, down into the essence of being a songwriter and being able to deliver a message. Take other people's songs and make them his own and give people the cold shivers and make them want to hear that song again. Tom is golden to me, he came back from Nashville and all of that. He told me one time, he said I thought I could do more good with the talents I have here in Oklahoma than I ever could have in Nashville chasing some big pipe dream that I might have had. I really respected that, that he got it. He understood that his enjoyment of his music didn't come from a big ol' royalty check. It came from a hundred friends standing around him, right up to the end, making music with him. That's pretty rare right there. That was Tom.

Marilyn Craig: I wasn't really ever starstruck, except one of the gigs I had in Nashville. I was working for Rob RC Bradley. He was managing Jim Lauderdale at that time and Juice Newton and Ray Wiley Hubbard. He had managed Dwight Yoakam in the past. He was in Manuel's building. The guy who made the nudie suits. Actually, Nudie was Manuel's father-in-law. Nudie Cohen. Manuel had his store in Nashville and of course all the stars would come in and get measured and stuff. Manny would always call me or yell up the stairs, come down here and meet this person. The only time I ever got just a little flustered was when I met George Jones. I met Merle Haggard. He'd been to NSU and I've done a couple of shows with him, but I don't know why. I was just like George Jones, man.

Austin & Three More Albums

Charlie Hollis moved to Austin in 1987, moving all his studio equipment there into a two-car garage. This converted studio became MARS, Mid-Austin Recording Studio. "When I moved to Austin, my old roommate in Stillwater moved down there about a year or so later, Charlie Hollis. We rented a nice apartment near LaFave's place, and Charlie set up his recording studio in the garage. Different artists like Randy Crouch and Childers would come down and record, and they moved in with us for a couple of weeks, you know? And they'd bring different musicians. I know we recorded at least one Bob Childers album in that garage," said Gene Williams.

The first project Hollis worked on in his new studio was with LaFave, *Highway Angels...Full Moon Rain*, which they released onto cassette in 1988. It won the Austin Chronicle Reader's Poll Tape of the Year Award that year. That award led to Tomato records noticing Jimmy and signing a recording contract with him. He recorded an album for them, but for some reason, it never got released. "Things kind of went sideways with Jimmy and Tomato, I don't really know the story. I don't know if they just didn't think it sounded like LaFave, or if it was just a big tax write off. I just don't know what the deal was. I think I have a copy of that record in my collection, but it never got out," said Williams. Unfortunately, LaFave's contract with Tomato records led him to be unable to release music for the duration of his contract, so he wouldn't release his next album until 1992.

MARS studio also hosted Randy Crouch and his band to do some recordings. "Randy's got such a wonderful personality. He's just a true Oklahoma music character. I've known him forever, like I said, he was bringing his whole band down to Austin to live with us for a couple of weeks to record. They'd bring a school bus or something, and I remember he used to bring these mason jars full of pot. One time, he brought this guitarist with the name Sparky Fisher. And you know, Jimmy and I was doing really good in Austin, and seeing a lot of great players. Sparky was one of the best players I think I ever saw. Just gifted player. Incredible guitar player. Sparky was just a full-blown alcoholic, and he died a few years after that. He died really young. But I'll always remember getting acquainted with Sparky and just his incredible talent. He was from Tahlequah. You know, that was a highlight of those years. When we talk about Randy Crouch. I love Randy and he and I are good friends. He's a wonderful violin player and a wonderful steel guitar player and guitar player and electric guitar player. Probably one of the most underrated song writers- somebody that can think out of the box. Very original writer and performer. Really a showman, you know. Which you know, Childers was a showman, too," said Williams.

Brad Piccolo made the move to Austin in about 1988. He played with a band called the Dickie Lee Irwin band. "I met some guys that lived on the same street as me. Back in those days the musicians could still afford to live in town in Austin. So, it was a very nurturing music scene. There was like three or four musicians on my street on Avenue D there in Austin. They had already kinda had a band, they asked me to join up with them. We ended up traveling the country, especially the east coast and what not, as the Dickie Lee Irwin band. That was another great place I got my musical education," said Piccolo.

Piccolo would also record an album called *Worldwide Roadside* with Charlie Hollis at his studio in Austin. "Of course, he was an Okie too. The Okies tended to congregate down there in Austin at that time. There was a group of people including Gene Williams, me. Bob Childers moved down there shortly after I did, Jimmy LaFave. It was just a whole group of Okies down there and we all played on each other's records that we recorded at Charlie Hollis' studio. He was such a nurturing thing that he didn't even charge me to record my first record. He just said, come on over, let's do it a little piece at a time. And so, I did that. I had some good luck with that cassette. In fact, many of the songs on it end up, once we started the Rangers, we started doing those songs too. That's the thing about our scene- when we formed the Red Dirt Rangers, from the very get go- we started doing original songs. Whereas most bands start out doing cover songs. We did our fair share of covers, but we were heavily doing originals from the very first gigs that we did," said Piccolo.

"I get a call from Piccolo, and he wants to do a solo CD. He needs a drummer and some guitar on that. I play both drums and guitar. So we went down to Charlie Hollis's place and Brad ends up doing a solo CD of his own stuff. Then *Circles Towards the Sun* gets recorded down at Charlie's place and I think I played three tracks on that," said Stan Woodward.

Brad James moved to Hollywood in 1987 at the age of 20, where he attended the Musician's Institute, and earned his degree from. "I remember when I was in LA, a lot of people had gone to Austin. Charlie Hollis was one of them, and I think Gene Williams was living with Charlie Hollis. He made a recording studio in his garage which was probably a four-track cassette set up. It was called MARS Studio in Austin, and three cassette tapes came out of there that are really pivotal to what we now call Red Dirt. Jimmy LaFave had one. The Brad Piccolo one that came out of there was *Welcome to the Worldwide Roadside* and the Bob Childers one that came out of there was *Circles Towards the Sun*. It was really pivotal, because you can hear- The Red Dirt Rangers did not exist yet- but you can hear John Cooper and Brad singing their special harmony on the whole record. So, Bob's *Circles Towards the Sun* was kind of profound as were the other two, the Jimmy record and the Brad Piccolo record. Cassettes. And I got these cassettes when I'm still 20-21 in Hollywood and I was like I don't even know what you call this, but that's what I want to do," said James.

James wasn't the only one who left for the Musician's Institute around this time. Eric Hansen had just turned 18 and graduated high school. He learned through Mike Shannon about the Musician's Institute program and decided that's what he wanted to do as well. Hansen packed up all his stuff and headed to Hollywood. While the program was just a year long, Hansen broke his arm halfway through and had to go back and finish it later, completing it in 1990.

Donnie Wood made it to Stillwater in about 1987 to attend OSU. Although Wood had been born in Stillwater, his family moved to both Bartlesville and Louisiana while he was growing up. They came back to Bartlesville, and he moved to Stillwater to attend college. Wood learned how to play piano as a child and eventually picked up the guitar. By the time he was in middle school he decided drums were the thing he wanted to play. Wood was taking some Television and AV classes at OSU. "Davy

Dyer and a guy by the name of Greg Morris, had some local bands around there and they were both sound guys and they used to do sound for a big annual event that happened every year that was called the Bennett Jam. Bennett Hall had set up a stage and had a battle of the bands. I was really not playing much anymore. I had started to play bass by that time, but any rate, some friends asked me if I would come play bass and sing for their set at the Bennett Jam. And through that I met Davy Dyer and Greg Morris. They were like, wow, this kid's a really great bass player and invited me to hang out," said Wood.

When Jimmy LaFave's Annual Musician's Reunion came along in 1988, LaFave had brought along his buddy Hank Sinatra, who hosted a variety of Austin Public Television shows and other programs revolving around music. Sinatra brought his TV crew with him to record the event.

Gene Williams, Hank Sinatra, David Dyer. Photo provided by Stan Woodward.

According to Rick McCord, Sinatra was only supposed to be filming in the state of Texas, nowhere else. During the recordings of the two days of the festival he would say, "We're shooting live from Willie's Saloon in Stillwater, Texas!" so no one would know he was out of state. "When the musician's reunion came around, Dave was like, hey, our buddy is coming up from Austin or something. They need some extra people to help run cameras and do some stuff. I did kind of get roped into doing that and it was that musician's reunion and all that where I first got drug out to the farm and witnessed all of that," said Wood.

The Musician's reunion would start on Thursday afternoon at the Farm, but by Friday more people would come pulling into town for the festival. Brad James, who had moved to Colorado, came back to town for the reunion that year. This is where he met Donnie Wood, who was helping Hank Sinatra with the Audio/Video components of the recordings. Wood had learned A/V all through high school and college and used that knowledge to help out the crew that was there for the weekend. "Donnie had an industrial strength, commercial grade mullet. I mean bangs to here, straight hair to his ass, and he was out there working with this crew. The guy's name was Hank Sinatra, he was making a documentary. David Dyer and Mark Lyon sat down. Mark Lyon was about to start playing. There would be picking parties all over at the Farm, just little circles of people doing things. David Dyer looked around at everyone playing and said he wished he had a bass so he could join in. Donnie Wood said he could go get one. Wood ran back into town and came back with an old Steinburg, which was headless and bodyless- it looked like just a neck. He also brought an extension cord, an amplifier and a bass, and he sat down and started playing along with Mark Lyon and David Dyer. At one point they played *Little Feat*, Lowell George's song from the album *Sailin' Shoes*. Wood was completely blown away by their ability to play together so well and asked if they played together all the time. Lyon and Dyer said no, not at all. He asked them, well how did they know how to play together so well then? "Dave was like, there's only like eight notes, and he was just using three of them. Donnie was just blown out by this," said James.

Stan Woodward and Brad James at the Farm. Photo provided by Sage Powell.

"For me personally, it was a life changing event. I'll tell you that. The reason being was at the time when I had come there, all of my interests musically were into very complicated prog rock and hard rock, stuff like that. So, the bands I had been playing in, we played stuff like Rush and Kansas and Yes. Just all of this crazy, really complicated prog rock from the seventies and eighties. That was my stuff. I really never put any focus into very simplistic,

G, A minor, D, singer songwriter, country Americana based stuff, right? I had spent my time learning this incredibly difficult music- hard to play, required a lot of dexterity on the instrument. So, I ended up going out to the farm and Dave Dyer was like, hey, let's go by your house and get your bass and your amp. I think maybe his was in the pawn shop or something. So, drug me out there because I had a bass and of course it was my stuff. They threw me in this ring of people to play with and these guys are playing all this stuff and, I mean, I couldn't figure out what they were doing as simple as it was. I just was lost. Just absolutely 100% lost. And it was just a very humbling experience. Like they're not nearly as good as I think I am. You know what I mean? I can't sit and play these simple songs with these hippies and rednecks around this campfire. I suck. You know what I'm saying? So, it was a very humbling experience and all at the same time, I just didn't really know what to think of it. I was slowly kind of indoctrinated into that, that whole gang of people. Began to play with various different people around town, Greg and Brad Piccolo. So, that's kind of where that started. I would say the farm had quite a life changing impact on me," said Wood.

The picking groups littered the farm grounds, and groups would get together and just play, perhaps for the first time ever together. There wasn't a set list or any rehearsal, it just happened organically. While the party got started earlier in the day at the Farm, soon it would be time for the actual event at Willie's. LaFave would be the emcee of the Musician's Reunions, getting up to talk and introduce the next act. The event would start at about five or six pm until The Night Tribe shut the bar down at closing time. "Night Tribe would go on last. Usually at Willie's, they would try to start shutting everything down about one-thirty AM because the cops would show up and they would make sure that the doors were shut, and they weren't serving anybody. But Jimmy would play, he didn't care. He would play up until two o'clock and then even sometimes more. And by that point, the place was packed," said John Buckner.

Willie's during a musician's reunion. Photo provided by Sage Powell.

"They had to build special plywood covers to put over the pool tables for people because there were people sitting on them. Just literally all the chairs, tables were full, and they were just covering pool tables up so people could sit and stand on them to see. This would go from six o'clock in the evening until two-thirty in the morning at the bar. And then it would kind of shift from there to the farm, and it would just be cars lining the dirt road in both directions, going north to south. It was just crazy. You would go up, there would be people out in the front of the house, the back of the house, inside the house, around the fire pit. There was people playing out front, people sitting on blankets in the yard just playing there. Hundreds of people. Probably in the heyday, I would say there would be a good 150 to 200 people when Jimmy was in town. Any other time when there wasn't stuff going on, there'd be 50 to 100 people," said Buckner.

Rick McCord moved to Stillwater in the mid-eighties and started playing music locally shortly after that as a drummer. His very first gig was at Willie's at the LaFave Musician's reunion in 1988. McCord was playing drums in the band Low Skies with Greg Morris. Low Skies played the song Suzie-Q by Creedance Clearwater Revival, and LaFave got on stage and told the story of singing that song with his nose closed and getting a knife pulled on him. Once the weekend was over and Sinatra went to edit his footage for the TV show, he left Low Skies in there playing followed by LaFave's story and then it cut into LaFave and the Night Tribe performing. This show was aired in Austin on the Public Access channels. "A friend of mine sent me a VHS tape of it many, many years ago because it was just so funny man. We're all so young and scared to death. It was just a really good time. But it was the only year that guy Hanks Sinatra came and did the tv thing. Man, he had some big old cameras. It was a beautiful thing too. It was fun. Jimmy told that story singing the song with us and he held one side of his nose and sang "Oh Suzie Q", I promise you that's the only reason our little band got edited to that program because it went from us to him, and to his group Night Tribe. It was my first bar gig. I was like a kid, just a baby. It was a hoot a man, wouldn't trade it for anything," said McCord.

In fact, that episode of Hank Sinatra's show has been archived with the Dolph Briscoe Center for American History and can be viewed either remotely for a fee, or at the center for free. It is listed under Hank Sinatra's archives, titled Jimmy LaFave Reunion, June 23, 1988 in Box88-110/17. You can go to https://collections.briscoecenter.org for more information.

Jim Dodrill (sax), Jimmy LaFave, unknown bassist, Mark Lyons. Photo provided by Stan Woodward.

In Their Own Words

Mark Lyon – Charlie (Hollis) plays a big influence in this whole Red Dirt thing before it was called Red Dirt. He had a studio in his attic, his studio probably got started in '79 through '80 somewhere right in there. Charlie recorded Jimmy LaFave up there. I don't know how many people he recorded up there, recorded Randy Crouch there. Ended up moving to Tahlequah for a while, recorded Crouch over there some more. But then Charlie moved to Austin, and this is where it really gets good. He recorded Jimmy LaFave's album that really helped him get into the scene in Austin. He recorded an album for Bob Childers down there. I think he might have done some work with Brad Piccolo, but basically any Okie that moved to Austin in those years, Charlie Hollis was the first place they would go. And he didn't charge much. Charlie almost gave his recording time away. But he's kind of one of these unassuming guys behind the scenes that while he didn't perform that much, he was a real catalyst in getting people's music heard, which is important. So, I wanna make sure that his name gets brought up in this because he's one of those behind-the-scenes guys that was really important and critical to all of it.

Jeff Parker - When I moved to Stillwater to start teaching, I was still going to college in Oklahoma City. So, I mean, you had Jimmy Lafave, Chuck Dunlap. Dunlap had been around, back when Jimmy was there, but had moved away. Bob Childers and Greg Jacobs were still there. They had moved to Nashville and moved back. I don't know the timeline on that. I remember hearing stories and then another guy, Randy Pease was another one, a part of that. Randy, I've done about every CD that Randy has done. We just finished up one last year. It was a buzz, you know, and it was kind of ironic because it was like when the Seattle music scene had blown up in the nineties. The same kind of thing was happening in a more of a songwriter, Americana way in Stillwater. And of course, Tom and Bob were heavily influencing the younger guys- Boland and Cody and Mike Mcclure and those guys- they were soaking it up, they were really soaking it up. So, you could tell, you could definitely tell that something bigger was gonna happen out of it.

Rick McCord- The farm just has a ton of memories from the naked Croquet tournaments and just good old farm parties. The campfires and back in the day when they used to set up the bands on the front porch. That was a hoot, those were good times. Man, watching the sun come up out there after playing Jimmy Lafave reunions, that was just kind of a staple. Everybody left the bar and went out there and on the weekend like that when you had musicians from all over the place coming in. That definitely would have to be the highlight of some of my best memories, were early days when the reunion was just still fresh, and people were just still coming out of the woodwork to hit that Jimmy LaFave reunion. The bar was a beautiful time, don't get me wrong. But after we left there, and everybody went out to the farm and scraped together a P.A. and hooked it up and watched the sun come up playing music with all those guys. That was a beautiful thing. That was a great time.

Bob Wiles - By hanging around the farm we ended up meeting Jimmy Lafave and Tom Skinner and, eventually Bob Childers. When we first started going up there, Childers lived in Nashville but eventually moved back to Stillwater. We just were in Stillwater at an Ideal time. There were a bunch of great songwriters in Stillwater at the time. And then Greg Jacobs, he had been out in Nashville. Jimmy Lafave used to have these musician's reunions once a year. He was living in Austin by then, and he would come back to Stillwater and have a musician's reunion at Willie's. All these great songwriters would find their way back to Stillwater- Chuck Dunlap and Greg Jacobs and Lafave and Childers. And, you know, it was just a great time to be in Stillwater. We didn't know it at the time, being mentored by some of the greatest song writers. You know, it was just really a great time.

Stan Woodward – Any time around these guys, everybody's super supportive and everybody's jabbing each other hard- that's an Oklahoma thing I think- like everybody's poking fun at each other. You develop this kind of thick skin, but you realize everybody's doing it because they like you. If they don't like you because you misbehave, it's like any other place- you're just not invited back. But everybody was just poking fun at everybody all the time. There were some people better than that than others, like Bob Wiles was always poking people and he had a great sense of humor.

Pam Potts - I think that the main thing about it is to impress upon what it really means- what Red Dirt means. A lot of people interpreted it in different ways. Of course, it's the melding of all these different genres, of whatever we feel like playing at that very moment- whether it's a jazz song or a folk song or country inspired, or bluegrass inspired, or just whatever it is. I mean, that all fits in there. But mainly, it's about the inclusiveness of the music and how we're a family of men – so to speak, you know, family of man, everybody from the past. I mean, when we would play on stage, if someone wanted to play with us, we would never tell them no. We would hand our instruments to drunks and let them get up there and have at it. But it's the inclusiveness and the idea that everyone has an equal amount of a chance.

John Buckner - The bands that were playing around there a lot, were not only Jimmy and Chuck, but the Skinner Brothers and the Cimarron Swingsters. They were kind of like the hot bands. And at that time there was early versions too of, the Red Dirt Rangers, they kind of sprung up out of that wild. Coop and Piccolo and them, they were there going to college, and they were kind of gelled out of that whole scene. Semi-controlled chaos. It was kind of like when Jimmy had moved at some point. He had left Stillwater. He had put out a record that I loved. It had a picture of him on the cover, between two speakers. That was the thing with everybody, you had to haul your own gear and back in those days, equipment- your PA system- was gigantic. And if you didn't have a good PA, you weren't really considered legit. But it had the picture of Jimmy, I guess he had been with Mike Hufford or something.

Newcomers

A round this time, the last of the musicians included in the first generation were just getting started. These last few would serve as a bridge that connected the older era to the next generation, a sort of transitional group as one era ended and another began. Scott Evans made his way to Stillwater in 1988 to attend college at OSU. Evans grew up in Bartlesville and picked up music as a hobby at the age of eight. He found that he wasn't coordinated enough for sports, and was already into books and drawing, so he decided to pick up music as well. "All of my dad's brothers- my uncles, and cousins- all played country western music and played the reunion every year for my grandmother's birthday. That's where my first exposure to music being made, the first place I was ever in a room while people were making music. So that's a pretty profound influence. Just that alone. It's totally different than watching a television and seeing somebody make music. When you're actually physically in the room with them, there's different thing that happens there," said Evans.

While at first Evans wanted to learn how to play the piano, he found obtaining a guitar would be easier and less expensive. "Starting at eight, I start figuring out the chords. And mom got me a guitar instructor. He asked me what I wanted to learn. I said, well, I like Puff the Magic Dragon, because that was a rocking song for me at the time. And he goes, well, I happen to have sheet music right here and he puts it up on the stand and shows me the little golf clubs on a fence and made me learn to read it. Said, go home and practice that, come back next week. When I came back for the second lesson, he put the sheet music up on the stand and said, ok, play it. I immediately looked from the paper down to my left hand because I had just figured it out by ear at home. The whole music reading thing wasn't taking and I just kind of pecked around on it until I found that melody and started playing it. He stopped the lesson right there. Said, ma'am, I'm not gonna charge you for this. This boy is never gonna learn to play guitar. He's not learning to read sheet music, and you know you can't learn that way," said Evans.

Evans went home at that point and started listening to whatever albums his brothers had around. He shared a room with his brother David, who was into Poco, Dan Fogelberg, and the Eagles. His brother Mark was into ZZ Top. One by one Evans learned to pick out the songs he was listening to, playing for hours and hours until he could get it right. "And then Stevie Ray Vaughan happened and that changed everything. I started, of course, listening to everything he put out. But all of the guitar player magazine interviews that he would give, he was real great about listing his influences, which were vast. He would go down these long lists of people that he'd listened to that were huge influences. Of course, I'd run out and go order those and buy all that stuff. So, I became a huge blues snob. In junior and senior year of high school, everybody else was listening to Rat and Poison and whatever hair band was cool," said Evans. He graduated high school in Bartlesville and stuck around for a year, working overnights in a grocery store before going to an art trade school in Phoenix, which he found disappointing. He left after a year. "My main creative outlet was drawing with graphic arts and more like cartooning, right? I wasn't much of a painter or sculptor, but just line drawings and illustrations. I would just constantly doodle all day long. I had spiral bound sketchbooks and filled those up. And that was my main creative outlet. Music was just something kind of fun and interesting. Like a hobby," said Evans.

He decided since his best friend from high school and his brother were roommates at OSU, he might as well head over there and enroll and get a Fine Arts degree. Evans found himself pulling out a guitar and entertaining his friends, making up novelty songs about various things, including Ted Bundy. He went to The Music Store and met Mike Shannon, who was then planning on quitting the store and opening his own store. At this point Evans was spending so much time at the Music Store that he was helping customers and showing them instruments if the other workers were busy. Sometimes they would give him a free set of strings if he would sit out front and play guitar to draw people in. Shannon asked Evans if he wanted to help him get his shop started. So, in 1988 Mike Shannon quit working at The Music Store and opened Backstage Music in an old house they fixed up and started finding equipment for.

"All the guitars we were getting from pawnshops. We take Sunday or Monday and go drive all over pawn shops just looking for good deals that we could sell for profit. Bring them back. We were learning to do guitar repairs out of the Don Teeter books and were mostly successfully. We did learn the hard way a few times. But he introduced me to Tom Skinner and Bob Childers and Ricky Peale and all those cats. Mike had been to Guitar Institute of Technology out in California. So, he was a real player and unbeknownst to a lot of people, Mike Shannon is also a math genius. People don't know that. I learned this one day. Well, he was always so good at explaining music theory to me, right? He was so much better at explaining it. I wasn't understanding so much of it, it just was over my head. I didn't have a foundation that would allow me to really understand what he was talking about. But me and Mike Shannon used to drive around Stillwater all the time. Working or going out partying, playing music with people. And one day we drive by the bank, and you know how they would give you the temperature in Fahrenheit and Celsius? Out of the blue we drive by the bank and he goes, oh, I got it! Like a eureka moment. I went, what do you got? What are you talking about? He goes, well, for the last year every time we drive by the bank, I look at the two numbers- the two temperatures in Fahrenheit and Celsius. And I'm trying to work out the equation that will get you from one to the other and it's hard. It's difficult. And he explained to me what the problem was like, it's a long technical thing. He goes, well, I'll wait till we get back to the shop and I'll show you. So, he grabs a piece of piece of paper and writes this all out in long form. It's an algebraic or whatever equation. It's completely over my head. But I'm watching all of this and looking at him like, you figured this out in your head? No wonder music is just a mathematical thing for you. Which is a very common thing. There's a lot of musicians that they just see the numbers and the way it all breaks down and the way the intervals are mathematical proportions of one another and that's how they understand it," said Evans.

Evans also had a job washing dishes at Mexico Joes, which would have live music featured from time to time. When he finished his shift, he would go out into the bar and his friend Tyler Forbes would give him a couple of free draw beers. But one day, Forbes decided that Evans needed to sit in with the band that was there that day- the Brownston Blue's Band. He wasn't going to give Evans any beer that day until he sat in with them. "I'm trying to protest. Like Tyler, you don't just walk up to a band and show him your guitar pick and they let you play, buddy. It's not how it works, man. I can't sit in with this band. I don't even know these guys. He just turned his back on me and walked away. Said, sorry, I don't know what to tell you. And I looked over and their guitar player had a wireless guitar

Mike Shannon and Scott Evans. Photo provided by Sage Powell.

rig and he's standing at the end of the bar playing with the band. There wasn't anybody in there yet. They were just starting. And so I literally did exactly what I described. I walked over showed him the guitar pick and without even mentioning it, without even missing a beat- AJ was his name- just takes the guitar off and goes, we're in A. So, the whole band heard the guitar drop out and saw and they didn't really care. They were just getting going. There were only a few people in there and I stepped up and played like the craziest overdone, just terrible guitar solo, right? Just way too much and took the guitar off, handed it back to him. Walked back over to get my beer very triumphant about it all. And that was kind of the moment where the way that felt, that was the first time I'd ever sat in with a real band. And it was exciting," said Evans.

Evans ended up leaving college after two semesters, deciding that music was much more important to his life. Backstage Music would eventually evolve into Daddy O's Music Co. in 1990. Daddy O being a nickname of Mike Shannon's. It would become another hub of music activity and a place where musicians could find jobs, gear, and camaraderie. Shannon also recorded music there, giving local musicians another easy access to lay down their tunes. It was located next to The Record Exchange, which was also a musician's hub, owned by Ken Sears. Sears was a big supporter of the local live music scene.

"He was just an old hippie, Ken Sears. He owned The Record Exchange forever and you could go in there and buy records and tapes. You could go in and trade ones you didn't want anymore. And it was just a place to hang out. Everybody that worked there was real cool and laid back. They always played great music. They had incense burning and it was just like a record flea market. It had been a bar at one time back in the day. I think it was called Toad in the Hole or something like that. And it just had that musty- still had that musty bar smell. But it was great. He had tie dye stuff hung up and posters and it was just a great place to hang out," said John Buckner. Buckner had just come to visit from Texas to Stillwater for his 10-year high school reunion, when he went into Daddy O's and Mike Shannon told him about a band, Loaded Jody, that was looking for a bass player. Shannon encouraged him to check it out. Buckner proceeded to buy a bass and amp from Shannon, got with the band, and decided to stick around and stay in town.

Monica Taylor arrived in the Stillwater scene somewhere near 1989. She had always been surrounded by music growing up. "I guess the first music that I heard was probably in church, gospel music, singing along with my mom at church. We would be holding the hymnal, and she would show me the notes that she was singing along to. She would sing the alto, and she would harmonize. She would show me what the melody was and as soon as I got it, she would drop to the harmony and I would feel the blending, the vibrations. That was really neat, I didn't know what to call it then. Then growing up my dad rodeoed, calf roped. I was always in the truck with the good ol' AM stations. I would hear George and Tammy, Conway and Loretta, Johnny and June, George Jones and Merle Haggard. I loved hearing them. They would leave the boot open, and I could hear the music. I loved it, and I think they liked that I appreciated it. Every once in a while, I would say, can you turn that up? I really got to appreciate good music through church and rodeos, rodeo dances too because I loved to watch my folks dance. Bob Wills is a big influence of course, Bill Monroe and Black Sruggs- blue grass," said Taylor.

In high school Taylor's parents gave her a Peavy sound system, speakers, microphone and a little eight channel mixer. She started calling up all kinds of places to see if she could come sing. Hauling her little system around, at the age of 15, all around Payne and Lincoln County. She would also go sing at the Oklahoma Opry and started singing on the Ben and Butch McCain show on the early morning TV show. Taylor raised and sold steer to help finance her way. She purchased a banjo in a Stillwater music store after selling two steer named Waylon and Willie. The music store had a bulletin board with announcements and advertisements all over it. She was looking for a banjo teacher and happened to see the name Bret Franzmann listed on the board. While she didn't end up getting his contact info for lessons, the name stuck in her head. Taylor had started college at OU for Broadcast Journalism, but decided she needed a break in about 1988.

Taylor's mom had read about a Country Music school called The Hank Thompson School of Country Music in Claremore at the Junior College, and suggested Taylor go there for a bit. Leon McAuliffe and Eldon Shamblin, players from the Bob Wills Texas Playboys, taught at the school. Taylor enrolled into the school and got a job teaching at a Baptist Christian School in town. About two weeks after she moved to Claremore, Leon McAuliffe passed away. Taylor had been disappointed; her love of western swing and McAuliffe's teaching was one of the main reasons she wanted to attend the school. She ended up taking steel guitar from Steve Collier who took over McAuliffe's position. Taylor attended that school for a year before moving to Perkins and enrolling into OSU for Elementary Education.

Before school even started in Stillwater, Taylor set out on a mission to find people to play music with. She had been having ear infection issues at the time and went to an Ear, Nose and Throat specialist. Taylor chatted with the nurse while being seen there, explaining she played bluegrass music and wanted to find a group to play with. The nurse said her son, Johnny Wright, played music with a guy named Bret Franzmann. Taylor remembered the name from the bulletin board in the music store a few years before and asked if Franzmann still played Banjo. The nurse said he sure did and gave Taylor Bret's phone number to get a hold of him. When Taylor called, Bret's mother Bunny answered the phone and Taylor explained that she was looking for people to play music with. Bunny got Taylor in Touch with Bret, who enjoyed learning that Taylor saw and remembered his name from the music store bulletin board. He invited Taylor to bring her guitar and come over that weekend to pick with him and some friends.

"I remember pulling up to the trailer out west of town and I knocked on the door and I was like- oh my God, this is gonna be so fun. I could hear the music playing in there and the door opened, and this real nice woman named Karen Knust answered the door. She was actually standing there with an upright bass in her hands, and I was like- oh, this is gonna be good. I said, I'm looking for Bret Franzmann and she said, well, you must be Monica. Well, come on in. He's in here. Bret stood up and when he stood up, I mean, he was just like a flash from the seventies. He probably wore the same thing all the time I knew him. He had the corduroy bell bottoms on always, never anything else and always an old pearl snap western shirt that he'd worn for years. This is how it is with people that you do end up knowing and are great friends with for the rest of your life. I shook his big hands. You know, you could tell he was a banjo player. He was a guitar player. And he smiled and said, well, it's so nice to meet you. Come on in and I'll introduce you to my friends," said Taylor. Taylor met Gene Collier there as well. She played so much music with them that evening that she didn't want to leave.

"I got a call from Monica Taylor. She had got my name. Met her and then she discussed, she wanted to kind of start putting a band together. So, me and her got together. I was working at OSU at the post office at the time, and a friend of mine that I actually met back in high school named Pam Potts- I've known her since high school basically. She was a secretary on my mail route, and we had kind of played music on and off before that. But I mentioned Monica to her one day and said we're putting this band together if she would be interested and she was. So, the three of us are getting together and we eventually added Mark Mars into it. Made it a four piece," said Franzmann. The four of them formed a group called The Wayfaring Strangers, four-part harmony, banjo, guitars, mandolin, and upright bass.

Pam Potts recalls having to meet Taylor's parents before she was even allowed to join the band. "Monica Taylor was in my band called The Wayfaring Strangers when she was a kid, before she was even old enough to be in bars or whatever. Her parents had to interview us to see if she could come over to my house to integrate into our band. We had to meet her parents, she was about 19," said Potts.

Mark Mars had gotten married and been musically dormant for about 10 years at this point. But he had met Bret Franzmann and decided to get back into

Monica Taylor and Pam Potts. Photo provided by Sage Powell.

playing with the Wayfaring Strangers. "We practiced a lot. That band didn't play very much out, Wayfaring strangers. I'm the guy that I learned by ear and I'm just woohoo and all, you know, space jam. Bret's the opposite. He's trained. He's a learned musician. He went to Claremore and he's real stringent. He doesn't bend strings, or he didn't used to before he met me. That was interesting, man. I think that's what made it so good. We were all four so different backgrounds, you know? Bret was more bluegrass, and I was country rock blues. Then Monica was country for sure, and Pam is more R and B blues. But I think we learned over 200 songs, I guess. We practiced a lot," said Mars.

Mark Mars, Kurt Nielsen and Bret Franzmann. Photo provided by Sage Powell.

In Their Own Words

Pam Potts – I played with Bob a lot through the years. Or he'd be doing something, and Monica and I'd be sitting in the audience, and all of sudden he'd drag both of us up there- we'd both sing. Monica and I both performed with him a lot too during whatever years, but it was very loose. Our band, Wayfaring Strangers, there were four of us- Mark Mars, Monica Taylor, Bret Franzmann and me. We didn't have but maybe one or two gigs. We did not perform very much. We had a spellbinding performance, this is weird. I mean, we put everybody in a trance at a Jimmy LaFave reunion one time and it kind of all fell apart after that. Jimmy got mad and didn't want to follow us because we sang this song that put everybody in a trance. I mean, this is the absolute truth. It was weird. I don't know what happened. It was like we did something to them- musically. And then everybody just took their purses and went home. Then Jimmy's like, I'm supposed to play and everybody's like, we don't need to hear anything else, you know? And he was like, what the heck? And he got real mad at us and we never got invited to play again. That was the end of it. But we played on television. The Wayfaring Strangers got a television gig. Just a weird day- a weird time in space. But we did. It was a good band. But we did like Indigo Girls songs, we sang a Ricky Lee Jones tune. We did Last Chance Texaco.

Scott Evans - I can't tell my story without including Mike (Shannon). He was the first person I met when I got there. He introduced me directly to Bob Childers, Tom Skinner, Randy Pease, Greg Jacobs- all these people- Gene Williams and Bill Erickson and on and on and on. Very early on, and that immediately, as a 20-year-old kid that doesn't know anybody that writes songs, that wasn't part of a musical culture. I didn't play in bands when I was in Bartlesville. It was just strictly something I did for my own amusement occasionally when I wasn't drawing cartoons. So that was the beginning of it. But you sit there and listen to somebody like Tom Skinner play an original one. 'Yeah, I wrote this one last week' and he plays this song, and you go- wow, that's really amazing. I can't believe it. That becomes the high-water mark. That obviously is, well, if I'm gonna write a song, it has to be at least as good as that. So, what does that mean? And so that influence thing, you're influenced by whatever you're exposed to. I just feel really fortunate about that. All that was just coincidence, and I got some really good role models to try and emulate.

Monica Taylor – Back when I was in middle school, there was this bluegrass festival down in McAllister- outside of McAllister, Oklahoma- that my folks and I been going to since I was in third grade. I loved it because it'd be like all the old guys, Bill Monroe, who were stars. They were the stars in my eyes. So, Bill Monroe and the Osburn brothers and different folks. But then at night, of course, it was just a family. This is not a wild and crazy bluegrass festival; this is family style traditional bluegrass. And in all the little campsites, of course, there's picking with all the old timers. And I remember being in the camp and these other young fellows were there, a little older than me, you know, like probably high school? They all played together in this group called The Signal Mountain Boys. And I remember this tall skinny guy playing the banjo, and he was funny, and he was cute. But he was probably, I figured too old for me. I was in middle school. Around that camp, around that picking group, I'm standing behind everybody with my guitar. You know, if you wait long enough, some old timer will say, hey, you got a song for us? And they'll bring you up and then you're sweating through your palms and you're just- you're sick to your stomach- and then you sing your song and they're so nice. Those older boys was the fellows Virgil and Glenn Bonham who played with Jim Blair all through their lives. But that cute and funny banjo player was Jim Blair. And also another, Travis, my husband, his family used to take him to things like that. And they went to the festival too when we were at about the same age. But he was at the festival, and I didn't know if I'd have known him. Boy, I'd have been like, oh, he's so cute. I was boy crazy. I guess. I think everyone is at that age.

Stan Woodward – I tell people, when I go to Woody Guthrie Fest, picture that going on like every other weekend out of the farm. That level of writing and musicianship, it was just going on all the time. We didn't really know what we had. It was just more of a party and it's fun. But you look back and just the sheer amount of songs that were written during that 1980 through all the way up into the 2000's really. There was a ton of stuff getting written.

Wrapping up the Eighties

The Red Dirt Rangers were just starting to form around this time. At this point Bob Wiles had gotten married and moved to Tulsa. John Cooper had moved out of the farm in 1986, although he stayed there off an off until about 1988. Cooper had graduated and gotten a job teaching high school in Oklahoma City, where he moved. Cooper gathered some musician friends and would get together once a week at his house near the Paseo District for jam sessions. This group would include Scott Buxton, Dave Clark, Charlie Pieden and K.C. Moon.

Oklahoma City musician Joe Baxter didn't start releasing music until the '90s but had been hanging out in Stillwater and Winfield for years. Baxter considers himself more of a rock sound, and not necessarily the folk and bluegrass sound that was more prevalent in the Red Dirt Scene at this time. "But you know, my sister went to school with John Cooper's first wife, and I met those guys. Shoot we'd go over to their house over by OCU for little jam sessions. When they were just getting rolling then. The first time I ever met Ben Hahn, I was like hell yeah. And I chatted with him a little bit. I ran sound for them for a little bit, because I had a system at the time. They asked me, said we needed someone to run sound, so I did that a couple of times. But those guys took it ran with it," said Baxter.

Dave Clark worked at the OU Health Science Center and met a guy at work who was going through a divorce and needed a place to stay. "So, Coop said- Well, he can stay on the couch for a couple of days. Dave brought this guy from work, and it turned out to be Ben Hahn. They didn't have any idea, but he was such a great guitar player. They were having these once-a-week jam sessions and started doing a few open mic nights in Oklahoma City. That year at the Musicians Reunion LaFave let them have a time slot. I think that was sort of one of the first really, sort of high-profile times, that they were on stage as the Red Dirt Rangers," said Bob Wiles.

Ben Hahn and John Cooper. Photo provided by Sage Powell.

Wiles was at the Farm listening to the guys playing that day before they made their way to the Musician's Reunion later that evening. "I went out there and listened to these guys practice. They were really excited, and then Hahn didn't show up. And they said hey, can you play some lead? I don't think Ben, our guitar player, is gonna show up. I lied, completely lied. I was like, Oh, yeah, you bet, man. Let me get my guitar. I'm not a lead player at all. But I wasn't about to miss out on the fun. So, I played with them at that Musician's Reunion," said Wiles.

Jimmy LaFave, John Cooper, Brad Piccolo. Photo provided by Stan Woodward.

Monica Taylor got to attend the Musician's reunion that night as well and met just about everyone else in the scene. The Wayfaring Strangers were practicing one evening during the weekend of the musician's reunion at Pam Potts' apartment, when there was a knock on the door. The group had told Taylor they had a friend of theirs who wrote songs that wanted to come over and meet the new girl in town. "The door opened, and I will never ever forget the very first glimpse I ever had of Bob Childers. I didn't even know anything about him. But I saw him, and he smiled and said- well I just had to come over here and meet this new girl that's singing around town. I had been there like two months or something. He shook my hand, and I knew I was going to know that man for eternity, like I would know this person. Then he sat down, and someone gave him a guitar and said do such and such. *Minstrel Boy's Howling at the Moon* was I think one he played- old, old song. I just said, you wrote that song? And he said yep. I didn't think then that I had ever really thought much about song writers, I just loved the song. But from that moment on I started reading all the liner notes in albums," said Taylor

That night they went down to Willie's for the Musician's reunion where Taylor met Greg Jacobs, Kurt Nielsen, Tom Skinner, and Jimmy LaFave all that same night. Afterwards they all went out to the Farm and stood out under the stars and played music. "I couldn't believe it There had to be like 50 cars of all shapes and sizes, and motorcycles and bicycles, all going out west to the farm. My heart was racing. I was so excited. I had been through three years of college. Nothing that I really wanted to do. I didn't even want to go to college. I just wanted to play music and that night I met, I really got to know these people, that tribe. I found my tribe- man and they accepted me. You know how it is when there are people that you look up to or you're just in awe of and all of a sudden- they turn to you, and you realize they have accepted you in that instance? They give you a nod in the circle. It's your turn to play a song, and then they love it. And they play with you, and they sing with you and, yeah. Yeah, that's it," said Taylor.

All in one night Taylor had met so many of the musicians in the scene. From the much respected and revered elders that helped start the scene, to the newcomers who were just making their way in it, like herself.

John Cooper, Brad Piccolo, Jimmy LaFave, Randy Pease, Farm crowd. Photo provided by Stan Woodward.

"I met all the Ranger Guys, the pre-Ranger band. John came over and spent hours picking on his mandolin and we sang *Rain, Rain, Rain*, that Beatles song. He said- we're starting a band. And I said, you are? Who else is it? He said, yeah, those guys over there. And he pointed to like eight-nine people. I said which ones? He said, all of them, all of those guys over there. It was hilarious. I was probably 20 years old. From there on my life changed," said Taylor.

When Monica Taylor first met Childers, they were playing songs and passing around a guitar and she asked him what kind of guitar he played. Childers told her what he had, but that he just sold his guitar. He said his boys needed dental work and he needed money for that more than he needed the guitar, so he pawned it. Taylor had an extra guitar and said she could only play one at a time anyway, so why didn't he just take it? "I felt so bad, and I had this extra guitar- a really nice one too- a Hummingbird. It needed a little work, but it worked fine. It had electric and I offered it to him. He said, you know what, that's a really nice offer, but I'll be alright. I said, well how can you be without a guitar? He said, remember this – guitars are just a thing. It's just a thing. Your kids and your family are what matters. Your friends are what matter. I have reminded myself of that throughout the years, over and over again," said Taylor.

The Walnut Valley Festival in Winfield rolled around that year and Bret Franzmann encouraged Monica Taylor to go. "I took off the whole week for Winfield not knowing anything about it. All I knew were these people, but they invited me to come up. They said, just drive into the pecan grove and start asking at different camps for the Stillwater camp. I got directed there and I pulled in. I had this big old 40 Econoline that was my folks, and I had nothing in it. It just had a big bed in it, and we had camped in for years. I met tons of people. We didn't sleep. I mean, I was up as soon as somebody was playing. There in this big camp, there were probably 30 or 40 people there at all times and then people would come in through the week. Then by the weekend- Friday, Saturday and Sunday- there were probably, I don't know, 70, it was twice that many. So that's where I met Kenny Parks and his wife Cindy who have always been kind of the Ramrod of that, and John and Jill Hunt. Just met just so many people who are still picking and still loving music," said Monica Taylor.

Also, at the Walnut Music Festival that year, Bob Wiles found himself hanging out with the still forming Red Dirt Rangers again. They mentioned to him that they were still looking for a drummer and a bass player at that time. "I said oh, I can play bass. Once again, totally lied. But I loved those guys. Looked like a lot of fun. They all lived in Oklahoma City. I lived in Tulsa. At Winfield, they had vendors selling stuff, and they had a guy up there selling instructional videotapes- how to play the banjo, how to play the guitar. I bought a 'how to play the bass' videotape by Rick Danko, who was the bass player for The Band. Then I went back to Tulsa and bought a bass. By the time the first gig rolled around, I knew just enough to fake my way through it," said Wiles.

Jeff Parker moved back to Stillwater in about 1989 and got a job at Daddy O's music teaching lessons and recording music there. He put together his own home studio where he lived at Maple and Lowry, which blossomed into his house becoming a studio for others in about 1990. It would eventually become Cimarron Sound Labs and would be instrumental in recording many of the Red Dirt artists in the next decades.

Bob Childers moved onto the Farm, into a trailer onto the property in about 1990, upon returning from Austin. All the local musicians around knew that it was the place to go for jam sessions at any time. Many bands that traveled through and played gigs in Stillwater stayed at The Farm in the process. "It was a great focal point for everything. And that made it good for songwriting, because you might write with somebody, rather than just one band writing all their stuff kind of in a tight little group. There was all this cross pollination going on. You know you might write with a guy from one band one time and somebody else the next, plus there was a lot of writing people you could pitch them to, to actually do the songs. That was what it was for me, a community," said Childers in a YouTube video about the Farm, that has since been removed from the site.

The Farm seemed to just expand and evolve even more with Childers living there. Childers was the one who decided the music needed to move from the front porch to the garage, which he decided to call the Gypsy Café. "We started having more music out there, and all of that. But then what got things really kind of moving to a different stratosphere was Bob Childers moving to the farm. Bob was always a good friend. Bob had left and gone down to Austin to be with his ex-wife and kids. And then one thing led to another, and he came back to Stillwater and needed a place to live. And he moved into the farm and once Bob moved into the farm, then the music thing, hits another stratosphere," said Danny Pierce.

Bob Childers at the Farm. Photo provided by Sage Powell.

Tom Skinner had also returned to Oklahoma sometime between 1989-1990. While he had moved back to Bristow, he still played and hung out in Stillwater regularly. "The Skinner Brothers, they were great. Of course, they had their big soiree in Nashville, with Garth. And we know that first trip didn't work out too well. I always kind of remember him saying, Garth wanted them all to be entertainers- put on cowboys hats and say yee haw and all this sort of stuff and they just were not entertainers in that way. They limped it on back to Stillwater and got things going again. But Tom, the amount of songs and creativity that he could come up with, with his brothers, all of that. I think we got the precursor to the Science Project. There would be times he just set up shop at the Gypsy Cafe and hosted events out there. Tom kind of hosted it and people just showed up- lawn chairs and music and rotate the stage around like the Science

Project. I think you can say the early Science Project began out at Gypsy Cafe before he took it to Tulsa out there. But Tom was always writing and always sharing songs. Always with the guitar and playing and it just was a great environment for that to happen and others to kind of chime in. And next thing you know there's Don Wood with the stand-up bass and there's somebody else over here with a couple more guitars and they're picking and working on songs and then it's three days later and here we are," said Danny Pierce.

In Their Own Words

Matt O'Meilia -As far as musicians- like the Red Dirt Rangers- those guys roll around, you know, Brad Piccolo, and John Cooper. They were just getting their thing together. All those people were gathering up at the farm. I didn't go up to the farm a lot, because I was mostly a rock and roll guy until I got into the Garth thing. I would go out there with my rock and roll buddies and there was all these kind of bluegrass guys. Other people I knew like Kurt Nielsen who's still playing around town and who I've known since I was a little kid. We grew up just up the street from each other. Kurt Nielsen is a funny guy. He was in my brother's class. He's just a real typical, Tulsa guy with the dry sense of humor. I got into the whole country scene and that whole scene just because- one thing I needed some money. But once I got in there, I saw they're all just great Oklahoma boys that are just funny- all of them are funny as could be. Tom Skinner was probably one of the funniest guys I ever knew. And so was Garth- all those guys. I always gravitated toward people who are funny. It's just they're a lot more fun to be around obviously, and everybody just seemed so normal to me- normal and funny even. But then they pick up an instrument and it's just like- whoa, you seem normal until you pick up an instrument then you just blow everybody's mind. Like the Skinners, or Garth or any of those guys, Red Dirt Rangers. I mean they were all just good, good friends. It just had the sense of community. It was such an organic formation for that, from that whole Red Dirt community. I never even knew the term Red Dirt when I was up there. That wasn't something that was talked about- we weren't categorizing ourselves. We're just playing music, man. I mean, John Cooper from the Red Dirt Rangers, Brad Piccolo, those guys were playing rock and roll. They were playing in rock and roll bands before they got into the whole bluegrass thing. I always thought it was kind of weird like that. They're playing bluegrass now. That's weird. Of course, they obviously turned out to be very, very good at it. But nobody perceived anything as being this type of music or that type of music, you know what I mean? It's just music. Hey, I like this song. Let's play this, and how do you play it? Well, you got to play it, it's really only going to sound good with a mandolin and a violin and guitar. We don't need any drums. There was no, I'm just going to do this style from now on. That's why it's such a melting pot of all that stuff. And Garth, he was such a prime example of everything. He was a total rock and roll fiend growing up. He liked the big stadium rock- Journey, Kansas, and going to all those big arena shows. He was into all that. I mean, so he obviously didn't grow up milking cows or anything. He's like- hey, I like this music too. It wasn't anything calculated as far as I can tell. It's just what you like to hear, and it also has to do with who you're hanging around. Guys like Bob Childers comes along and people are like- hey, man, this guy's writing some cool songs. That's how he became such an influence on all these guys. I didn't know Bob that well, really until after the Santa Fe band and when I was writing the book, he was very helpful.

John Cooper - Everyone's got their own personal definition. I don't think you can get a dictionary and look up Red Dirt and have something say this is what it is- there's no definitive thing. It's personal, everyone has their own definition. For me, what I call Red Dirt- and I don't even call it music- it's really more of a scene. The scene started at a particular place at a particular time, and that would be Stillwater Oklahoma, that would be at The Farm. The genesis of it, that's where the people that I think started what is known as the Red Dirt scene or Red Dirt music came from. And that would be Bob Childers, Tom Skinner, Greg Jacobs, Chuck Dunlap, and my band was there. So, I think The Farm was really- that was the place for me, and I think for a lot of other people as well. That was actually where it started. To me it took many other people, you can define where Red Dirt music started, not only to a particular town but to a particular place in that town. Which is kinda weird but not really. A lot of different music scenes started that way. There was a certain- it was just a place where everything came together. As Bob Childers said, our music scene needed a place to grow, and that's what the farm provided. It provided a really fertile setting for the music to become a thing.

Monica Taylor - To me, it is Oklahoma first. People who grew up in Oklahoma or spent a lot of time in Oklahoma. Really got to know the people– old people, young people, the country roads, the little towns, the history of Woody Guthrie and Will Rogers. And then Red Dirt really did start at the farm and different places in Stillwater - the yellow house, where Jason and Stoney and Cody were. But it's like there's this big kettle, this big black kettle that I see, sitting on the campfire at the farm. I don't really know how I see it, but everybody comes and sits around that campfire. They come from some place in Oklahoma, where they heard different kinds of music - gospel to straight country, to your Hank Jr like Jason, to your southern rock, to your AC/DC to all kinds of different things. Tex-mex, cajun, everybody brings a little bit and plays their songs, and that music falls into the kettle and gets stirred around just a little and you dip it out. Because you have heard everybody else's music, and you dip it out and put it in a coffee cup and you drink it. Or you take it and put it on your dashboard and off you go, down the road with your music. I think you take a little bit of whatever you hear, and sometimes you can't help it.

Bob Wiles – It's kind of amazing, you know? For one of the guys in the band to say- hey, I've got this friend that's going through a rough time, and needs a place to stay, you know? Do you think he could crash on the couch? And it ends up being Ben Hahn. It just lined up without even trying. Every step of the way, you know? It wasn't like there was a plan- just having fun and living day to day. Great things happened, nobody got rich. But Golly, how could you trade all that for money?

Scott Evans – Jimmy LaFave and the band that he brought, my God, that's the biggest impression on me was how good the guys that Jimmy brought up with him from Austin, Texas. I was just blown away and very intimidated by it as well. It was just obviously these guys are serious pros. We need the woodshed. I need to practice, I wanna play like that. And Jimmy was just such an amazing singer, right? Like a really gifted vocalist. That's my main memory and impression of it. Medicine Show barely got in on the last one or two of those. I think we did. I think we did make the cut. We actually got to get up and play. Which, you know, you wanna be acknowledged by your peers. That's as much acknowledgment as you can possibly get. Like here's this group of musicians; Pam Potts, Bret Franzmann, Gene Williams and all these older generation guys, you know, than me. And they've been doing this a long time. They were pros, they played gigs for a living. and we had just started and wanted to be that good.

And then when you get invited to go do that, it's that validation of like, yes, these are our peers, and they accept us and appreciate us and that's really what that's about. That's my impression of it. Was that validating thing. Yes, we can do this. We're legitimate musicians. Yes, we've been accepted by the old guard.

John Buckner- My God- Bob. Bob is kind of like interwoven with everything. Bob lived at the farm. Bob was like everybody's spiritual guide. Bob was always there and always happy to see everybody, he was just like your older cousin at the family reunions. Bob was a celebrity unto himself because Jimmy just thought, Bob was it. Bob was a thinker, a deep thinker, and he was in the vein of Dylan. Bob Dylan. And Bob just had a whole different outlook on life, and he just believed that life was short and that you should pursue what makes you happy. No matter what it is- it's ok if you wanna do this and other people don't like it- it's ok. It's about what you want, it's about what makes you happy; not what makes your parents happy, not what makes your significant other happy. What makes you happy. Stay true to yourself. And Jimmy loved that about Bob. Jimmy, he and Bob were close lifelong friends. Bob was just kind of like- he didn't really have anything. He didn't want anything. He lived in a little trailer out there by the farm, even when they closed the house down. I guess it was on the verge of collapsing or something. Bob had a little trailer out there and any time anybody showed up, he was just like- yeah, let's do it up. He was always ready to go and get up and play. Everybody would say Bob- you gotta get up here and speak a few words. We'd play and then we'd just kind of stop and Bob would step up to the mic and just something totally awesome would come out of his mouth. Just something profound and would make you think. So, everybody loved it when Bob was there.

Passing the Torch

Scott Evans, Donnie Wood and Kenny Early started a jam band called Skeleton Crew inadvertently while learning how to play more music. "Scott and I had gotten to be friends, which is another weird thing because I met him at a party from some guys from Bartlesville. He had come home and was back playing in the bedroom. I'm like, who's that guy? Yeah, that guy's pretty good back there playing some stuff. Went back there and I kind of hung out with him. Of course, I'm a little older than Scott, but I was like, you're from Bartlesville? How do I not know you if you're from Bartlesville? Apparently, he was just a guy that didn't go out and play, just played in his bedroom. I bent his arm and said, well, we should jam together. I've got a drummer buddy and we kind of started this thing. Our friend Kenny worked someplace. I can't remember if it was Garfield's or whatever, but basically, they'd give us free beer if we'd come play. We didn't sing or anything. We just went up there and made a racket. That's all Skeleton Crew was- we just made a racket. People would yell out some song and we'd try and play part of it and then drink more beer," said Donnie Wood.

"Skeleton crew was just this jam band with Donnie and Kenny and that started when Donnie had come over to see my roommate at the time. I had finally upgraded my little 15-watt practice amp- this terrible little solid state practice amp. I finally upgraded it. I worked hard. I had three jobs. Glen Townsend told me about a Music Man 410 that he had sold to a pawn shop- Golden Pawn on Sheridan. And if I went in there and dropped his name, maybe they would make me a good price on it. Well, I did. I had just brought that thing home and was baptized by decibels, is the way I described it. Like all of a sudden, all these guitar things that were very difficult to do with a tiny little quiet amp- it did not have very good sound- all of a sudden, now at big rumbling volumes, now you can get those tones and it's all now right there at your fingertips. I was just, you know, very obsessed with this. Donnie came by, had to come back there and go- 'what the hell are you doing? That's very loud. You having fun?' He suggested, man, I know this drummer from Bartlesville. If you guys wanna jam together, sometime. His name's Kenny Early," said Evans.

Evans had gone to high school with Early in Bartlesville and already knew of him. Donnie and Evans got together with Early and the first time they got together, they just jammed together for an hour, and everyone got excited. Someone called their buddy that owned Three Frogs, which was caddy corner to Willie's, and got them an in to play. "And we threw our stuff in the car and drove down there and set up in the basement with just a room full of drunks and just jammed with no lyrics, no expectations. No nothing, just for the sheer joy of it and for free beer. And that turned into somebody else asked us to come and do it somewhere else. And so we had a couple of gigs going on," said Evans.

Brad James came back to Stillwater from Colorado for the Musician's Reunion in 1990 and met Scott Evans who was with Donnie Wood. Greg Morris was looking for a new bass player for the band Low Skies. James had heard Wood play at Willie's and told Morris he knew a guy. "That's really another weird thing of how I met Brad even- was just very, very odd.

I had played with these guys, this group of guys at the jam. Then all of a sudden there were some other guys in town that were like, hey, man, that guy's pretty good. So other bands were asking me to come join them or whatever. I'd go play with this band or I'd play with this band just for a night or whatever. I was playing at Willie's one night with some band, and in the bathroom- of all places- and this guy damn near seven foot tall is like- hey, man, can I talk to you for a minute? I'm like, can I get finished here? And he's like, hey, I've got some friends of mine that are looking for a bass player. I mean, you're really good. You obviously don't play with these guys full time. I can tell that. This other band is a lot better. And so that was Brad trying to get me to go play with Greg Morris and these other guys," said Wood.

"I was bad broke and didn't even have gas money, and Greg said- well, I'll pay you to go hang out. You know my arrangements, you know my music, I don't have time. Because he lived in Oklahoma City. He said go hang out with that bass player and teach him my stuff. So that puts me and Donnie on a couch with instruments," said James.

"He (James) had come back for the summer. He was back for a couple of weeks or something from Colorado. He said, well, I'll come over and show you some of this stuff. And long story short- Brad showed up in my house and just never left for like a week. He just parked his van in the driveway and we kind of jammed for a few hours. Like, dude, I gotta go to work. He goes, ok, man, what time are you gonna get back? And I'm kind of like, nicely- like you wanna leave because I gotta go to work? And he says, but what time are you gonna be back? Uh, probably around 10? Mind if I just stay here and watch some TV? Yeah, he squatted for a week and the funny thing was, is instead of teaching me really any of that material, he and I ended up just playing a bunch of stuff that we both liked," said Wood.

Soon they got together with Rick McCord and started having jam sessions. James and Donnie would go to Daddy O's and hang out and jam with Scott Evans as well. Soon it was time for James to get back to

Breckenridge. James was in a band called Buckwheat Groats in Colorado, but they had recently lost their bass player to another local band. James didn't really relish the idea of spending another winter in Breckenridge and thought about the guys in Oklahoma still trying to find their places in bands. He called Evans and Wood and got each of them on the phone and asked if he moved back, would they want to start a band? "Start a band where we make basically every song an epic like, brothers of the Grateful Dead or something. I was already playing Red Dirt stuff. I mean I was playing Bob Childers, and Jimmy LaFave and Brad Piccolo music, out there. I was doing like The Band, and Little Feat, and the Allman Brothers, all of that stuff, that I still like to play. It's kind of my wheelhouse. This Red Dirt stuff and The Band and Little Feat, and the Dead and Allman Brothers, Leon Russell and JJ Cale, I could live there, and just do that. So, I came back, and we started The Medicine Show. They already had a little thing going with Kenny Early that they called Skeleton Crew. So, we just basically expanded that outfit and started Medicine Show in the fall of 1990," said James.

It was an easy transition from Skeleton Crew to Medicine Show. "Brad was kind of the ramrod of all that. He was the one that had the band name because he really loved this song by The Band called *Wes Walcott's Medicine Show*. And so, we learned that song, became like our moniker namesake song. And yeah, the rest is history. Started little by little. He had some original songs. I started writing some original songs. Little by little, we went from being a real terrible Grateful Dead cover band to within just a few months, we were doing fairly sophisticated arrangements by Little Feat. And it's kind of remarkable," said Evans.

"My house was always the band house through all of the years until the very end. We just did that, became very popular locally and then in Tulsa. I never could figure it out myself because I had come through playing prog rock and very disciplined styles of music than just free for all stuff. I'm coming out of having been in band, all state drum, all this kind of stuff.

Gone to college on a jazz scholarship and somewhat- I guess you would say- traditionally trained in music. And I'm playing with these guys who are just self-taught for lack of a better word. To me, it was very frustrating a lot of times because my God- these bands were horrible. This is very sloppy. It's just like you guys need to learn. I just never could figure out why that band became so popular. I mean, from my perspective, we were horrible. But it was just the realness of it all. We are talking about a time when jam bands were really coming back in. The Grateful Dead was having a resurgence of popularity, and the Allman Brothers and then a whole new offshoot of new jam bands like Pearl Jam, just all kinds of stuff. So just that kind of free form, loose, organic, non-commercial approach to playing music was really kind of a thing, especially in the nineties. I learned a lot from it, probably a lot about not being so constrained and trying to put a formula to things. I guess you would say is just kind of let music be music and quit trying to put it in a box. Which is kind of kind of how- if you're being classically trained and stuff- it's kind of how you're almost geared to think," said Wood.

Amazingly enough, Medicine Show recorded all of their shows through the soundboard, and they are archived at https://archive.org/details/MedicineShow. You can go listen to any one of the shows they performed from 1990-1997, which includes other bands and musicians that played with them on the shows. It's a treasure trove of the time and history of it all.

The Red Dirt Rangers were still fairly new as Medicine Show began and the two bands became close and started working together to build each other up. They would swap gig information and try to work together.

Scott Evans and Brad Piccolo. Photo provided by Sage Powell.

In Christmas of 1990 they played the Hideaway Christmas Party together. "That's where we really started saying, well let's not have an opener. Let's not have it be who's opening and who's the headliner or whatever. Let's just kind of change out one band member at a time and we'll do like the Vulcan band meld. We'll change out and then change back. That night, they called it the Iron Halo. Bob Childers sat in a bunch. There were literally people hanging from the ceiling. People that were there that night remember that even after we couldn't play electric rock and roll in the dining room of the Hideaway anymore, the staff went back and started beating on pots and pans. It was basically like a drum circle- it was absolutely tribal. I remember a guy- you know those spring-loaded plate things, in a restaurant that holds plates- people were playing that, like ca-chow, ca-chow. People are beating on pots and pans, plates, glasses, literally hanging from the ceiling. That was like my first chapter, me getting to Stillwater and starting Medicine Show," said James.

James started working at Daddy O's where Evans already worked. James taught lessons and learned guitar repair. "Other catalysts other than the family type encouragement - Daddy O's was certainly one. Mike Shannon was great at allowing us to learn. He really began teaching me the craft that is how I make my living today. I think a luthier actually builds instruments from scratch, so I'm probably more of a guitar mechanic. But I'm almost 30 years into being a guitar mechanic and Mike would have started me on knowing how to do that," said James. Like many of the "elder statesman" of the scene, Mike Shannon is well loved and respected by the younger musicians that he helped, mentored, taught and inspired along the way.

Daddy O's music was heavily involved with the formation of the Red Dirt movement.

Brandon Jenkins also hustled onto the scene at this time, a Sociology student at OSU from 1987-1992. He played his very first gig at Eskimo Joe's at the age of 18 in 1989. When he turned 21 in 1990, he played his first bar gig at Willie's. "I guess officially, my first official gig on my own at a bar was at Willie's Saloon in 1990. I had played a couple of other things at Eskimo Joes before that. Just for these little things, kind of songwriter nights- but it wasn't my own gig. So, when I turned 21- which happened to be in 1990- I could finally play in the bars, and I started playing Willie's Saloon. I remember after the show, there was some house where Scott Evans, Donnie Wood, Brad James, Kenny, and all those guys were just starting. I kind of got to be in the crossroads of a couple of different groups of Red Dirt. A lot of people in their mind if you say Red Dirt- there's kind of different generations of Red Dirt. Back then when I was up there, the big draw or big act of Red Dirt was Jimmy LaFave. He had this thing called the Jimmy LaFave reunion weekend, and that's kind of when I first met the Red Dirt Rangers and those guys, was around a Jimmy LaFave weekend thing. That was my first introduction to The Farm was going to that reunion thing and then afterwards everyone went out to the farm and played and partied. I wasn't a singer/songwriter, I was more just the stagger on dude that came out there. I was just in school, and nobody knew me from Adam. Everybody just wanted to get their turn playing guitar around the campfire. That's where I met Bob Childers and those guys. Thinking back to that time, around that same time 89-90 I went to Winfield Bluegrass festival. Stillwater had their own camp there which was actually a really big camp, and it was all the same who's who of all these people that sat around and played guitar. I think that was the first place where I really met the Red Dirt Rangers and got to know them," said Jenkins.

Jenkins was born in Tulsa. His father was a Tulsa radio DJ, so he grew up immersed in music. In his youth he played in the school band, sang in the choir, and taught himself how to play guitar. Jenkins, known as Brandy to those close to him throughout his youth, took ballet classes as a child and spent some time growing up in a hippie style commune with his family. He graduated high school in 1987 and did a short stint in boot camp and school for the Army Reserve before starting school at OSU.

"Well, he was a pretty good kid. Rarely got in trouble. Cute as a bug. Always. Had beautiful long eyelashes. Everybody would notice when he was really young, thought he was a girl all the time. He was just smart as a whip. Right off. One of my funny stories is when he was four, he called Walmart all by himself. Called information, got the number, called them to find out how much a GI Joe was so that so that he could tell his grandmother. I laugh about it because the kids these days, young kids, they hardly know how to use a phone, right?" Said Wilma Jenkins, Brandon's mother.

Brandon Jenkins in the Tulsa Central Jazz Band in 1987. Photo provided by Wilma Jenkins.

David Teegarden Jr., son of drummer and studio owner David Teegarden Sr., was childhood friends with Jenkins. They grew up in the same

Boy Scout troop and soon started playing music together. "I first met Brandon Jenkins- I think we were both six or seven. His mother, Wilma Jenkins- wonderful, beautiful woman, hippie. She was a den mother. And my mother was a den mother as well, Vicky Teegarden. We were both cub scouts and I walked in and there was Brandon and only a few people are able to call him by this name, Brandy. He went by Brandy and in our adult life, only his mother or my mother were allowed to call him Brandy. And so, we were in Cub Scouts, then we were later in Boy scouts. We played soccer together while all this was going on. My father is involved in the music industry and my father had a studio. I had a drum set and an amplifier and a little PA system and stuff going on and we were able to go play music. Brandy and I would go in the studio with some other friends of mine, another gentleman by the name of David Kelly, who is a music educator. He taught at NSU, he lives in the Pennsylvania, New Jersey area right now. But we would get together and play songs. Probably eight years old. But one of the most amazing things was we weren't mimicking anything. Brandon was writing his own music. We probably had about ten songs, nine songs worked up easily that we would just kind of jam around and work out. Work out the music because he had the lyrics already. And one of them comes to mind, the song title was *Roller Coaster*. Not to be confused with the Ohio players or Red Hot Chili Peppers version, but he had a song- *Roller Coaster*. His lyrics were already deep by the time we were eight or nine and Roller Coaster seems light. But I remember one of the lines was, I'm on a roller coaster, I'm on a roller coaster headed for nowhere. Kind of sounds like *Finger on the Trigger* a little bit. His music always had a deepness and that's just me, a drummer, you know," said Teegarden.

Teegarden would come to play drums with Jenkins down the line, as well as have his own successful music career during the next era of the Red Dirt movement.

In Their Own Words

John Cooper - Asking me about the Red Dirt scene and Red Dirt music is like asking a fish about the properties of water. I'm in the middle of it. I can't tell you exactly what it is, I can just tell you what I think it is. I think it takes someone on the outside of it to figure out exactly what it is. I think you really nailed it well by saying there's a Red Dirt scene and then there's a Red Dirt sound. I still don't know what that is really, but I think they are different. I think they are different but in the same family in the same way. I think it would create more interest if you could come up with more of a definition of it, but I also think part of the beauty of it is that you can't quite put your thumb on what it is. We've been trying to explain to people what it is for thirty years, and I still can't do it. It started really as a singer/songwriter thing- the real nut of it with Jimmy and Bob and Skinner, early Red Dirt Rangers, Medicine Show. We were all writing our own tunes. I guess when it hit Great Divide and Ragweed it kind of took a left- become more of a ballroom, raucous rock and roll, shit kickers, break a beer bottle over your buddy's head, get drunk kinda thing. Which whatever, the thing is we've never had a gatekeeper. There's no one standing at the gate saying you are Red Dirt, you aren't. You can be in, and you can't. We never had that, which I think that's what makes it so broad, but like I said that's also what gives it a certain magic. Because you can't define it, which I think is cool. That's the thing, we've always as a scene been very accepting of everything, because there's only two kinds of music; good and bad. If you're good come on, if you're bad, get good and then come on.

John Buckner - It was more, everybody kept trying to figure out what we fit into and everybody at the time said- oh, it's Americana, that's what we were. They were trying to figure it out, people that started trying to get played on the radio and making some stuff. They were labeling it as Americana, and Red Dirt really hadn't come up yet. I think everybody started to call it that because of the Red Dirt Rangers- that name kind of fused and the fact that everything came out of Stillwater. And if you ever been there, everything around there when it rains is just red mud. The oil rigs and all that, all the trucks that come and go, they're just stained. Even the houses and the housing additions, when they were being built- the bricks, the bases of them are stained red and it never comes off. And you can drive to the neighborhoods and in the brick houses they've got red mud stained still on them and they've been there for 30-40 years. But that's kind of like how it came out of that, and everybody just started calling it, well, it's just Red Dirt. And they're like, what is Red Dirt? It's like Red Dirt is every musical genre except rap- basically- that you can think of, thrown in a pot. Some of it stirred slowly and some of its run through a blender, but it always comes out the same. It's good, it's smooth, it's intense. It's kind of like describing a food or a sauce or a wine, you know. It's like you take a sip and you go- what are you picking up? Like, I don't know- that drummer's got kind of a jazzy swing to him and that bass player just something straight ahead. Like, he's a ACDC and that guitar players got- wow, I've heard some chicken picking, I've heard a couple of Zeppelin licks, I've heard a Hendrix lick. The keyboard player- man, he's rolling all over it like Chuck Berry's keyboard player. It's great and it's just you can hear the different influences of it and it's hard to put your thumb on it, but that's what makes it up. And each one of those musicians, because they were so varied, and because there was really no straight core rock bands at that time. Straight core blues band, Straight Core Jazz. They are just like- hey, I wanna play, I don't care what the music is. I just wanna play. I wanna get up on stage and I wanna play and they're like, ok, grab your stuff, get up here. That's kind of basically how it started. And Jimmy was like the maestro of that because he was doing original music. Chuck was doing original music. And Jimmy especially fostered that community because he loved Stillwater. He loved Stillwater more than anything. And whenever he would come back, he was just always so happy. He was always walking around talking to everybody. He was just so friendly and such a good soul. And then you see other people that were like that too, that you would meet out at the farm. Once you became known at the farm and you were hanging out there, you were a good person. Yeah, if you came to the shows - and these people wouldn't just come once a year to the farm - they would come, you see a lot of these people, these faces at gigs regularly.

The End of the First Era

Two decades in and the first generation and era of the Red Dirt scene was wrapping up. Back in Tahlequah, Bobby Martin had just gotten married and decided to sell his half of Master Tracks studio. Sparky Fischer, guitarist extraordinaire, bought it and move it into a trailer on his property. Martin helped Fischer get it up and going, but Fischer never seemed to take to it very well and the studio died out within about a year. Martin went back to school at Northeastern. "I decided to go back to school. I started at Northeastern in Tahlequah and dropped out. I was out trying in my music and rock star phase, recording studio phase and then decided, I think I just wanna go back to school and really concentrate on art. Because I was really getting kind of reacquainted with the art creation side. Graduated, got my undergrad degree in fine art and Indian studies because I'm on the Muskogee Creek. And I was really interested in kind of rediscovering who I was as a native person," said Martin. Martin would move onto a career in Art, working with Kevin Smith who also had turned to Art at this time. They each created successful careers in art.

K.C. Moon, who played accordion for the Red Dirt Rangers, was also a journalist and wrote for the Daily Oklahoman. During college at OSU, he had been the editor of the campus newspaper. Moon got to work writing up press releases for the band and worked at getting them into any place he could. While they had gotten a few gigs around Oklahoma City at this point, soon they landed a gig in Tulsa. "We get a really good gig put on by the city of Tulsa at Chandler Park- was a pretty high-profile thing with several thousand people. Man, the timing couldn't have been worse. One of the accordion players, I believe K.C. Moon's wife was having a baby. Coop had promised a guy he would help him move to New Jersey and it happened to be that weekend. Dave Clark had something going on, and I just panicked, you know, because we traded off the singing. We each would sing four or five songs, and it was pretty hard for me to sing and play bass at the same time- I just wasn't good enough. All of a sudden, all the singers are flaking out. So, I called Austin. I called Brad Piccolo. I said, man, is there any way you can come up and play this gig with me? About half the songs we did at the time were songs he had written. He had a cassette tape album. He said, Yeah, man. Okay," said Wiles.

On his drive from Austin to Tulsa, Piccolo stopped and was able to pick up Dave Clark and bring him as well, who was also one of the singers. They played the gig at Chandler Park in front of several thousand people, and soon Piccolo decided to join up with the Red Dirt Rangers, making the trek from Austin to Oklahoma to play gigs until he decided to move back in about 1991-92. "And that was when the line-up really solidified; Coop, myself, Brad and Ben Hahn really started to play a lot together. Seems like everywhere we went, people were nice to us and never threw stuff at us. Throughout it all, all those older guys really encouraged us, Tom Skinner and Jimmy LaFave. We'd go to Austin. There are so many bands in Austin, it's really hard to even get a gig in Austin. Jimmy LaFave would let us warm up for him and helped expose us to a ton of people. It really helped us a lot," said Wiles.

Ben Hahn, John Cooper, K.C. Moon and Dave Clark at the farm. Photo provided by Sage Powell.

The local music scene was so deeply rooted and connected at this point that it never took long for everyone to meet everyone else, and end up playing music together in some way, even if it was just picking together around the campfire at the Farm. Everyone knew what venues to show up to, what places to go, anytime they wanted to catch some music playing. "Willie's was really the place to go in the beginning. I remember Wednesday night open mic nights. I saw Brandon Jenkins when he had hair, and he was a sociology student, he looked the part. He'd get up and then he'd start singing and I'm like, how did that sound come out of that body? His voice is very, very country, and kinda high twangy country. So, there was Brandon, and the Medicine show was just forming, or had kinda formed. They had been playing together, and Coy Mouser would bring in this huge Hammond B3 and this Leslie- you know this speaker- which would take up the whole left side of the stage. He would sit over there. And we would dance and dance and dance, and the Rangers would take up the whole entire stage. Dale Pierce was playing Dobro with them at the time and Benny Craig was playing fiddle at different times. Kenny Early was the first drummer, crazy boy, I mean wild man. He was a wild man, and Donnie Wood and Scott Evans, Brad James," said Monica Taylor.

By 1990 the Red Dirt Roots were firmly planted. The first generation were revered for what they had accomplished so far and were mentoring and inspiring the newcomers. Things kept moving right on along. While at this point the term Red Dirt music, or the fact that it was its own little genre, hadn't been fully established or realized- the previous two decades was where it all started. In fact, many people commented that by the Red

Dirt Rangers naming their band, they were the first to really market the name Red Dirt and start it on its way to being recognized by that moniker.

The entire history of the Red Dirt scene will see this common theme; the older musicians mentoring the younger ones, and the younger ones finding new ways to branch out even more and take it farther.

Brad Piccolo, Bob Childers and John Cooper. Photo provided by Stan Woodward.

"Greg Jacobs was teaching in the summertime with this low-income youth program on campus- a sports program. I was going to school so I would see him. I worked at the Colvin center, and he'd come by, and we would visit about music. He would tell me what he was going to do that night. I was like 20, and it was usually somebody's house. I would go over, and he would be playing songs that he had written, and I was just amazed. And one time he said- hey, a friend of ours is coming in from Tahlequah, Randy Pease, and so we're going to swap some songs. Then I'm just blown away by them. So those are really the first people I really heard; Bret Franzmann, Pam Potts, Mark Mars, and then I met Doug Hawthorn, and Kenny Parks. It was just all-night pickings with these people that you're meeting when you are young. You are so thankful, so thankful that you are meeting older people that are cool and would take care of you a little bit," said Monica Taylor.

Taylor went with the Wayfaring Strangers to see Tom Skinner in Bristow and to record a few songs with him. "We would hover around this microphone and just record- we got some pretty good stuff. I remember that time, the first time I ever heard *Turn this Train Around*, was right there. We had just recorded *Route 66*, and we had taken a break and Tom said- hey, listen to this song Bob and I are working on. I'll never forget it. I just said, that's a great song! And everyone else was getting more of the political undertones and I just thought it was a great song. Then I started listening to it again you know- politically. And you aren't stepping on any toes, not saying any names- it's just great. I think I might have heard *Water your own Yard* at the same time and sang along with him immediately. Because it was just one of those songs you couldn't help but sing along to. Tom used to make me mixed tapes. I remember Tom always saying- hold up, hold up, I got a tape for you. When Jeremy was just a little whippersnapper, not even in kindergarten I think," said Taylor.

The most prominent feature of the Red Dirt scene as it formed seemed to be its mentoring aspect, which fostered a family feeling versus a competitive atmosphere, as many other music scenes seem to have. The early musicians didn't have a lot of grand business plans of making it into the "big time"- they just wanted to play music because it was a part of who they were.

Gene Williams, Jed Lindsay. Greg Jacobs, Tom Skinner. Photo provided by Stan Woodward.

Because there were so many places to play -so many opportunities for anyone and everyone who wanted to play music- there wasn't fierce competition to try to secure gigs. There was plenty to go around, and everyone was more than happy to help everyone else find their footing. The musicians were encouraging, supportive, and genuinely wanted to help others who were trying to achieve the same things that they themselves were.

"One of the things about me personally, during my day, I would never ever not play with somebody. I didn't care if it was the first time they had ever played, I would sit down with them. And that's come back in several different ways to me. About six years ago, this great big, huge guy- he was just a giant. He came up to me and said- You don't remember me do you Mr. Collier? I said, no, I don't man. I would remember you. He said, at

Winfield one year you showed me my first song on the mandolin- *Liberty*, a little bluegrass song. You stayed there three hours until I had the whole song down. I said I do remember that. He was just a little bitty kid. He just hugged me, and to me that's the full circle and the Red Dirt. It's the best you can feel when somebody's done you like that, and he lifted me off the ground when he was hugging me. I would always make sure- I didn't care if they wasn't any good, or if they sounded terrible, or if I would rather be in another jam. To me, mentoring a child or playing with somebody that doesn't feel good about the way they play- that spirit to play- it's not just about performing, it's about building friendships. I can tell you one thing, if you'll show a child a little bit of attention, that little bit, even if it's just three hours, they will never forget it. Somehow or another you'll be some kind of special in their eyes, just a little bit, even if it's just that. So that is real important to me, that feeling. Not only just that, I want to play with every single person I can in my life. And I have gotten to play with a lot of different people. And it's just been so much of a blessing, and fun for me to do. I never worry about a dime or what I can make playing; I just want to experience meeting new folks and jamming. To me, jamming and making music is as close to making magic us human beings can get. You just can't get any closer to true magic than that. Because something happens, whether it's a 440 or a vibration or whatever it is- it gets in your soul. I tell ya, I have just been a blessed guy for making so many friends. It's a family," said Gene Collier.

The pioneers of this scene were now firmly planted- they formed the roots- which were strong and sturdy and starting to produce a thriving organism. There were young blossoming artists who sat at the feet of these pioneers- raised on the culture that was being created- who would come into their own in the next era, such as Eric Hansen and Jeff Parker. Then there is the group of transitional artists, that came towards the end of the first era, but before the next generation. Red Dirt Rangers, Monica Taylor, Medicine Show and Brandon Jenkins are a part of the transitional group of musicians that helped connect and bridge one era to the next. The second generation would include names like The Great Divide, Cross Canadian Ragweed and Jason Boland, who came in blazing and creating much more movement for the scene. Each group of artists continued to help make the entire scene thrive as time marched on.

Bob Childers and Jimmy LaFave. Photo provided by Sage Powell.

The pioneers continued with their careers and provided the 'elder statesman' aspect to the younger generations, even as the younger ones continued to expand the Red Dirt movement beyond what the pioneers were able to do.

The first years of this scene mainly was about establishing a philosophy, culture and community. The first generation had no idea they were creating something entirely new that would be a springboard for the next generation to jump off and expand even further. It was something that formed organically, without thought or planning. But without these first years and first players, there would never have been a foundation or a place to grow from. While these musicians were just doing what came natural to them- creating music that stirred their souls, encouraging and supporting one another and fostering a community that worked for each other instead of against one another- what they were really doing was creating and defining the culture that would form and shape the entire music scene that came after them. Many of the first musicians on the scene said they had no business plan- no plan at all really. They were just doing what they loved to do. It would be the new musicians and bands that came onto the scene as it transitioned from one era to the next, that found a way to label, package and market it. Which would allow the scene and the newly formed genre to grow and expand. While it would take years for these first musicians to even realize what they had really accomplished- they had formed an entire new culture of musicians and music that would become vastly important to Oklahoma and the careers of so many that followed in their footsteps. It was all born and built up out of dirt and spirit.

"I'm not sure that it is a sound so much as an attitude. You know there probably is a certain sound to it, but for instance- I kind of was in that Bob Childers group of people and I don't think I sound anything like Bob Childers. I don't think the two of us sound anything like each other, but we're both classified like that, you know? So, I think it's a friendship and a spirit of cooperation and brotherhood, that's got a lot to do with it," said Tom Skinner in a 2012 interview by Sterlin Harjo (Youtube : *Tom Skinner Interview*, Sterlin Harjo).

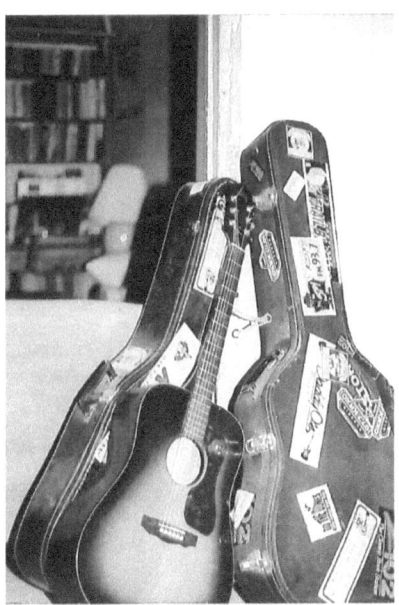

Photo provided by Sage Powell.

In Their Own Words

Wilma Jenkins - Brandon went to Central high school and played in the jazz band. Mike Medford, who was a friend of his until he passed, was his band director. And that's when he started loving the guitar. He had several throughout his young life and he studied very hard. He knew chord changes and all that kind of stuff fairly early. He wrote some songs when he was that young and they were pretty funny. He was very serious though. Don't get me wrong. They were serious songs. But looking back, they were just funny. But he started writing probably in the ninth grade, and he wrote lots of things that were interesting, stories and stuff. Then he graduated from Central. Well, here's the deal. They were in a talent show- oh, maybe his junior or sophomore year. And he played in a band- and these were all just young people, not necessarily in the jazz band- that he put together and dressed all up for it. He looked great. They were a mess. I mean, they were good. They were ok. And after that he was going to be a musician, you know? It was the girl factor. I guess everybody in school noticed him finally and he liked that.

John Buckner - I got Brandon Jenkins started playing. One of the waitresses at Willie's had the hots for him. I said, well, let's just get him up. I kind of coaxed that whole thing and told him how good he was. Which he wasn't that good at the time- he was a college boy. He was going to college at OSU and he's like, well, I sing a little bit, and I can play guitar. I was like, why don't you come for open mic night? We had an open mic night on Thursday nights at Willy's. He's like, well, I don't know if I'm ready for that. I said, well, when do you think you're gonna be ready? He said I don't know if I'm ever gonna be good enough. He just wore a baseball cap. He just looked like a kid. And I'm telling this girl that worked there- I was like, yeah, I'm gonna get him here for open mic night. And then so I was working both ends of that deal. I was telling her that I'd do whatever I could to get him in the bar. And then I was telling him, hey, you know, a couple of girls come up to me and ask me if you were ever gonna play. He was like, girls wanna hear me play? And I was like, yeah, that's the whole reason we do this is to get girls. Jesus where you been? And so, I finally got him- he came and did it. I just remember him doing it that first night, just seeing after he got done playing. His first time on stage, the look on his face is that it looked like he had just run a marathon. Brandon, I have great memories- just that memory. Especially of just getting him up to the open mic night when he was just- he was so scared, he couldn't do it. But then the night that he did do it, he thought that was the greatest. I mean, you could just tell, like a kid that got their first Christmas gift. Opened his first present, you know? It opened up and their eyes were just wide and smiling and he just- yeah, he was riding the high. And people liked it and clapped and the song he did was called *Big Legged Woman.*

Brandon Jenkins -We always like to say it started in Stillwater- it did, it has its roots. And it was because of guys like Tom, you know, and then there's a whole other era of Tom that people don't even think about and talk about. He and his brothers were the band for Garth Brooks. The beginning of this thing that became the biggest act in the whole fucking world. Bob Childers went out there with them too, I mean, it was like they were all in Nashville and went together. They all lived together in two houses. Maybe Garth is that link- that's something we don't really talk about because he became so big. But to me, Red Dirt music was never country. It was the Grateful Dead meets Allman Brothers. It was always that kind of sound. But then even though we don't really connect Garth with it, after Garth, then it started having this country connection there like with The Great Divide. They all of a sudden are wearing cowboy hats singing and saying they're Red Dirt. It was an interesting time. And to me, it was all exciting. You know, that was something I hung my hat on when I played. My first place I ever played was here at Eskimo Joes in 1989, because they could come here and not be 21 and play. But my first real gig- that was MY gig, a real over 21 bar- it was at Willies. And they used to have, I don't know if they still have it, but they had a plaque. That said Garth Brooks played right here. And then this was like just around the time when he just had been there- he just left and gone. So, I was always like- Oh, I'm playing the bar where Garth Brooks was playing. Yeah, he became so popular that we don't call it Red Dirt. But still, it was still forged here. But in the midst of it all, without The Skinner brothers and without Bob Childers and all these guys we're talking about there would be no Garth Brooks. So, is that Red Dirt? You know, just the Red Dirt that became really successful? Greg Jacobs, he was really popular back then, he was on the same level as you know as Tom and Bob and all those.

Greg Jacobs – I never thought of Red Dirt as a particular style of music. To me Red Dirt- and now it's gone to Texas, and Texas red dirt- to me you say Red Dirt and I think Stillwater. To me, there should be some kind of Stillwater connection, in my mind, for it to be Red Dirt. Those Texas people got it from Oklahoma people. Jimmy LaFave was the trailblazer, and he took it to Austin. Jimmy was a fantastic singer. He was just a great guy. I felt guilty. Jimmy was one of those guys, that there were two different Jimmy's. There was the public Jimmy LaFave whenever you would see him at a gig or a festival or something, and that was the showman Jimmy LaFave. And I know there was a private Jimmy LaFave that I never really knew, and after he passed away, Ashley Warren, who helped run his record label- she's archiving all of Jimmy' stuff. She sent me a copy of a song of mine that Jimmy recorded, that he never released. A song called *A Little at a Time*, which Tom Skinner used to do also. It was the closest that I've ever had recorded by an actual top 40 artist. Earl Thomas Conley, he was a big country music guy in the 80's. My publisher called me one day and said now I don't want you to go out and buy yourself a new car or anything, but Earl Thomas Conley is going in the studio, and they got 20 songs that he's going to pick 12 from. And your song *A Little at a Time* is on the list. Now of course, if he does it, you're going to have to give up half your songwriting credit. He's going to want songwriting credit and you're going to have to give half your publishing for him to do the song. Which is the way it works. I said sure, I don't have a problem with that- I'm trying to get a foot in the door. He didn't do it, but that's the closest I ever came. So, Ashley sent me a copy of this song, and I'm listening to Jimmy singing this song. I didn't even know Jimmy was even familiar with this song, and I'll be honest with you, it almost brought me to tears. It made me feel extremely guilty that I didn't make more of an effort to actually get to know Jimmy better than I did. I knew Tom and Bob very well- we were like brothers. We were very close for years, but Jimmy was always a little bit of an outside guy. In Stillwater there were two camps, Jimmy was the red-hot rock and roll band in town, and the Skinner boys were the red-hot eclectic band in town. I was in the Skinner boys circle, and we just didn't get to know Jimmy as well as I wish I would have. Now that it's all said and done, that's one little guilt trip I carry over from those days. I just didn't make the effort. Now Jimmy didn't make the effort either, but that doesn't matter. I didn't make the effort, and I wish I would have. I just didn't know that Jimmy actually respected my music that much, I never got that impression from him. My stuff was different than the stuff Jimmy did. I always thought, yeah he appreciates what I do. He thinks I'm pretty good, but I didn't know he really thought highly of what I did, he never told me. I wish he would have. I still feel guilty over that. Maybe he knows.

Don Morris (on how the Red Dirt Scene has evolved) – What I can tell from all the players around? It's in good hands now. The difference is- is the business part of it. It's not here but it's, you know, the music and the camaraderie. But that's still the same. They're generous people, generous and helping each other. So. that's what I like about it. It wasn't so cutthroat. Sometimes it can get a little cutthroat. Tom, really helped for that. He really welcomed me into the scene, and I'd known Tom for 15 years before I really met him, you know. So, I knew who he was, but it was always a pleasure working with him.

Mike Skinner - Bob was different, Tom was different, Crouch is different. Losing people like Bob and Tom, I'm never going to be able to laugh like I've laughed with my older brother. There were lots that didn't get his humor, that just missed out. We had a good time I guarantee you that.

Resources & Reference

The bulk of the content of the book came from oral or email interviews from contributors, dating from 2015-2024, additional information was found through these sources, in no particular order.

Moore, Aaron, *PLAYING IN THE DIRT: STILLWATER AND THE EMERGENCE OF RED DIRT MUSIC*, July 2010, Bachelor of Arts in Education in History Northeastern State University Tahlequah, Oklahoma, Submitted to the Faculty of the Graduate College of the Oklahoma State University in partial fulfillment of the requirements for the Degree of MASTER OF ARTS. https://openresearch.okstate.edu/entities/publication/2ceb0a26-b427-42b6-993f-689649e2afed

O'Meilia, Matt. Garth Brooks: The Road Out of Santa Fe. Norman: University of Oklahoma Press, 1997.

Hyde, D.(Producer) (2008) *North of Austin/West of Nashville: Red Dirt Music* [DVD]

Tyler Mahan Coe (Host), January 16, 2018, "CR013- Rusty & Doug Kershaw: The Cajun Way", *Cocaine & Rhinestones*. https://cocaineandrhinestones.com/rusty-doug-kershaw-cajun-way

Payne County Promotions website. Texas Troubadours Interview with Bob Childers, https://www.paynecountyline.com/interviews/bob_childers_2004.htm

Laka Documentation and Research Center on Nuclear Energy website. https://www.laka.org/music-from-anti-nuclear-movement/usa

Global Nonviolent Action Database website. https://nvdatabase.swarthmore.edu/content/oklahomans-prevent-completion-black-fox-nuclear-plant-1973-1982

O'Bannon, Ricky, "Remembering the Farm, the Oklahoma Commune where Red Dirt Music was Born", Dallas Observer, April 17,2014, https://www.dallasobserver.com/music/remembering-the-farm-the-oklahoma-commune-where-red-dirt-music-was-born-6432428

Donovan-Wallis, Cindy. "48 Hours in Atoka", The Chronicles of Oklahoma, article, vol 91, number 1 (Spring 2013); Oklahoma City, Oklahoma. https://gateway.okhistory.org/ark:/67531/metadc2017000/: The Gateway to Oklahoma History, https://gateway.okhistory.org; crediting Oklahoma Historical Society.

KIDS Radio Show, Carolyn Meyer and Kel Pickens, https://creators.spotify.com/pod/show/kids-radio-show

Eskimo Joe's Website https://eskimojoes.com/our-story/

Tumbleweeds Website https://www.calffry.com/about

This Land Press, "A Day with The Rangers", YouTube, July 24, 2012, https://www.youtube.com/watch?v=OEwcuoOgkQQ

Red Dirt Nation, "Tom Skinner Interview". YouTube, June 10, 2014, https://www.youtube.com/watch?v=4bx8mogtA9Q&t=183s

Red Dirt Nation, "Chuck Dunlap: Meeting Randy Crouch for the first time", YouTube. April 18, 2014, https://www.youtube.com/watch?v=kSXbcBgVciE&t=39s

Harjo, Sterlin, "Tom Skinner Interview", YouTube, October 1, 2015, https://www.youtube.com/watch?v=-a2Y1qidfC0&t=4s

Rockvision, *"The Tulsa Sampler Story",* YouTube, November 26, 2023, https://www.youtube.com/watch?v=EMUE0NvgF68&t=383s

Wikipedia (various subpages) https://en.wikipedia.org/

Author Page

Lost in the music on stage at the Mercury Lounge in Tulsa. Photo by Tom Harris.

Tonya Little is an Okie with a passion for music, arts, creative expression, cooking, reading and writing. A military brat who was born in Midwest City, Oklahoma, her family also lived in Japan and California while growing up. She settled her roots back into Oklahoma at the age of 12 and has never had a desire to leave since. While she does have a Bachelor of Science in Education from the University of Central Oklahoma, she believes most of her wisdom, knowledge and skills have come from life. Tonya is the mother of three amazing grown children, and two lovely daughters-in-law. She has been writing in some shape, form or fashion since the 4th grade, when she decided she wanted to one day write books. An avid reader, she knows books are portals into other lives and worlds and can teach and mold us in substantial ways.

www.ingramcontent.com/pod-product-compliance
Lightning Source LLC
Chambersburg PA
CBHW030104170426
43198CB00009B/487